Black Women, Agency, and t
New Black Feminism

Davidson sometimes carves out a concept from her observations of the lived experiences of black girls and women, and names it, thereby providing a superlative reflecting tool—a splendid memento—through which black girls and women can proudly recognize themselves, and each other.

Janine C. Jones, *Associate Professor of Philosophy, The University of North Carolina Greensboro, USA*

The powerful Beyoncé, the formidable Rihanna, and the incalculable Nikki Minaj. Their images lead one to wonder: are they a new incarnation of black feminism and black women's agency, or are they only pure fantasy in which, instead of having agency, they are in fact the products of the forces of patriarchy and commercialism? More broadly, one can ask whether black women in general are only being led to believe that they have power but are really being drawn back into more complicated systems of exploitation and oppression. Or, are black women subverting patriarchy by challenging notions of their subordinate and exploitable sexuality? In other words, "who is playing who?"

Black Women, Agency, and the New Black Feminism identifies a generational divide between traditional black feminists and younger black women. While traditional black feminists may see, for example, sexualized images of black women negatively and as an obstacle to progress, younger black women tend to embrace these new images and see them in a positive light. After carefully setting up this divide, this enlightening book will suggest that a more complex understanding of black feminist agency needs to be developed, one that is adapted to the complexities faced by the younger generation in today's world.

Arguing the concept of agency as an important theme for black feminism, this innovative title will appeal to scholars, teachers, and students interested in black feminist and feminist philosophy, identity construction, subjectivity and agency, race, gender, and class.

Maria del Guadalupe Davidson is Director of the Women's and Gender Studies Program and Co-Director of the Center for Social Justice at the University of Oklahoma, Norman, Oklahoma, USA.

Routledge Research in Gender and Society

Black Women, Agency, and the New Black Feminism

Maria del Guadalupe Davidson

Routledge
Taylor & Francis Group

NEW YORK AND LONDON

First published 2017
by Routledge
711 Third Avenue, New York, NY 10017

and by Routledge
2 Park Square, Milton Park, Abingdon, Oxon OX14 4RN

Routledge is an imprint of the Taylor & Francis Group, an informa business

Library of Congress Cataloging in Publication Data
Names: Davidson, Maria del Guadalupe, author.
Title: Black women, agency, and the new black feminism / Maria del
Guadalupe Davidson.
Description: Abingdon, Oxon ; New York, NY : Routledge, 2017. |
Series: Routledge research in gender and society ; 56 | Includes
bibliographical references.
Identifiers: LCCN 2016042057 | ISBN 9781138843677 (hardback)
Subjects: LCSH: African American women–Social conditions. | African
American feminists. | Feminism–United States.
Classification: LCC E185.86 .D3776 2017 | DDC 305.48/896073–dc23
LC record available at https://lccn.loc.gov/2016042057

ISBN: 978-1-138-84367-7 (hbk)
ISBN: 978-1-315-73092-9 (ebk)

Typeset in Times New Roman
by Wearset Ltd, Boldon, Tyne and Wear

For Scott

Contents

Acknowledgments

This book has been a long time in coming. I would like to begin by thanking Linda Perkins, who, after hearing me give a paper on this topic at the National Women's Association annual conference, invited me to speak at Claremont Graduate University. Linda, thanks for giving me the spark I needed to write this book. I would also like to thank my friends at the University of Oklahoma for their continued support of this project, especially Kirsten Edwards, Elon Dancy, and Melli Velazquez. And, a special thanks to my dear friend and brother, Dr. George Yancy. I'm so fortunate to have you in my life.

It has been a pleasure working with Routledge Press and I want to say a special "thank you" to Max Novice and Jennifer Morrow, who began this project with me, and to Elena Chiu and Emily Briggs, who got me to the finish line. I could not have asked for a kinder and more supportive team of professionals. Finally, I'd like to thank my friend, partner, *mi vida*, Scott Davidson, for walking through this world with me. Our kids (Yannick, Kolya, and Yelena) are so lucky to have you as their father.

Introduction
Agency Born of Struggle

In 2014, I was presented with the Feminist Teacher-Mentor Award from the Organization of Communication, Language and Gender (OCSLG). Although I could not attend the award ceremony, I sent along a note to share with those in attendance. A sampling of my comments read:

> I'm very sorry that I am unable to join you tonight. I am deeply humbled and honored to receive OSCLG's Feminist Teacher-Mentor Award. I grew up in an immigrant family where my Afro-Caribbean mother, sisters, aunts, and cousins did not talk about feminism, intersectionality, or the importance of mentoring. Nevertheless, I learned to be a feminist from those women who never let me forget that dark-skinned black girls from the hood were just as good as everyone else. They did not give me the language of intersectionality. They didn't have to because they lived it. What they did give me was the will to resist all forms of intersectional oppression.

Before I knew its name or knew that black feminism ever existed as a *thing* that one could read about, black feminism as an *act* of living and as an *act* of resistance saved me from a world that I knew did not value my existence. Time and time again, I have been given material proof that little girls who looked like me did not get the chances or positive attention other little girls got. The saying, "If you are white (or light), you are alright; if you are brown, get down; if you are black, get back, get back, get back" held real meaning for me, then and now. It is no wonder that early in my teaching career, I felt that it was my duty as a black feminist souljah gal to impart the relevance of agency to my students, especially my black women students. I saw the discourse of agency as a weapon given to me by my black feminist foremothers to be used against the forces of white and black male patriarchy, racism, and classism telling me that I could not act or resist. Those forces telling me to "get back, get back, get back." Agency was not only a weapon, it was also a command, as if my black feminist foremothers (both unpublished and published) had impressed upon me that the fight for black women's agency continues and that it is my responsibility to move ahead, never ceasing until every black woman has claimed agency as her birthright.

So, a few years ago, when I walked in to teach a class on African American Women, bearing the concept of agency—Prometheus-like (what arrogance!)—to my students, I took it for granted that although the black males, the white females, the white males—all of the *others* in the room might not know or understand everything that I was going to say (although many were certainly allies) that the black women would really *get it*, because, like me, they have really lived in a world that did not hear their voices and did not perceive them as legitimate actors. To my surprise, many of those young women sat there staring at me uncomprehendingly. I was astonished to be told by several of them that they did feel like agents, they saw black women enacting agency all the time, and that this agency thing didn't seem like a significant issue any longer.

After much deliberation, I would argue that my perspective—i.e. walking into that classroom and believing those black women would understand the import-ance of agency in the lives of all black women—was not a naïve one. My per-spective is firmly grounded in traditional black feminist discourse, that sees black women as sharing a unique standpoint because "black women's political and economic status provides [us] with a distinctive set of experiences that offers a different view of material reality than that available to other groups."[1] Based on our shared standpoint it was no stretch for me to believe that the black women in the room would understand the power of the gift that I placed in their hands. Black women far younger than I, whom I assumed based on our shared position as black and as women, should know where I am coming from. They would accept the gift of the discourse on agency that black women have passed down one to another for generations and then in their turn share the gift with others. They would be eager and willing to pick up the mantle and carry on with the struggle for black women's agency. My goodness, how wrong I was, but why? What the hell happened?

A simplistic answer is that I got a disconnected group of students, and if I had presented the material on agency to another group, that would have yielded results that matched my understood outcomes. Sensible, yes, but I don't think that is the case. The reception I got from those women actually is what I have found in countless other groups of young black women that I have presented this material to over the years.[2]

The difference is best summed up in the lyrics presented by juxtaposing the lyrics to "Sisters are doin it for themselves," sung by Annie Lennox and Aretha Franklin and those from Beyoncé's "***Flawless."[3] In "Sisters are doin it for themselves," Lennox and Franklin celebrate womanhood and powerfully command women to be proud of who they are. On the contrary, in "Flawless," Beyoncé sends mixed messages. On the one hand, the listener is uplifted by the message of Nigerian writer, Chimamanda Ngozi Adichie, reading from her essay, "We Should All be Feminist," while at the same time listeners may be taken aback and even offended by hearing Beyoncé calling women "bitches," and telling them to "bow down" before her. From these two examples we can see how traditional black feminists[4] set agency within a larger framework that includes individual freedom as well as the "conscious liberation of the female state." The cry that "sisters are doin it for themselves" is seeped in a second-wave feminist understanding of sisterhood as well as a third-wave feminist understanding of girl power. The lyrics—sung powerfully by Annie Lennox and that diva Aretha Franklin—and the sentiments espoused stand in stark contrast to the Beyoncé song "Bow Down/I Been On," in which Beyoncé tells women "this is my shit, bow down, bitches." What, on the surface, seems troubling is that Beyoncé has called herself a feminist (discussed in detail in Chapter 5) and she has been called the potential new face of feminism—feminism for a young generation—a woman not afraid to "fuck with the grays" (shout out to Joan Morgan, see Chapter 6). How do traditional black feminists, or for that matter younger black women, reconcile Beyoncé the potential new feminist icon and the Beyoncé of "bow down, bitches?" Do Beyoncé and others finally reveal the iteration of the long-awaited fourth wave of feminism—a feminism that is bad ass and is not working for the conscious liberation of the female state? Are we looking at a feminism where one of its key features is *agents without agency*?

The Struggle Is Real

I would be untruthful if I did not admit that I struggle with the concept of agency in Black Feminist Studies and black women's lives, and, at times, thinking about agency makes me feel unsettled and confused—in large part because of what seem to be divergent black feminist paths articulated by the following troubling questions that, for example, the persona of Beyoncé calls to mind. Namely:

1   Am I your "sistah" or am I your "bitch?"
2   Is it possible to occupy both roles or have both articulate black women's existence?
3   Is this all right?
4   How can we learn to sit with this tension?

The idea of occupying the unsettling space of both sistah and bitch feels, in a word, yucky. It is not as if Beyoncé singled out one imaginary black woman to throw shade at; she didn't name a name, she didn't give black women an out by allowing us to say "Oh, she's talking about so and so, not me." No, she called everybody a "bitch" and then had the nerve to tell us all to "bow down." Conversely, in her other song, "Run the World (Girls)." she talks about girls (a complicated category) running the world. Beyoncé's brand of feminism reads a bit too close to the virgin–whore dichotomy. Articulated in psychoanalysis, the virgin–whore dichotomy explains the limitation placed on (some) women. Because of the complexities and neurosis of male sexuality, women are not allowed the full range of their being. Freud wrote: "Where such men love they have no desire and where they desire they cannot love."[5] Either women are saintly, Madonna-like figures or they are jezebels. Similarly, the conflicting messages that we receive from Beyoncé's different songs: "Bow Down Bitches" and "Run the World (Girls)" point to a complexity and perhaps even neurosis of black women's relationships with one another and how we are portrayed in society. On one hand, we are "bitches" (think about the character of New York from the VH1 series *The Flavor of Love* or even NeNe from the *Real Housewives of Atlanta*) and the running the world image from Twitter hashtags like "blackgirl-magic" and Beyoncé herself. With these two very contradictory songs, Beyoncé puts these two images (and her conflicting feelings about) black women/girls in tension. Commence with the thought experiment.

I admit that I may be perplexed (but also intellectually engaged) by what I see as a new enunciation of black feminism (the elusive fourth wave). This stems from the fact that I am a traditional black feminist trained to see agency in a particular way—respectability politics seeping in here, but, hell, is it bad to expect people to act right, because when they act wrong, it reflects on all of us? Or, it may be that I am afraid that younger black women will articulate agency in a manner that I find threatening and damaging to the cause of black women's liberation. I mean, come on, Beyoncé, fuck! Words matter, and, like it or not, you are a black woman and people listen to you! Finally, it may be that I am so deeply invested in the concept of agency that I cannot bear the thought of it morphing into something that lies outside of my horizon of experience. So many questions ..., and, I don't know, maybe agency as it relates to black women's lived experience is just too damn complex for a thought experiment.

In addition to these queries, *Black Women, Agency, and the New Black Feminism* is rooted in twin semantic struggles. The first of which is the endeavor to comprehend the meaning of agency in young black women's lives today. Second, the struggle to bridge the apparent gulf that exists between traditional black feminists and younger black women centered on the following questions[6] related to black women and agency:

1   What does it mean to be an agent?
2   Are women like Beyoncé, Rihanna, Solange, and Nikki Minaj new incarnations of black feminism and black women's agency, or are they only pure fantasy in which, instead of having agency, they are in fact the products of the forces of patriarchy and commercialism?
3   Are young black women in general being led to believe that they have power but are really being drawn back into more complicated systems of exploitation and oppression?
4   Are young black women "flipping the script" by challenging notions of their subordinate and exploitable sexuality? In other words, "who is playing who?"

Consequently, *Black Women, Agency, and the New Black Feminism* explores what I see as a generational divide over such questions. While traditional black feminists may see new images of black women negatively as a retreat and an impediment to progress, younger black women may embrace these new images and see them in a positive light. After carefully setting up this divide, the book suggests that a more complex understanding of black feminist agency needs to be developed, one that is adapted to the complexities faced by the younger generation in today's world. In order to accomplish this, *Black Feminism After Agency* does the following:

1   Provides a historical perspective on the black feminist search for agency.
2   Postulates a gendered and raced phenomenology of the black female body in contrast to the gendered body in feminism and the raced body in black studies.
3   Compares and contrasts the perceptions of agency by traditional black feminists and young black women today.
4   Analyzes the connection between different perceptions of agency and different perceptions of black female sexuality.
5   Develops a new black feminism that resonates with younger women's conceptions of agency, sexuality, and race. For this, I use José Esteban's Muñoz's (1999) work on *disidentification* as well as reviving and rearticulating radical feminist interpretations of androgyny.[7]

Agency: Success and Failure

Traditional black feminism is the term I use to describe black feminist theory and criticism articulated from about 1960–1990. Much of the work done during this era highlights the following concepts and concerns (by no means an exhaustive list): black women speaking their own truths; resisting white and black male patriarchy; calling out white women's racism; the importance of black women's sexuality; coercive reproductive technologies; the role of the state in women's lives; and finally agency as the linchpin holding all these concerns together.

From a traditional black feminist perspective, it is indisputable that the many gains that have been achieved by black women are based on black women never being "passive victims nor willing accomplices to their own domination."[8] Agency is the foundation that black women's resistance to systems of oppression is built on. Agency here is simply defined as having *the ability to act and to be recognized as an actor*. Before going much further, it is important to note a few things: first, there is no *one* action that constitutes agency. Agency is reflective of a multiplicity of actions undertaken by black women with the intention of defying systems of oppression and domination. Second, we should see black women's actions in the context of a non-hierarchical, multiple, interconnected system of response (many of which are not recorded) to the brutalities they still face and have faced in America. In this way black women's agency is rhizomatic and, as such, it defies western knowledge systems based on hierarchical order.

For Deleuze and Guattari, the rhizome is a way to talk about *becoming* "with no prescribed form or end."[9] U.S. Black women enacting agency does not have a beginning point, that is to say that there is no one action on the part of one black women (or a group of black women) to which all the other acts can point back as the origin of black women's resistance—i.e. the moment where black women reached for agency. Thus, there are incalculable moments of black women asserting their agency some documented, like Harriet Tubman leading an insurrection against the US government, or Harriet Jacobs choosing who is to be the father of her children, or Mamie Till choosing to open her son's casket. These are documented points in black women's quest for agency. And, though we are happy to have these artifacts, many more instances of black women claiming their agency are lost to history because they involved everyday acts of defiance and everyday assertions of will that did not get recorded. Knowing or not knowing these everyday acts of agency seems, on the one hand, inconsequential, not because they are unimportant, but because they were so *everyday* they don't rise to the level of exceptional. What does seem important is that we recognize that those unrecorded acts of claiming subjectivity have laid the groundwork for black women making bold proclamations of agency on the most public of stages. For a more recent example of a black woman reaching for agency in a public way, because she was influenced by everyday black women performing agency, we need look no further than Shirley Chisholm and her remarkable political career.

Chisholm was the first black woman to be elected to Congress and the first black person (of any gender) to run for president on a major Party ticket when she sought the Democratic nomination in 1972. Though she did not secure the endorsement, Chisholm successfully garnered 172 votes and won primaries in Louisiana, Mississippi, and New Jersey. Throughout her presidential campaign and tenure as the Congresswoman from NY, Shirley Chisholm provided a perfect example of black women's public struggle for agency. Chisholm, the daughter of immigrant parents, represents, as expressed in a *Black Feminist Statement*, all that white capitalist patriarchy sought to subjugate, yet there she stood as an agent—acting, rather than being acted upon. Take, for instance, when Chisholm was first elected to Congress and was given a seat on the House Agricultural Committee. As she represented New York's 12th District, which included parts of Brooklyn, Manhattan, and Queens, Chisholm felt that she would do her constituents little good in that position.

Chisholm then did the unthinkable for a junior Member of Congress. She asked to be reassigned to a different committee—and was. Chisholm was placed on the Veterans Affairs Committee, which, though not her first choice, she accepted, noting that: "There are a lot more veterans in my district than trees." Later, Chisholm was assigned to the Education and Labor Committee, which was her first choice. One of the greatest moments of her presidential campaign came when she visited George Wallace in hospital after an assassination attempt on his life had failed. George Wallace, also running for the Democratic nomination, was a notorious segregationist, who upon being elected Governor of Alabama, stated in his inaugural speech:

> In the name of the greatest people that have ever trod this earth, I draw the line in the dust and toss the gauntlet before the feet of tyranny, and I say segregation now, segregation tomorrow, segregation forever.[10]

Visiting Wallace took great courage. Chisholm knew that her supporters would be angry, and she knew that the media might try to turn the visit into a spectacle. Nevertheless, she visited Wallace out of compassion, stating that she wouldn't want what happened to Wallace to happen to anyone. In that moment, we again witness Shirley Chisholm *daring* to be herself. Women like Shirley Chisholm embody the black feminist demand for agency, and we should note that one does not reach the heights that she reached without the support of a community that told her she could. Chisholm saw herself as a "catalyst for change." Speaking later about her tenure in Congress and her running for the presidency, Chisholm writes:

> I want history to remember me not just as the first black woman to be elected to Congress, not as the first black woman to have made a bid for the presidency of the United States, but as a black woman who lived in the 20th century and dared to be herself.[11]

To some, Chisholm's words—especially the comment that she "dared to be herself"—may sound like bravado or braggadocio, but, other than Sojourner Truth's question "ain't I a woman?," there may be no truer articulation of the black feminist struggle for agency since struggle to *be one's self*, the struggle *to self-define*, the struggle to be seen as having the ability to *self-name*—these are the hallmarks of agency.

Circling back to the original issues this book began with, namely, the tensions between older and younger black women on the question of agency, we might ponder the following "with women like Chisholm and those everyday sista souljah, why would young black women today look to Beyoncé, for example, as a black feminist agent?" This is the central question this book hopes to answer.

The Structure of the Book

Chapter 1 The Constructed Agent: Postmodernism, White Feminism, and Black Male Agency

Chapter 1, "The Constructed Agent: Postmodernism, White Feminism, and Black Male Agency," provides an in-depth analysis of agency, while at the same time complicating postmodern feminist models of agency by Susan Heckman, Rosemary Tong, Luce Irigaray, and Teresa de Lauretis. Many postmodern feminist thinkers regard agency, not solely as a natural capacity, but as constructed or developed out of social relations. As such, one becomes an agent in relation to another agents or non-agents. Through the opposition of one agent to another, the characteristics of agents are determined. From this point, the chapter analyzes how black male theorists like Charles Johnson, Frantz Fanon, and other prominent black male theorizers have defined agency. Particular attention is paid to how Charles Johnson explains agency in his (2001) essay, "A Phenomenology of the Black Body."[12] What needs to be called into question is Johnson's narrow focus on the black male body and how it is objectified by white society. Either Johnson incorrectly assumes a universal experience that encompasses black men and black women, or his attempts at inclusion are disingenuous. Indeed, there is no point in his essay where black women can see their full selves. The chapter concludes by arguing that while white female and black male interpretations of agency provide beneficial and necessary resources, they do not fully account for the specificity of the black female experience and expressions of agency in the socio-cultural history of American society.

Chapter 2 Historicizing Agency in the Black Feminist Tradition: A Phenomenology of the Black Female Body

Chapter 2, "Historicizing Agency in the Black Feminist Tradition: A Phenomenology of the Black Female Body," begins with the argument that achieving agency for black women has been long and arduous. The chapter goes on to present various challenges to black women's articulations of agency. This first section spotlights the ways in which the black women's agency was challenged through silencing their voices and marginalizing their bodies. To be more specific, black women's attempts to gain agency during the first wave of black feminism focused on the issue of silencing, and concluded with how black women sought to deflect attention away from their bodies. One way that they did this was by making sure that their language was referential—that is, directed toward others. In this way, black women were able to gain agency by speaking about and for their concerns for others, thereby redirecting society's attention away from their bodies. Indeed, the strength of the early black feminist movement was its ability to *downplay* the body of black women.

The second section presents black feminist constructions of agency through reference to theorists like Alice Walker, bell hooks, Audre Lorde, Francis Beale, Angela Davis, Alice Walker, Beverly Guy-Sheftall, and Patricia Hill Collins. Here the focus is placed on black women's return to and reflection on the black female body as a place of agency. Most important to this section is Audre Lorde's use of the erotic. Lorde believed that the erotic was indeed a site of power and that black women needed to tap into the erotic and see it as a critical site from which to challenge racism and patriarchy. Based on this analysis, over time it can be seen how black women activists and theorists have developed the following markers of agency: voice, resistance, community, and piety; elements that are unique to the black feminist tradition. The third section concludes by discussing the challenges to traditional notions of black female agency. The final section of this chapter views how younger black women are redefining the body as they argue for viewing the commodified body as a site of agency. This section provides a sharp contrast to early black feminist desires to disassociate agency from the marginalized black female body.

Chapter 3 Worrying the Feminist Line

Chapter 3, "Worrying the Feminist Line" presents the generational divide between traditional black feminists and younger black women today on the question of agency. The first section discusses the following issues that challenge traditional black feminists' notions of agency: the culture of commodification; the reclamation of once inflammatory words like "bitch," "ho," "badass," and "ratchet;" blurred gender lines; the rhetoric of racial and gender inclusion; emotivism; the new sexual liberation. The second section poses the question of whether new articulations of agency reinscribe black women as other and deviant or whether young black women are *flipping the script* on agency by offering innovative and exciting ways of being a black woman that indeed liberate black women from past objectification, by claiming objectification as a site of resistance. The chapter concludes by discussing why this new articulation of agency may be seen as problematic, i.e. the tension that it causes with older black women, and how the two sides can find, if not clear consensus on what constitutes agency, at least a middle ground that acknowledges difference in black women's theory of agency.

Chapter 4 Millennials: Black Women Forming and Transforming Agency

Chapter 4, "Millennials: Black Women Forming and Transforming Agency" focuses on how traditional black feminism can reach out and engage those young women who are looking for, in the words of Joan Morgan:

> a feminism that would allow them to explore who [they] are as women—not victims. One that claimed the powerful richness and delicious complexities inherent in being black girls now—sistas of the post-Civil Rights, post-feminism, post-soul, hip-hop generation.[13]

If we seek to validate young black women and also affirm the traditional black feminism that got us here, the dilemma is as follows. On the one hand, if black feminism simply gives up its prior occupations and reaches out to young black women where they are today, then it risks losing some of the key insights and critical tools that have defined it. On the other hand, if black feminism does not redefine or reconstruct itself at all, then it runs the risk of losing touch with those young women or not reaching them at all. The second section proposes a possible solution to this dilemma, though it is likely to be almost as controversial as the problem that it is trying to solve.

To do this, first, I engage José Estaban Muñoz's (1999) discussion of *disidentification* where Muñoz importantly shows how theorists of color can balance conflicting positions. So, on the one hand, we understand the power, for example, in the colonial gaze and how it frames bodies of color; yet, on the other hand, we do not deny the pleasure we may receive from the framing of such images as well. Disidentification allows us the opportunity to hold conflict in tension, and from this tension, a new more liberatory discourse can emerge. Second, I turn to an important insight from the Radical Feminist Movement of the 1960s and the 1970s. While I do not agree with all of their views, what intrigues me is their notion of androgyny. In this section I link androgyny and disidentification to a new black feminist agency. The third section discusses the disidentificator force of the word "bitch" (and also playing with Beyoncé's refrain "bow down bitches"). I see this as an affirmation of a different kind of ambiguity from the one that Joan Morgan seems to valorize in her (1999) book, *When Chickenheads Come Home to Roost* and the rigidity of traditional black feminist thought when it comes to the question of agency. Within the context of hard core hip-hop and young black women's play with agency, I think that Joree Freeman's disidentified androgynous bitch can provide a good model of how the new black feminist theory can begin to "fuck with the grays" of agency, to borrow Morgan's phrase, without playing into the hands of any power structure. To spell out the compromise more concretely: while, for Morgan, it may be a matter of gaining benefits by sacrificing power, and, for traditional black women, it might be a matter of claiming power on a par with others, under the new black feminist articulation of agency, the "bitch" is about getting benefits *and* power conventionally and unconventionally—with neither representing a privileged path.

Chapter 5 Troubling the Water: Black Feminist Theory and the Hegemony of Thought

Chapter 5, "Troubling the Water: Black Feminist Theory and the Hegemony of Thought ," presents a broader vision of the future of black feminism. At stake here is whether or not black feminists will have a guiding hand in shaping "a new gender politics" for younger women today, who exist in between hip-hop culture and Michelle Obama. This can only happen if traditional black feminists are willing to open the door for other expressions of agency to enter into the discourse. They must be willing and open to addressing it in a way that creates dialogue with younger women who, like Joan Morgan, ponder (non-jokingly) questions like: "Can you be a good feminist and admit out loud that there are things you kinda dig about patriarchy?"[14] They need to invite a discussion with the woman who may have just come back from the club, who wears a multi-colored weave and has long, painted nails, and who calls her closest friends her bitches. Or she may be a college student with a high GPA, who by day is the president of the student government and at night blogs about all of the guys she slept with, giving us the play-by-play of where they did it, how good/bad he was, and whether or not it was worth her time.[15] Or she may be a black lesbian biker chick, who is a member of the Tea Party. In any case, they are the ones who will eventually forge this new black, gender politics—and it is important that the politics that they shape is rooted in feminism not fantasy.

Chapter 6 Conclusion: On the Grayness of Gray

This book makes it clear that traditional black feminists must realize that younger black women are entitled to structure and define the struggle for agency and agency qua agency from their own embodied position. Although I firmly believe in the importance of agency in black women's lives, and I remain committed to the concept of agency in black feminist studies, I also acknowledge that the only way that agency will remain relevant to young women is if they are allowed to create a space where they can engage agency theoretically and through their lived experience without getting checked too much by old heads like me.

Notes

1 Patricia Hill Collins, *Black Feminist Thought: Knowledge, Consciousness, and the Politics of Empowerment* (New York: Routledge, 2000).
2 Special thanks to Linda Perkins, who after hearing me present for the first time on the issue of black women and agency (all of eight pages back then) at the 2011 National Women's Studies Conference, invited me to Claremont Graduate University to present on a panel.
3 Beyoncé released this song in 2013 under the title "Bow Down Bitches/I Been Down." She rereleased this song (now titled "***Flawless") in 2014 on her self-titled album. This new version included the speech, "We Should All Be Feminists" by Nigerian writer Chimamanda Ngozi Adichie.
4 I use this term throughout the book to describe black women scholars from the 1960s to the 1990s and those of us who remain heavily influenced by their work.
5 Sigmund Freud, *Collected Papers*, vol. IV (London: Hogarth Press, 1949), trans. Joan Riviere, p. 207.
6 These questions are not exhaustive. I chose them because they are directly related to the problems presented in this text.
7 José Esteban Muñoz, *Disidentifications: Queers of Color and the Performance of Politics* (Minneapolis: University of Minnesota Press, 1999).
8 Ibid., p. 184. Patricia Hill Collins, "The Social Construction of Black Feminist Thought," in Beverly Guy-Sheftall, ed., *Words of Fire: An Anthology of African American Feminist Thought* (New York: The New Press, 1995). p. 339.
9 Charles J. Stivale, ed., *Gilles Deleuze: Key Concepts* (Montreal: McGill-Queen's University Press, 2005), p. 100.
10 George Wallace spoke these words during his inaugural address as the Governor of Alabama on January 14, 1963.
11 Shirley Chisholm, *Unbought and Unbossed* (Boston: Houghton Mifflin, 1970), p. xiii.
12 Charles Johnson, "A Phenomenology of the Black Body," in Beverly Guy Sheftall, ed., *Traps: African American Men on Gender and Sexuality* (Bloomington, IN: Indiana University Press, 2001).
13 Joan Morgan, When Chickenheads Come Home to Roost: A Hip Hop Feminist Breaks it Down (New York: Simon & Schuster, 1999), pp. 56–57.
14 Ibid., p. 57.
15 This example is related to the stir created by 2010 Duke University graduate, Karen Owens, who gave a PowerPoint presentation called the "Fuck List." For more on this, see "Karen Owens Shatters the Glass Ceiling," in Duke's student newspaper, *The Chronicle*, online edition, October 4, 2010. See also "College Girl's PowerPoint Fuck List Goes Viral," on the website *Jezebel*, September 30, 2010.

1   The Constructed Agent
Postmodernism, White Feminism, and Black Male Agency

Defining Agency: Choice, Rationality, and Recognition

There are three principal intersecting markers of agency. The first is having the ability to choose. The distinction between the human agent and the non-human actor resides in the ability to be led by deliberation rather than instinct or ignorance, it is the ability to determine oneself rather than be determined by another. Being an agent, in the simplest terms, means that one has the *capacity* to choose *to do* or *not to do* something. So, for example, a dog may not choose if it wants to take a walk, but presumably the human walking the dog exercises great choice including the time of the walk, the route, the distance, etc. Human agents are therefore different from non-human actors, since, as one commentator puts it, actions by human actors are in "control" over what they do while non-human actors are guided "by innate or conditioned reflexes and instinct."[1] The second marker of agency is rationality. To be an agent means that our choices are guided by rationality. Thus, "Rational actors always act out of a well-defined interest in their own personal welfare."[2] Rational actors are clear about their desires and have what it takes to achieve a particular end goal. This view of agency is significant because it understands agency as based on ability—meaning the ability to think in a rational way and the ability to use rational thoughts to one's own advantage.

The final marker of agency is having one's agency recognized by others. Of the three, recognition may be the most difficult marker to explain, since we might argue that as long as one sees oneself as an agent, it does not matter what others think of you. To a certain extent, we might agree with this, especially when we think of the recognition that comes in the form of "praise and esteem."[3] Nevertheless, there are forms of recognition that are consequential to one's humanity. Or put more firmly by Cillian McBride, there are forms of recognition that "some are willing to sacrifice their lives for."[4] Martin Luther King Jr. and other civil rights warriors provide obvious examples of a form of recognition one is willing to sacrifice one's life for. King and others knew that speaking for black people's humanity was tantamount to suicide, yet they spoke out nevertheless, because being seen as human was worth the cost. Characters like Patsey in the film *Twelve Years a Slave* also provide us with examples of forms of recognition that are worth great sacrifice. In the film, the viewer cannot help but feel sympathy for the way she fights for recognition of her basic humanity and disgust at how she is treated. In one dramatic scene, Patsey is accused by her enslaver of disappearing without telling him. He accuses her of running away, but we learn that she has gone to get a piece of soap to wash herself, because her enslaver's wife, Mary Epps, denies her this basic dignity. The desire for personal care, to have a clean body, to be recognized as human to Patsey, is important because it prevents her enslavers from reducing her to an "animal." Though she is severely beaten, her demand for recognition in that instance was worth, it seems, dying for.

In addition to this example, Charles Taylor also provides us with clear discussion of the recognition that "some are willing to sacrifice their lives for," in the seminal text, *Multiculturalism*. Taylor writes:

> Our identity is partly shaped by recognition or its absence, often by *mis*recognition of others, and so a person or group of people can suffer real damage, real distortion, if the people or society around them mirror back to them a confining or demeaning or contemptible picture of themselves. Nonrecognition or misrecognition can inflict harm, can be a form of oppression, imprisoning someone in a false, distorted, and reduced mode of being.[5]

As cited by Taylor, two powerful examples of the dangers of misrecognition or nonrecognition come from feminist scholars' explanation of the internalization of patriarchal beliefs about women's inferiority, and from the impact of white supremacy on the black psyche. The examples that Taylor offers are similar to our understanding of the stereotype threat where those in minority groups are "placed at risk of confirming, as self-characteristic, a negative stereotype about [their] group."[6] One well-known study shows that if girls are told that they will perform worse on math tests before they take a math test, their scores will be lower. In this case, the girls' performance conforms to the negative message. The statement "girls score lower" acts like a trigger causing the low performance.

Misrecognition, and I would also add nonrecognition, have serious consequences for out-groups not simply because there is an inherent "lack of due respect" but moreover because misrecognition, and nonrecognition, "can inflict a grievous wound, saddling its victims with a crippling self-hatred," lowered performance, feelings of not belonging, and the negative effects of the imposter syndrome. Thus, "Due recognition is not just a courtesy we owe people. It is a vital human need."[7] We might say that due recognition is *the* ethical imperative of our time.

Constructivist Understanding of Agency

As we continue to contemplate agency in terms of choice, rationality, and recognition, I would suggest that we should likewise consider the possibility of conflict between agents. Stephan Fuchs provides insight into this subject with his discussion of constructivist agency. Since an individual is unaware of what other individuals are doing or thinking and likewise are (unless otherwise told) typically unable to discern why an individual acts one way rather than another, this can lead to conflict. For this reason, Fuchs advocates a constructivist rather than a realist approach to agency, which would simply assume in advance that not everyone has agency. In this way, agency is something that can be granted or denied and various "societies" and, to paraphrase Fuchs, "cultures" decide independently how to grant agency and to whom.[8]

Constructivism of this kind seems to suggest that the granting or withholding of agency can be seen as arbitrary. Though I largely agree with the constructivist approach to agency—i.e. that agency is something that may or may not be ascribed—nevertheless, I would challenge the manner in which Fuchs and others shy away from discussing concrete and, more importantly, controversial ways in which society constructs agency, based on the intersecting markers of choice, rationality, and recognition, all of which correspond (directly or indirectly) to the interlocking categories of race, class, and gender. As an illustration of his claim, Fuchs examines the benign examples in which societies may ascribe agency "to our pets" but not, for example, to an amoeba. Or, how we might see a fully functioning adult as an agent but not an adult who is in a temporary or permanent vegetative state or one who suffers from mental health issues.[9]

Instances of this sort are not without merit, but they do not come close to dealing with the substantive struggles over agency that take place in the social world between actors who are not "insane or comatose" but fully capable of expressing themselves in such a way that their intentions should not be misconstrued. Furthermore, when we examine genuine conflicts in the social world, two basic observations emerge: first, agents have conflicts with other agents; second, as a result of these conflicts, some agents (including some groups of agents) are sometimes deprived of their agency. These observations become apparent when we consider a social world made up of gendered and raced beings.

Constructing Agency from White to Black Feminism

In approaching the issue of gendered and raced agency within a social context, our first cue can be taken from the work of white feminists who have deliberately historicized and gendered their treatments of agency. White feminist interest in the issue of agency is best understood when placed within the broader framework of subjectivity. Susan Heckman writes of subjectivity: "[T]he feminist argument is that the subject as it has been conceived at least since Descartes is gendered, not generic."[10] Thus, feminism has sought to challenge the masculinity of the subject, since the masculine subject is at the heart of women's oppression. Like the Cartesian subject, we should also see that the agent as gendered male. Also like the Cartesian subject, a marker of male agency is rationality or the ability to reason. As explained by Rosemarie Tong, liberal feminists tend to accentuate the "moral" or the "prudential" nature of reason. "When

reason is defined as the ability to comprehend the rational principles of morality," writes Tong, "then the value of individual autonomy is stressed." On the
other hand, "when reason is defined as the ability to determine the best means to
achieve some desired end, then the value of self-fulfillment is stressed."[11]
Though there is a difference in whether emphasis is placed in regard to moral or
prudential reasons, liberal feminists from both camps agree that: "A just society
allows individuals to exercise their autonomy and to fulfill themselves. Liberals
claim that the 'right' must be given priority over the good."[12]

White liberal feminists clearly understand that positioning women as incapable of rational action continues their subjugation while also denying them the
right to exercise their autonomy. Indeed, "Our entire system of individual rights
is justified because these rights constitute a framework within which we can all
choose our own separate goods, provided we do not deprive others of theirs."[13]

To see women as without agency is tantamount to stripping away the basis
for all other rights (e.g. life, liberty, the pursuit of happiness) *guaranteed* to individuals by society. What are these rights without the ability to *act* and to *self-
determine*?

As we move forward in our discussion, it should be noted that though the
agent and the subject are similar in function the agent and the subject remain
distinct in that the category of subjectivity entails a far broader discussion, as it
encompasses not only agency but also issues related, for example, to transcend-
ence. The agent is a particular facet of the subject and manifests the subject's
capacity to execute and be recognized as an actor. This is important because we
are dealing with whether one is a *free* person with the ability to act or whether
one is a person who is *determined* and thus lacks the said ability. This may be
read as an essentialist understanding of agency, and I'm fine with that because
simply too much is at stake.

Since agency is embedded in subjectivity, white feminists are not merely
interested in critiquing the transcendental nature of subjectivity, they are also
analyzing the subject's ability/inability *to realize its agency*. And much like subjectivity, white feminists are not interested in dismantling or displacing the
notion of agency; rather, they are interested in how women come be seen as
agents.

Attempts to shift the discussion away from subjectivity continue to be problematic for white feminists, especially since it is primarily white male postmodern thinkers who have professed the death of the subject. "French theorists
have boldly declared the 'death' of man, the subject … despite their difference,
[they] have all called into question the major tenets of the subject-centered epistemology of modernity,"[14] as if the discussion of subjectivity were *passé*.
Heckman explains that calls to decenter the subject are varied. So, for example,
Derrida asserts that the subject-centered theory of modernity "fails to describe
the play of meaning in language." Lacan, on the other hand, "criticizes a fixed,
transcendental subject as inadequate to explain the psychological process by
which a 'self' is created." Yet, it is Foucault who, as stated by Heckman,
presents us with the strongest analysis of subjectivity. Foucault, Heckman writes:

"argues that the transcendental, constituting subject of the Cartesian tradition is inadequate to describe the conditions of the subject in the contemporary world, subjects who are constituted by the powerful forces of modern life." She continues, for Foucault: "The subject of modernity has been a means, if not the means, of the subjection of subjects that characterizes modernity, that is, that subjectification entails subjection."[15] Although I am sympathetic to arguments that support the decentering of the subject (especially arguments advanced by Foucault), however, like Heckman, I believe that not only has the Cartesian subject been generally oppressive to those on the outside of its sphere (and this encompasses a wide range of people), for white feminists the subject of modernity has always: "been conceptualized as inherently masculine and thus has been a significant factor in maintaining the inferior status of women."[16] Where among our esteemed postmodern male scholars is the gender critique of the subject?

It makes little sense to decenter the Cartesian subject without first analyzing and challenging those attributes of the Cartesian subject that made it not only a dominant force in the world but also a prevailing force in the lived experience of women (of all hues), who were not just left outside of its definition but were figured (at least in gender terms) as its antithesis. In response (and resistance), Heckman writes that, for feminists, "the postmodern attempt to decenter the subject is both unfair and premature"[17] particularly since women have not had the opportunity to claim the subject position. Heckman continues, "Braidotti expresses this sentiment very precisely in her statement that 'in order to announce the death of the subject, one must first have gained the right to speak as one.'"[18]

Though it is not my intention here to go much further into this broader debate, however, I want to suggest that feminists, both black and white, are likely to agree with aspects of the above observation, including the important point that "in order to announce the death of the subject, one must first have gained the right to speak as one." And, I would further add, that black and white feminists are likely to agree with Heckman and Braidotti, precisely because they connect the question of subjectivity with the question of agency (which Braidotti's point alludes to).

In fact, Heckman herself observes this theme when she notes the connection between agency and the Cartesian subject. As cited by Heckman, Teresa de Lauretis is at the forefront of such an inquiry, since de Lauretis seeks to "retain agency by grafting elements of the Cartesian, constituting subject onto a constituted subject."[19] Some feminist thinkers tend to regard agency as constructed out of social relations. As such, one becomes an agent in relation to another agent or non-agent, and the marker of agency in both cases is the ability to assert one's self. Through the opposition of one agent to another agent or non-agent, the characteristics of each agent are determined. Taken concretely, white feminists have figured the agent (those having the ability to act) as male, and they have depicted the category of female in opposition to male agency. It is through such relations to male agents, in the feminist analysis, that women (a worrisome category) are limited or deprived of their ability to act. The role of misogynist ideas and discriminatory practices against women is precisely to further limit or deny women the power to act or be recognized as agents.

Black Feminists' Critique of Agency

Like their white feminist counterparts, black feminists are also apprehensive about the displacement of the postmodern subject, and like de Lauretis, our apprehensions are linked to the importance we give to agency. After all, what is the point of white feminists supporting the postmodern party line in dismissing subjectivity or considering it no longer relevant, if all women to various degrees have been denied one of its core features? Agency—understood as the ability to act and to be perceived as an actor—for traditional feminists (white and black) is valued as a site of resistance. Where the traditional black feminists' treatment of agency will depart from that of white feminists, however, is in their emphasis that the construction of agency is not only *gendered* but also *raced*. To the white feminists' figuring of the agent as male, traditional black feminists will add that: the agent is not only *male* but that the agent is also raced, that is, the agent is a *white male*. Inasmuch as the black female stands in opposition to the white male in race (read power) and gender (read power), traditional black feminists recognize that it is the black female who stands most in opposition to white male agency. For this reason, it could be argued that black women fare the worst in a society structured in terms of gender and racial hierarchy. Since black women "have always embodied, if only in their physical manifestation, an adversary stance to white male rule and have actively resisted its inroads upon them and their communities in both dramatic and subtle ways,"[20] it should also come as no surprise that black women scholars were some of the first to emphasize the "interlocking system of oppression"—race, class, and gender and how this system of oppression works to limit or deny black women's agency.

The most notable and articulate in a long history of black feminist protestations directly related to agency is "A Black Feminist Statement" by the women of the Combahee River Collective (1978). The black women of the Combahee River Collective positioned themselves as sister outsiders, and they saw themselves as outsiders as the result of the historical agential antagonism between themselves and white men. Traditional black feminists never acquiesced to being placed on the periphery of society (where they often found themselves and their discourse); nevertheless, they have used their marginal position to argue for societal change and to assert counteraction. In subversive articulations like "A Black Feminist Statement" and Michele Wallace's "A Black Feminist's Search for Sisterhood," there is no doubt that agency is framed as a crucial site of resistance. Traditional black feminists understood that power was needed to change *the system*, and the site of power for black women was their lived personal experiences. From their individual experiences and from acknowledging not only the everyday indignities but also the everyday acts of defiance came the realization that black women's agency was fundamental to challenging their subordinate status in society. As stated by the women of the Combahee River Collective: "We believe that the most profound and potentially the most radical politics come directly out of our own identity ..." They go on to make it clear that no one else's struggle should supercede that of their own and that all they demand is for black women to be seen as "levelly human."[21] Here we see a direct transfer from the formal constructivist account of agency to the concrete situation in which it is raced and gendered. Rejecting the arbitrariness with which society can give or refuse agency, traditional black feminists see the affirmation of agency as nothing less than an ethical and moral call to be seen as human—neither above nor below other agents—just *levelly human*.

A tangible example that helps to demonstrate the danger of a black woman being *or being perceived as* without agency from a traditional black feminist perspective is provided for us by Dorothy Roberts. In her well-researched and thought-provoking book, *Killing the Black Body*, Roberts recounts the narrative of an enslaved black girl under the age of 10, who was raped by another enslaved person named George. During the trial for this crime (a surprising event given the time), George's lawyer did not argue that George suffered mentally or physically, nor did the lawyer argue that his client was falsely accused. Rather, as Roberts recounts, the lawyer "argued that the criminal code did not apply because the victim was also a slave."[22]

One way to interpret this is that a ruling in favor of the little girl would undermine the slaveocracy because it might grant enslaved women (girls) some legal recourse to sexual abuse by other slaves (although none against white males). Yet a more compelling interpretation from a traditional black feminist perspective would suggest that ruling in favor of the little girl would be tantamount to *recognizing her agency*. The little girl would be seen as a person with the *ability to act* rather than only being determined by situations. Saying that the criminal code did not apply because she was a slave meant that any atrocity—no matter how cruel or brutal—could be done to her. She was classified as a non-agent, without choice, reason, or recognition in the face of brutal circumstances. Just as a table cannot sue you for kicking it or a wall cannot sue you for punching it or a bug cannot sue you for squashing it, so too the court found that the little girl could not say *no* to her rapist and technically, she could not be raped at all. Due to her station, she lacked agency altogether that is, the power to act, reason, or to resist, as well as the power to choose one thing or another. The court's ruling defines the slave girl who is raped as having no ontological resistance, as simply being a thing. Importantly, Roberts reminds us that, at that time, the crime of rape "committed against a white woman was a capital offense."[23]

Instances like this illustrate the lived experiences of black women and help to clarify why traditional black feminists have emphasized the importance of agency in their writings.[24] In the face of brutal enslavement, traditional black feminist are responding not only to cases like the one above but also to laws like *partus sequitur ventrem*, which translates as "the child follows the condition of the mother regardless of the race of the father."[25] Such laws virtually enshrined the condition of enslavement, at the same time as allowing white men to rape black women with impunity. In traditional black feminist theory, then, the call for agency—to act like an agent and to be perceived as an agent—is a call to be more than an object. It is a call to gain the power of bodily and representational resistance against others.

Agents Without Agency: One Manifestation

The ability to discern the difference in agency between white men and black women is not challenging. History gives us myriad examples of white men acting as agents in *flesh* and in *mind* and black women's bodily and representational agency being denied, ignored, questioned, or placed in peril. Phillis Wheatley's experience when trying to get her first book of poetry published provides yet another instance of the dichotomy that exists between white male and black female bodily and representational agency. Before Wheatley could have her book of poetry published, Wheatley had to stand before a group of white men to answer questions about the legitimacy of her text. This shows that it is one thing for Wheatley to *see* herself as a poet (agent), yet it is very different thing for white society to recognize Wheatley (a formerly enslaved black woman) as a poet (agent). The idea of agency (humanness) being connected to a critical imagination, as well as the belief that producing art requires a higher level of being, have a long history.

A recent articulation of this can been seen in Saul Bellow's often quoted culturally insensitive questioning: "Who is the Tolstoy of the Zulus? The Proust of the Papuans? I'd be glad to read them." What he seems to be getting at is that these cultures have not produced high literature. We might also read Bellow as implying an evolutionary hierarchy that places western culture at the top and black and brown non-western culture at the bottom. Bellow attempted to clarify his remarks later in a *New York Times* op ed., by arguing that his comments were taken out of context and that he "was speaking of the distinction between literate and preliterate societies." Bellows then goes on to explain that "preliterate societies have their own kinds of wisdom ... The fair thing, therefore, is to make allowance for what we outsiders cannot hope to fathom ..." On Bellow's account, since wonder and violence exist in all societies, we should expect "primitive" people to behave like others.[26]

Unfortunately, the explanation is almost as bad as his original comment. Bellow's clarifying remarks reek of paternalism, cultural superiority, and indeed an attitude that still seems to privilege white, male, western voices above others. There is also a failure on Bellow's part to critically interrogate the lens he uses to evaluate western and non-western peoples. This failure (blindness) leads Bellows—and has led so many others—to occupy a space from which to argue universal truths as if it were ever possible to reason from nowhere.

Thomas Jefferson provided yet another example of the historical tension between seeing one's self as having a critical imagination, yet not being perceived in this way by others when he wrote:

Among the blacks is misery enough, God knows, but no poetry. Love is the peculiar oestrum of the poet. Their love is ardent, but it kindles the senses only, not the imagination. Religion indeed has produced a Phillis Wheatley; but it could not produce a poet.[27]

According to Jefferson, it seems poetry is not produced through sorrow, for if that were the case, then blacks and First Nations people might well be considered among the greatest poets this country has ever produced. What produces poetry is love, as Jefferson says that "love is the peculiar oestrum of the poet." According to Michael Beran, what Jefferson means by this is that:

[L]ust is transformed by the *oestrum* of poetry—its frenzied sting, what the Greeks called its "divine madness"—into the higher passions known as love. It was an overcoming (or mending) of mind through art. Art made possible the higher forms of order such as love. It supplied the techniques that enabled men to turn what Jefferson called "eager desire" into something that "kindles" not the "senses only" but the "imagination" as well. These processes changed lust into love, passion into noble architecture, bloody revolution into liberty, and so on.[28]

Although we might appreciate Beran's thoughtful and articulate interpretation, it is important not to read Jefferson's musings on black people's inability to produce poetry as merely an enunciation on the idea of love itself, rather we should read it as a critical reflection on race, gender, and agency. Likewise, as "love is the peculiar oestrum of the poet," Jefferson believes that black love cannot bring forth poetry, because black love "kindles the senses." Black love is debased; it is contained at the level of the body and results from blacks interacting with their senses (taste, touch, sight, smell, hearing). Since blacks are embodied creatures, Jefferson believes things that the body cannot sense or that are on a higher plane, such as the creative imagination—where poetry presumably comes from—are impossible for blacks to understand or enact. Given this assessment, what are we to do with black poets like Phillis Wheatley? In order to adequately address this question, some background on Wheatley is necessary.

Phillis Wheatley's America

Wheatley, the first black women to publish a collection of poetry in America, was abducted from her home in Senegal when she was around 8 years old and enslaved by John Wheatley of Boston, MA. It is often said that Phillis Wheatley was an incredibly talented child, so much so that the Wheatley family allowed her to receive an education—a rare and illegal activity at the time. Wheatley's collection, *Poems on Various Subjects, Religious and Moral*, was published in 1773. Although it is held to be one of the great literary achievements of black African people, the publication of Wheatley's collection was not without issue. For his part, Henry Louis Gates calls the publication of Wheatley's book of poetry, "One of the most dramatic contests over literacy, authenticity, and humanity in the history of race relations in this country."[29]

In his lecture, "Mister Jefferson and the Trials of Phillis Wheatley," Gates tells a riveting tale about how Phillis Wheatley (all of 18 years old) had to stand before some of the leading male figures in Boston who, as explained by Gates, "had one simple charge: to determine whether Phillis Wheatley was truly the author of the poems she claimed to have written." Gates is certainly correct when he sees Phillis Wheatley's trials as a "contest over literacy, authenticity, and humanity," but we should also see the questioning of Phillis Wheatley as a contest over her agency. In this case, Phillis Wheatley was not recognized as a actor or as a person with the ability to speak for herself *and* be believed by others—she was not an agent in the traditional sense or her authorship would not have been called into question. The white men in the room called there to question her were agents. Upon completion of their inspection of Phillis Wheatley, the six white men wrote the following judgment:

> We whose Names are under-written, do assure the World, that the Poems specified in the following Page, were (as we verily believe) written by Phillis, a young Negro Girl, who was but a few Years since, brought an uncultivated Barbarian from Africa, and has ever since been, and now is, under the Disadvantage of serving as a Slave in a Family in this Town. She has been examined by some of the best judges, and is thought qualified to write them.[30]

Although Phillis Wheatley was able to publish her poetry, first, in London and finally in America, the fact of this statement being issued does not afford Wheatley agency, since she was unable to act on her own and have her actions seen and respected by others. Those elements of agency: choice, rationality, and recognition, were denied to her.

The examples of Saul Bellow's unfortunate comments about Zulus and Papuans and the disheartening case of Phillis Wheatley speak to the precarious position of being an agent without agency. While there seems to be a certain acknowledgment of the humanness of Zulus, Papuans, and Wheatley, what Bellows and Wheatley's inquisitors cannot fathom is a sense of intentionality embedded in the being and action of black people and people of color that would allow them to create art. The concept of intentionality, because it is connected to agency, literally seems to baffle Bellow, Jefferson, and Wheatley's white male inquisitors when intentionality is applied to non-whites and non-white women. That body x could produce art on par with body y seems disturbing to fathom. Black women in particular have over a long period of time had to craft tools to resist whites' rejection of the intentionality of their actions.

Complicating Agency, *Still Brave*

Phillis Wheatley is but one individual in a long line of black women whose agency has been questioned, thus from this perspective her case seems fairly easy to analyze—white men working out of their own whiteness and maleness deny a specific black woman her agency—from a traditional black feminist perspective, it is open and shut. What is more difficult to examine is how agency is *differentiated between* oppressed groups who at times *work together* to resist white male racism and patriarchy. In this case, I am referring to black women, white women, and black men.

Because black women and white women can typically coalesce around the issue of *gender* discrimination, and black women and black men can align on the issue of *racial* discrimination, there is a danger of failing to comprehend how these points not only of alliance but also of shared history, suffering, and resistance can cloud and complicate our understanding of agency. Traditional black feminists, like Gloria T. Hull, Patricia Bell Scott, Barbara Smith, Beverley Guy-Sheftall, and Kimberlé Crenshaw, have all argued that black women's position *as blacks and as women* and many times *as poor* gives black women a unique history and socio-historical viewpoint that white women and black men do not have. The necessity to make this history and black women's difference from white women and black men not only clear but also distinct, precipitated the need for Black Women's Studies, which is not a subfield of women's studies or race studies but its own unique discipline.

The editors of *Still Brave* put it succinctly when they write:

> Although Black women had been instrumental in helping establish Black Studies, the field remained male centered, while Women's Studies privileged middle-class white women as the norm for what it meant to be female. Because Black Studies and Women's Studies *failed* to adequately address the unique experiences of women of African descent in the United States and around the world, a few brave women created a new field—Black Women's Studies—to provide a conceptual framework for moving women of color from the margins to the center of Women's Studies: for incorporating gender analysis into Black Studies...[31]

Although one purpose of *Still Brave* is, as the subtitle suggests, to show that Black Women's studies is dynamic and ever evolving, we should also note the way that the title also suggests that black women are still fighting for a place. Hearkening back to its predecessor *All the Women Are White, All the Blacks Are Men, But Some of Us Are Brave*,[32] *Still Brave* reminds us that black women are not only *still brave* primarily because they have to be, because there is a real sense that all the "women are [still] white" and "all the blacks are [still] men," so not much has changed. This is not to say that white women and black men have not experienced limits on and even denial of their agency, because they certainly have, or that the struggle is not real for them as well, but it is to suggest that there exists not just a *hierarchy of agency* but also a *gradation of agency* in society. The ability to distinguish between these two positions is critical if we are to understand black women's unique struggle for agency and the tension black women's unique struggle may pose to the concept of alliance.

Although Miri Song notes: "There is no one definition or indicator of racial hierarchy (or inequality) which is used consistently in either the USA or Britain,"[33] nevertheless, based on US and western racial history, it is possible for us to map a *racial hierarchy*. Post enslavement and post our traditional understanding of Jim Crow, our understanding of a racial hierarchy has certainly become more complex and nuanced, since the master–slave dichotomy that existed under slavery and the quasi-feudal system that existed under Jim Crow no longer provide the primary systems of racial stratification in society, making it unquestionable who was at the bottom of the racial pyramid. In today's post-civil rights era, markers such as access, equity, wealth and trait desirability help delineate racial hierarchy in society. In Figure 1.1 we can see that the apex of racial hierarchy continues to be white, simply because whites fare best in US society because, as a group, they tend to have greater access, to be wealthier, and to continue to have their physical features privileged. And while a much longer and more nuanced discussion needs to happen on this issue, we might conclude that to a varying degree Native Americans,[34] Asians, and Latinos all occupy subordinate positions to white identity. At the bottom of this racial hierarchy is

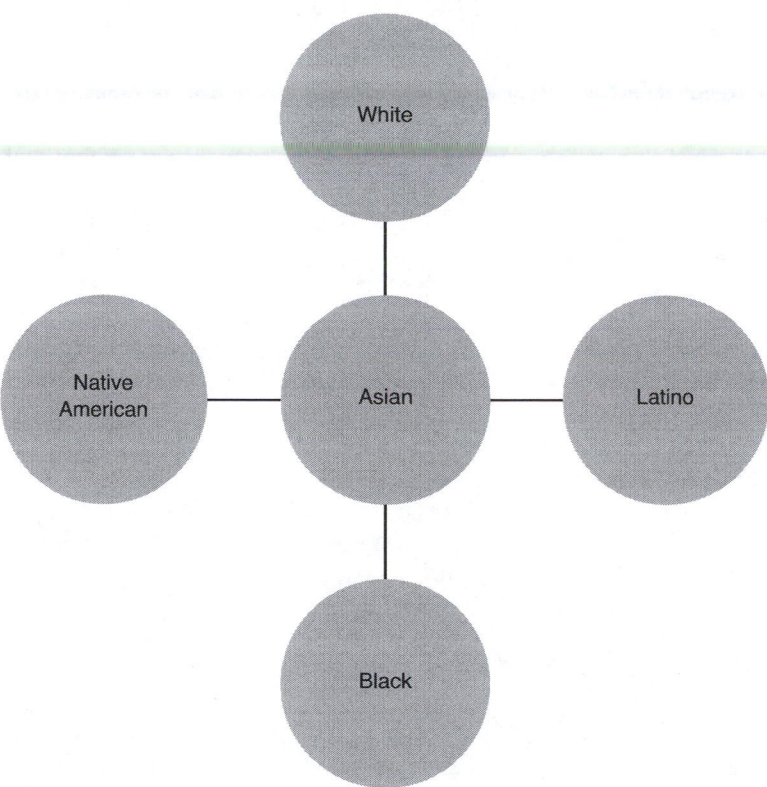

Figure 1.1 American Racial Hierarchy.

black, which means that when comparing markers like access, wealth, and desired traits, blacks by and large fair poorly to whites. Blacks' position at the bottom of the racial hierarchy has remained stubbornly fixed for over 200 years.

Citing Joe Feagin, Song "notes the high level of white effort and energy put into maintaining antiblack racism" as one of the many reasons why African Americans are at the bottom of the racial hierarchy.[35]

As mentioned above, discussions of racial hierarchy help us understand group participation in or exclusion from society, as well as access and treatment or mistreatment of one group by another. Yet, if we are to understand the full impact of agency on a person's life, we need to have a more complex discussion that takes into consideration things like gender as well as race, class, and nationality. Indeed, these particular indicators can further help us assess who is able to enact agency and *to what degree* that agency may be enacted. Moreover, paying attention to these particular indicators allows us to be responsive to the different experiences of subgroups. Large, monolithic categories such as GENDER, RACE, and CLASS may be false and deceptive ways to discuss marginalization, difference, and hierarchy because these categories suggest that intersectional dynamics are not at play. Large, monolithic categories also suggest a solidarity between and even equality of members in such groups—this is the point about alliance that is being made. Black feminist scholars have time and time again argued against the way we structure race and gender specifically, because such structuring is not reflective of black women's lived experience. In other words, black women are not *just* black or not *just* women, they are deeply impacted by both categories. And simply because we share one aspect of our identity and history with another out-group should not mean that privilege between groups is eliminated. One way to illustrate this is by depicting agency in terms of the Venn diagram (Figure 1.2).

As shown in Figure 1.2, white men in society sit at the apex of agency and this has to do more with them being white and male. Based on the markers of agency discussed earlier, white men also have the following characteristics that solidify their agency:

- White-men have the ability to choose to do or not to do something.
- They are perceived as rational actors.
- Their agency is recognized by others and is rarely placed in jeopardy.

Although white women and black men do not exercise anywhere near the agency of white men, we can see how each of these out-groups share important characteristics with white men that allow them, if not full agency, certainly partial agency, based on the degree to which they intersect with the racial and gender characteristics as embodied by white males.

To simplify, white women gain advantages and in-group status based on their whiteness *and* proximity to white males (as mothers, wives, daughters, etc.). Scholars such as Tim Wise and Peggy MacIntosh have spelled out the benefits of whiteness and white skin privilege.[36] How white women benefit from white

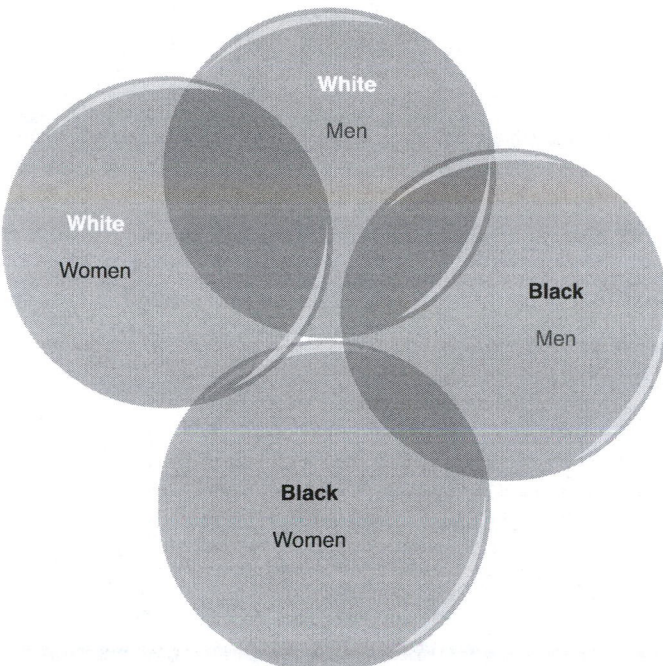

Figure 1.2 Relational Agency.

male patriarchy may be more difficult to flush out, as white feminists like Betty Friedan have illustrated how dangerous white patriarchy has been for white women.[37] Yet, unpleasant as it might be to hear, white patriarchy protects white women as well and offers them benefits that women of color do not have access to. My colleague calls this the "daughters of the plantation syndrome."[38] What this means is that white patriarchy will protect what it perceives to be its own. This protection may come in the form of affirmative action or diversity programs at a university that benefit white women disproportionately. Or, protection may come in the form of violence against non-white males who threaten white women's purity. Take, for example, the following verse from black folklore:

Black Man: Oh Lord, will I ever?
White Man: No, nigger, never!
Black Man: As long as there's life, there's hope.
White Man: And as long as there's trees, there's a rope.[39]

One way we might interpret this is black folks warning black men to stay away from white women. Conversely, we might read it as black men's supposed desire for white women; their inability to leave white women alone because white women's bodies mean something that black women's bodies could never articulate.

For Eldridge Cleaver, the *something* that white women's bodies represented was the idea of freedom. Cleaver writes:

> I know that the white man made the black woman the symbol of slavery and the white woman the symbol of freedom. Every time I embrace a black woman I'm embracing slavery, and when I put my arms around a white woman, well, I'm hugging freedom. The white man forbade me to have the white woman on pain of death. Literally, if I touched a white woman it would cost me my life. Men die for freedom, but black men die for white women, who are the symbol of freedom.[40]

Yet to complicate this matter further, in the case of Cleaver's and others' suggestions about why black men prefer white women, it seems that all the attention is placed on *black male* desire or what *black men* should (not) do with this supposed desire. Might we, instead, focus on white males and what makes the white female body worthy of protection? Doing so turns the focus away from black male desire and places it squarely on white patriarchy which—admittedly, to an extreme—sees white women's bodies as precious enough not just to control, but to kill for. No one, to my knowledge has ever gone to this extreme for a black woman's body. Black women's bodies on a whole do not inspire this kind of perverse fidelity.

Alternatively, black men have an advantage over white and black women based on their maleness or proximity to patriarchy and other forms of male power. In a society supported by patriarchal principles, one way we might see black maleness benefiting from patriarchy was during the 2008 race for the White House when Barack Obama won the presidency. That President Obama certainly had a sense of history on his side and a charisma that is not often seen is an understatement. Nevertheless, Senator Clinton was the victim of sexism and misogyny throughout her campaign from the press and the men she competed against. In his book about Clinton, Shawn J. Parry-Giles noted:

> When an unidentified woman asked John McCain, "How do we beat the bitch?," Ed Henry of CNN's Election Center charged that McCain "laughed it off, instead of slamming it for being demeaning." Barack Obama would likewise be condemned for his jest that Hillary Clinton was "likable enough" after a moderator from a New Hampshire debate asked Clinton "why some voters seem to like Obama more." Henry framed Obama's words the following way: "Sexist? Not really. But condescending? Bigtime."[41]

Some of us might take issue with the last part of this statement, by stating that many times men enact condescension when they are working out of a sexist orientation. During the election, Obama's gender and his ability to enact patriarchal authority played a role in his winning the presidential election. In so much as white women and black men both occupy out-group status, nevertheless each have proximity to white male privilege. As a result, white women's *whiteness* and black men's *maleness* provide them with the ability—even if it is limited—to enact agency and be perceived as agents in ways that black women simply cannot.

In saying this, traditional black feminists not only contribute to the ongoing critique of agency (and subjectivity for that matter) but they do what black male scholars who see *race to the detriment of gender* and white female scholars who see *gender to the detriment of race* do not—they show that by combining both gender and race in the body of black women, it is the black female who truly stands in opposition to white male agency, and, therefore, it could be argued that they fare the worst in a society structured in term of gender and racial hierarchy. Not having white skin privilege or being gendered male, or by and large having access to personal wealth place black women not only outside of the subject position, but also on the margins of agency (i.e. their ability to act in their own interest and to be viewed as self-constituting, and having their agency recognized by others is severely curtailed).

Even as we work to better understand not only the racial hierarchy but also issues of proximity and power, this presents us with an opportunity to flush out the complexities of agency between black women and black men. The bond as allies between black men and black women by virtue of their shared history and shared kinship is stronger than the bond between white women and black women (gender) or white men and black men (patriarchy). While we discussed white feminist approaches to agency earlier in this chapter, at this point it would be beneficial to turn our attention to black male agency and the difficulties associated with black men's agency and black women's being in the world.

The Complexities of Black Male Agency

Like all forms of agency, black male agency is complex. Going back to our original definition of agency in the Introduction, agency is the ability to act and be seen as an actor. Like white women and black women, black men have had to face particular and unique challenges to their agency, challenges that become more complex when patriarchy is introduced. In so much as white women can define the idea of womanhood, so too, white men embody the totality of maleness. It goes without saying, but like black and white women, black male agency has had to develop in the social, political, and historical context of white male agency. What makes black men's struggle for agency different from that of black women and white women is that black men (as shown in Figure 1.2) share a gender affiliation with white men, but although this gender affiliation does not always translate into full access to patriarchal power, it does provide black males with status and at times access.

At this point, two issues come to the forefront. First, black men's struggle for agency is not merely a race-based struggle. it is a gender-based struggle as well—with both race and gender being equally important to black men's social, economic, physical, and political existence. As a consequence, whereas black and white feminists are fighting so that those gendered females are deemed equal to those gendered males—thereby disrupting the gender binary that favors male over female—though black men have fought to disrupt and destroy racism, it can be argued many black and white feminists have engaged in committed and thoughtful struggle to dismantle patriarchy, however, black men by and large have sought to fully participate in it.

Thanks to the history (and sometimes heroics) of photojournalism, we are fortunate enough to have iconic images from the Civil Rights Movement. One such image that remains a part of America's cultural iconography is that of an African-American man holding a sign that reads, "I am a Man." In fact, this is not an isolated image, there are several instances of black men, as recently as during the protests in 2014 in the Missouri town of Ferguson, bearing signs that read, "I am a Man." One way to "read" these signs is to say that *man* stands in place of *human* so that black men holding such signs are signaling their humanness to a society. The "I am a Man" signs reference slavery but also pre-slavery when black (and brown) people were seen and treated as less than human. The philosopher Charles Mills provides insight into the positing of black and brown people as less than human in his seminal text, *The Racial Contract*. Mills writes:

> By virtue of their complete nonrecognition, or at best inadequate, myopic recognition, of the duties of natural law, nonwhites are appropriately relegated to a lower rung on the moral ladder (the Great Chain of Being). They are designated as born *unfree* and *unequal*. A portioned social ontology is therefore created, a universe divided between persons and racial subpersons, *Untermenschen*.[42]

The sign "I am a Man" confronts blacks' social position as "*Untermenschen*" while at the same time it works to shame white society for its abuse of black people and for creating a two-tiered system made up of free and unfree "citizens."

To be sure, this analysis represents one way that the historical bearers of the sign "I am a Man" intend their message to be interpreted—again that "man" stands in the place of "human"—however, I would point out that I have never seen someone who identifies as a woman carrying an "I am a Man" sign. If this were to happen, would we so readily make the connection between the sign "I am a Man" and the call to a universally understood meaning of what it means to be human? Highly unlikely. For all its good intentions and its promotion of a simple but radical idea, the "I am a Man" sign, nevertheless, is a deeply gendered image with profoundly gendered motives. Since this is the case, what we should then ask is: *who is the sign for?* Much like its historical predecessor "Am I Not a Man and a Brother?," which, in 1787, became the seal of the Society for Effecting the Abolition of the Slave Trade, the "I am a Man" sign is designed to appeal to white male-dominated society. It is a plea as well as a demand for white male patriarchal society to see and treat black men as equals, and equality here means allowing black men the ability to fully participate *as men* in patriarchy.

Manning Marable's "Grounding with My Sisters" supports this analysis by looking at the way that black men strive to fully participate in patriarchy. Marable writes: "Black social history, as it has been written to date, has been profoundly patriarchal. The sexist critical framework of American white history has been accepted by Black male scholars …"[43] In his essay, Marable does an excellent job exposing the history of black male patriarchy, not only on slave plantations but also in the black churches post-enslavement, which were "dominated by Black men, who served as pastors, evangelists, and deacons," as well as in black newspapers and the "New Negro Convention Movement."[44] Turning our attention back to the "I am a Man" sign, we see the continuation of black male efforts to fully participate in patriarchy, based on their gender affiliation with white men. What we also see is the frustration that occurs among black men, including some black male scholars, when their protestations are not heard and their maleness is not recognized.

Essentializing the Black Experience

In his very compelling book, *Black Bodies, White Gazes*, George Yancy shows us not only how bodies speak but are also encoded with particular meaning.[45] He also reflects on how bodies are defined in relation to one another. This is not to say that "I" am not capable of self-definition, but it speaks to a truism, namely, that I am also defined by how the *other* sees me. This binary is simply inescapable. Consequently, when dealing with the racial history of this country, one reason that problems arise is because the black body historically finds itself *on the business end of the black–white binary*—i.e. minoritized and exploited. Yancy goes on to explain that because of the nature of white supremacy, there is the unsupported argument that the white subject exists outside of its oppositional social construction, which posits blacks as "inferior." This means that white identity is not dependent on anything for its identity, which, to Yancy, is simply not true. The positioning of the white subject outside of signification and marking is certainly made more problematic since black identity is based on its historic position as other to white subjectivity; and it is this that "informs [his] sense of agency,"[46] and Yancy concludes that "the black has been confiscated." This confiscation has occurred historically, for example, as part of the forced enslavement of blacks, lynching, experimentation on the black body, as well as medical iconography that showed how the black brain was less developed than the white brain, the prison industrial complex (where now there are more black men of a certain age imprisoned than are in college), etc.

It is because of this historical confiscation of the black body that Yancy feels comfortable in making an analysis about a situation that once occurred while he was riding an elevator with a white woman. He states, "I feel that in their eyes I am this indistinguishable, amorphous, black seething mass, a token of danger, a threat, a criminal, a burden, a rapacious animal of delayed gratification."[47] Yancy goes on to assert that in certain social spaces not only the *history* of white racism but also *actions* can communicate racism to blacks, creating a situation where one suffers internally from the external manifestation of racism (e.g. feelings of discomfort). Blacks may also suffer from existential manifestations as well which may "result in a form of self-alienation, where the integrity of one's Black body is shaken, though not shattered. Self-alienation can assume various forms, self-doubt to self-hatred."[48] This is not the alienation that Marx referred to where one is alienated from one's work, it is the kind of alienation that Charles Mills refers to where "under white supremacy, one has an alienation more fundamental; since while one can always come home from work, one cannot get out of one's skin."[49]

Yancy's discussion follows a long line of black male thinkers, like W. E. B. Du Bois, Frantz Fanon and Charles Johnson, engaged in a qualitative assessment of the lived experience of blackness under white supremacy and patriarchy. Like Fanon's description of riding the subway in Paris before the little white child accosts him, and Du Bois' eloquent story of the well-educated Tom who returns to the South a new man, Yancy sees himself as neat, clean, "well dressed" and under no circumstance a threat to anyone, especially in a public space. Although Yancy has the trappings of success, he is wearing something more meaningful than clothing or more important as a marker of his being: he is wearing his race. To Yancy, the white woman's body communicates to him "look at the black."[50] Again Fanon is instructive, as he explains how the white person looks at his black body, not to ogle it, but rather to mark it as different and dangerous. For Yancy, the only language the woman sees/hears communicated by his black body is that "I'm threatening." She sees him (so he believes) as a criminal, "she sees me as a threat."[51] Yet for Yancy, "She is one of the walking dead unaware of how the feeling of her white bodily upsurge and expansiveness is purchased at the expense of my black body."[52] This is the lack of empathy that Janine Jones cites in her powerful work; the woman could not see Yancy as anything other than a potential perpetrator but as a consequence she also doesn't see how her false positive identity is purchased at the expense of the black identity.

For Yancy, there is no issue of deed; a question of whether his black body did something to elicit this white response to it—meaning, was he threatening in some way, did he make a false move? This kind of questioning puts the onus on him to be still, to self-regulate in the face of the white woman's gaze, as if he has to be aware of his black body so that it is not perceived as a threat. For Yancy, "the question of deed is irrelevant. I need not do anything."[53] All things thought of as black are bad, Satan is black, etc. So Yancy says: "It is as if my black body has always already committed a criminal deed … there is not anything as such that a black body need to do in order to be found blameworthy."[54] It is this that curtails freedom. The woman in the elevator does not see him; if she saw him, she would have to challenge her own racism (and this is something that most white people cannot do).

Like Fanon on the Paris metro, Yancy's experience presents us with a opportunity to unpack a few things related to racism, patriarchy, and essentialism. White men (or white people in general) might look at Yancy's discussion and question his thoughts about his "maleness" and the threat it has posed to women in general. For example, they might say, "Well, any woman might clutch her purse tight at the sight of a man she did not know." Though certainly a possibility, we might interpret this response as deflection away from what Yancy sees as a matter of race to one about gender and women's general concern about their public safety, especially around strangers. Eliminating race from the equation invalidates Yancy's concerns, but it also suggests that white women interface with all men in the same way, regardless of race. More darkly, a white man (person) may be tempted to think, "Well, black men are more violent," thus it makes perfect sense that a white woman would be afraid. But does it? Black men on a whole are not more violent than any other males in society. How black men are framed in the media may account for this assessment. Furthermore, this analysis supports Yancy's and Fanon's argument that a black man is never taken as an individual, that the group represents the individual. Black people, *in general*, will appreciate Yancy for calling out the banality of racism expressed not only in the white woman's actions but the responses to Yancy's critique because many black Americans suffer daily from the everyday indignities of racism. These everyday indignities include not being able to get a taxi and being followed in stores. Black people can agree with Yancy's exasperation with "not doing anything" or of always already being thought guilty.

Yancy's "the elevator effect" seems like a well-staged play where all the actors know their parts, but who is the star of this twice-told tale? This question is deliberately asked. Because Yancy is the teller of this tale, his perspective dominates, thus it is "easy" to see him as the protagonist and the white woman as the antagonist. Yet there seems to be another character whose role is as important as Yancy's or the white woman's and that is the role played by black hetero-patriarchy. Like the narrative told by Fanon, Yancy's story (full of sound and fury) is written from a black male perspective that seems to dominate most discussions of race and race analysis. In this way, it becomes difficult if not downright impossible for black women *as a group* to *see* themselves in Yancy's scenario, since there is little space to theorize black women's lived experience in such examples. We might sympathize with Yancy, as well as stand in solidarity with him and other black men, but truly seeing ourselves in the place of Yancy, perhaps, is more challenging because patriarchy, maleness, the masculine gendered nature of the narrative are barriers.

Black Women's Distinctiveness: Pivot This Way[55]

As discussed earlier, black feminist scholars have tried to situate black women's struggle for agency within the broader struggle for racial and gender equality, so that, in order to liberate themselves, black women believe that they must combat racial, gender, and more often than not class discrimination. Because they are called to fight battles on several fronts, black women correctly see their struggle as unique, intersectional, and interlocking. Yet, getting others to acknowledge black women's unique, intersectional, and interlocking position has been a challenge since black women have historically been (for lack of a better term) *claimed* as comrades by black men who correctly argue that black women and black men have a shared racial history. Conversely, white women have also *claimed* black women as allies (though to be sure, not to the degreem that black men have done so), based, they argue, on shared gender affiliation—again which is true.

Yet, and here is the navigational challenge for black women, when those who are not black or women choose black women's group affiliation, or make claims about black women's group affiliation based on the argument of *sameness* (racial, gender), or decide using any other criteria which group black women *naturally* fit into, an important part of black women's agency is lost, i.e. the ability to choose which group best serves their needs without being pressured. What is also lost is black women's assertion that their experiences (e.g. herstory, interaction with sexism, racism, and white supremacy, and racialized patriarchy) are in fact distinct from the experiences of white women and black men and should be treated as such.[56] Anthologies such as *All the Women Are White, All the Blacks Are Men, But Some of Us Are Brave* speak to the historical silencing and sublimation of black women's experiences. It is a shame that 20 years after the publication of that historic text, Beverly Guy-Sheftall and others believed it necessary to release the follow-up anthology, *Still Brave.* And they did so because black women's experiences are *still* not seen as unique. The reason why black women's struggles are subsumed into those of black men and white women is complex and multi-layered. A less complicated (and perhaps cynical) way to address the sublimation of black women's struggles into the struggles of others is to say that this occurs merely because black men and white women *benefit* from the addition of numbers, in this way, black women become bodies in the room who help bolster a cause that does not altogether fit their needs.

Influential critics like Ann duCille discuss how black women's bodies are constantly used as support structures for others' causes or used for the purpose of building the academic careers of non-black women. There is a sexiness about studying black women, perhaps as duCille alludes, because embedded in black women's bodies and social position is so much *tangible wrong*. duCille writes: "Within and around the modern academy, racial and gender alterity has become a hot commodity that has claimed black women as its principal signifier ... Why are black women always already Other?"[57] A consequence of this always already "othering," black women's voices are typically silenced and our stories are co-opted. The irony, as shown by duCille, is that when placed in *any* dichotomous relationship, black women's bodies are devalued, yet black women's bodies, narratives, and lived-experiences are also a valued site of inquiry for non-black women. Furthermore, duCille questions how we should think about non-black women producing much of the present-day scholarship about black women and reaping more "commercial success than that of the black female scholar who carved out a field in which few 'others' were then interested."[58]

In this way, black women's bodies, lives, etc. take on a certain functionality, serving to bolster academic careers as well as social movements. We saw this most profoundly during the Black Power, Civil Rights, and Women's Rights Movements. In each case, black women's bodies served different functions and were used to support the claims for others. For example, in the Black Power Movement, not only do we see a clear and violent articulation of black male patriarchy, we also see clear articulations that black women's place in the movement is, in Stokely Carmichael's estimation, "prone." Recounting her experiences with the Black Power Movement, Michelle Wallace states: "As I pieced together the ideal that was being presented for me to emulate, I discovered my newfound freedoms being stripped from me, one after another."[59] Wallace's article, "A Black Feminist Search for Sisterhood" shows how it is not black women's voices but their bodies that served a critical function during the Black Power Movement. And the way that black women were positioned— mothers, cooks, tools for sexual gratification, and in some cases as an enemy of black masculinity—did much in the way to silence black women altogether, or, at the very minimum, limit their choice of expression. As Wallace's essay shows, the co-dependent relationship that black women and black men have developed over the long history of racism has been the most difficult to critique, challenge, and sever.

The feminist movement, which we should code as mainly white and middle-class, also used similar tactics to the Black Power Movement, in that white feminists too desired to count black women in their ranks, based on a limited and uncomplicated notion of "sisterhood." Yet time and time again many white feminists fell back on marginalizing and silencing black women based on race. One example of this is when white women held a strategizing meeting at Sandy Springs, where they did not want black women to be present because black women would complicate the meeting by bringing in race, make the meeting unproductive, and make those present feel bad. On the other hand, white women also saw how important it was to have some black women support the movement. What these examples show is that black men and white women take a utilitarian approach to dealing with black women; black women benefit movements only to the extent that they serve to push a particular agenda. And, as has been shown, the agenda is typically not one that advances black women's needs or acknowledges their *difference* in a way that does not commodify their difference.

Where You Sit and Stand

To say that black women's experiences are distinctive is in some ways similar to feminist standpoint theory, which argues, that "society is structured by power relations that generate unequal social locations . .. The different social locations that women and men occupy cultivate distinct kinds of knowledge."[60] By highlighting "power relations," feminist standpoint theory provides an avenue to critique patriarchy. For women of color, standpoint theory (even if it did not set out to do this) also opens up a space for fruitful questioning to take place over the different "power relations" that exist between people of different racial categories as well. Thus, not only can we look at how the "different social locations that women and men occupy cultivate distinct kinds of knowledge," we can also analyze how the "different social locations" that blacks and whites "occupy cultivate distinct kinds of knowledge." A limitation of feminist standpoint theory is that it does not offer a suitable way to address the complexities of living in a body marked by race and gender difference.

Taking what I see as a more overtly and consciously intersectional approach than feminist standpoint theory, Patricia Hill Collins posits what she refers to as "an afrocentric feminist epistemology." Much like standpoint theory, "black feminist thought ... reflects the interests and standpoint of its creators."[61] Hill Collins advances "four tenets of black feminist epistemology."[62] Hill Collins' first argument is that a subject's knowledge is built on lived experience. So knowledge is never divorced from one's own personal involvement. Another way to think of this is as situated and experiential knowing—knowledge is developed out of specific situation and context. The second tenet of Hill Collins' black feminist epistemology is that knowledge emerges from interaction and dialogue with others. Like Paul Ricoeur and Jürgen Habermas, there is a clear sense that black feminist epistemology sees the *self* as dialogically constructed and emerging from interactions with others. Third, since knowledge is never divorced from one's values, Hill Collins argues for an awareness of self and an *empathetic* approach to dealing with others. Finally, a black feminist epistemology "requires personal responsibility," since "knowledge is simultaneous assessment of an individual's character, values and ethics." In this way, Hill Collins shows that knowledge is never divorced from the knower; knowledge is embedded not in systems but in people who act. Consequently, black feminist epistemology requires that subjects take responsibility for themselves and their assumptions. So, for example, it is not for the *other* to either confirm or deny the subject's assumptions, rather it is for the subject to see how she/he imposes his/ her assumptions on another, and how these assumptions can endanger or challenge—in our case—the other's *agency*. This is the *pivoting* mentioned earlier; it is a turn toward the direction of the other. When we turn toward the direction of the other, we acknowledge the other's position as opposed to always demanding that the other turn to face the subject's position. To pivot or to turn toward the other is to acknowledge the situatedness of the other. This may not necessarily disrupt the balance of power between the *subject* and the *other*, but it does open up a space of respect as the subject acknowledges that the other is embedded in his/her own narrative.

Another way to think about black women's distinctive social location and lived experiences is through the perhaps unorthodox lens of *Miles's Law*. Coined by Rufus E. Miles—who worked as an Assistant Secretary under three American presidents—the saying "where you stand depends on where you sit" is typically used in the field of management primarily to describe advocacy of issues based on one's position and relationship in a given organization. Miles's Law has been called both "intuitive" and limiting for various reasons. Rufus E. Miles actually developed this saying:

> When an employee left the bureau [of the Budget in 1948] to work for another federal agency, Miles observed that the departed employee would soon become a staunch defender of his new agency and a vocal critic of the bureau because "where you stand is where you sit."[63]

Miles, perhaps unbeknownst to him, not only hit upon a bureaucratic truism, he also presents gender-race scholars another way to analyze the importance of positionality where we might equate "standing" as one's position (political and social) on a given issue, and "sitting" as one's actual physical, metaphysical, and philosophical social location. To put Miles' Law "where you stand is where you sit" more concretely, we need look no further than the women of the Combahee River Collective, who in a "Black Feminist Statement," do a superb job explaining where black women stand. They write:

> The most general statement of our politics at the present time would be that we are actively committed to struggling against racial, sexual, heterosexual, and class oppression, and see as our particular task the development of integrated analysis and practice based upon the fact that the major systems of oppression are interlocking.[64]

As expressed by the Combahee River Collective, where black women's "sit" (physically, metaphysically, and philosophically) is directly related to their oppositional *stand* against racism, sexism, and patriarchy. Speaking in a collective voice they state:

> [W]e would like to affirm that we find our origins in the historical reality of Afro-American women's continuous life-and-death struggle for survival and liberation. Black women's extremely negative relationship to the American political system (a system of white male rule) has always been determined by our membership in two oppressed racial and sexual castes.[65]

Yet, here is the rub—despite these passionate, eloquent, and historically grounded articulations of black women's epistemology and lived experiences, which clearly articulate where black women "sit" and "stand," black women tend, nevertheless, to be figured together with either black men or white women. Consequently, black women are called to sacrifice either their gender or their race for causes that may not align with their own interests or support the development of their agency. Given this, perhaps three of the most pressing questions we must answer are:

1   What does it mean to be a black woman in the hierarchy of race and gender politics?
2   What will it take to have black women's agency to be acknowledged specifically by their allies?
3   What would a phenomenology of the black female body look like?

The End of Subjugation

Before we move too far into our analysis of these questions, perhaps we should begin by starting with what we know to be indisputable about black women: namely, being neither white nor male, black women stand in opposition to white male ontology. This does not make black women the *yin* to the white male *yang*, which would imply a complementary or even mutually beneficial relationship. Rather, what is implied is that black female identity is the *fun-house mirror* image of white male identity. When placed in contrast to white male identity, black women's identity appears to the world opposite and distorted. One might be tempted here to make a connection to W. E. B. Du Bois' double-consciousness, where double consciousness implies a twoness to one's identity. Du Bois writes:

> It is a peculiar sensation, this double-consciousness, this sense of always looking at one's self through the eyes of others, of measuring one's soul by the tape of a world that looks on in amused contempt and pity. One ever feels his two-ness, an American, a Negro; two souls, two thoughts, two unreconciled strivings; two warring ideals in one dark body, whose dogged strength alone keeps it from being torn asunder.[66]

When placed in opposition to white male identity, black women do not necessarily experience, I would argue, a sense of "warring ideals." For Du Bois, there is certainly an external struggle that takes places between black bodies and white society. But I would argue that in *The Souls of Black Folks*, blacks struggle with white society usually manifest *internally*. Moreover, the struggle than Du Bois so powerfully spoke about is a deeply gendered struggle—that is the struggle is primarily between the black male psyche and white society. Contrariwise, Patricia Hill Collins' controlling images expertly explain what we can see primarily as an *external* struggle between black women and white society where the images of the mammy, the matriarch, the jezebel, and the welfare mother transform the black female body in forms or tropes relatable to white society.

Another way to say this is that controlling images frame the range of performance that black women's bodies can engage in, based solely on the white and male gaze. Since controlling images are a more physical (external) rather than a psychological (internal) assault on black women, it should be of no surprise that black women's resistance to controlling images has been in the form of bodily resistance rather than psychological. So that, the more wanton white society says black women are, the more black girls are told to "close their legs."

The more "loud" black women are, the more black women seek to temper their justified rage and their joyful expression so as not to be labeled "ghetto," "angry," and "disruptive." Based on the firmly established gender and racial binary as well as white men's historical mistreatment of black women's bodies, it becomes rather simple to point the finger at white men as the sole and main source of black women's oppression. When closing "A Black Feminist Statement," the authors state:

> In her introduction to *Sisterhood is Powerful* Robin Morgan writes: I haven't the faintest notion what possible revolutionary role white heterosexual men could fulfill, since they are the very embodiment of reactionary-vested-interest-power.[67]

Given the history of racial, gender, and class oppression that black women have endured at the hands of white men, it is extremely difficult for black women to find points of intersection with white male identity (and vice versa). On most things, black female and white male issues simply do not align. Nevertheless, this does not mean that black women do not face challenges and even subjugation from groups that they we might consider their allies. Indeed, black women have also worked as opposites in the Manichean divide to the whiteness and racism of white women and to the patriarchy and sexism of black men. It seems that no matter with whom we are paired, black women often find themselves at the end of subjugation. The reason for this is complex, yet, first, I think it is best examined in terms of the struggle for agency mainly by out-groups or *marginalized* groups, and, second, how the struggle for agency is connected to what I mean when I say that *black women are the end of subjugation*.

The *end of subjugation* means that Black women represent the perfect foil or identity of contrast to many groups. Black women's role as counter or contradictory to the identity of others further complicates black women's agency, since, it would seem, black women are incapable of action without the help of groups like white women or black men. Or, another way to say this is that black women's agency can only be contextualized and realized if they associate their cause with another— that is they must see themselves as intricately linked to the other's struggle for agency.

Gendering Race and Racing Gender

In most presentations I give, I talk about the importance of racing our discussions of gender and gendering our discussions of race. One of the most difficult issues, then, is to tease out the difficulty some white women and black male scholars have in *racing* their *gender* discussions and *gendering* their *racial* discussion. In fact, race theory and gender theory offer us a plethora of examples of black women being subsumed into the cause of both black men and white women with nary an acknowledgment that black women are indeed different from either of these groups, and that black women have suffered at the hands of both. We can take, for example, critical theory that focuses on the black experience, black identity, or what it means to be black in the world. Many black male scholars, like Charles Johnson—whom I greatly admire—fail to acknowledge that black women and black men experience racism differently—they just do. Because of this blind spot, Johnson, for example, provides readers with several racialized instances where he assumes a shared perspective between black men and black women. It is fine and incredibly important to write about the experiences of black men, to focus on their bodies and to critique gender from their perspective; it is not fine to offer a missive on racism and assume a universal experience. For theorists like Johnson and more recent theorists like Yancy, their work implies a universal "I" in which black women are symbolically included, but in the real world, black women are nowhere in their texts. I would argue that this is a common mistake made by many black male scholars. In his widely anthologized "The Phenomenology of the Black Body"—*the black body*—Johnson's attempts at inclusion are disingenuous. Indeed, there is no point in this essay where black women can see their experiences partially or fully addressed.

An Agential Reading of the Black (Male) Body

Charles Johnson's canonical "The Phenomenology of the Black Body"[68] is a masterfully written piece that shows a great level of thought, raw physicality, and cutting analysis of a black male body walking through the world. One way to read Johnson's essay[69] is simply based on the title. Johnson is engaging in a phenomenological reading of the black (male) body, which means that in this piece Johnson is focused on how awareness of self, or the first person point of view structures consciousness. To say one is doing a phenomenology of the black body is to imply that one is studying: "Various types of experience ranging from perception, thought, memory, imagination, emotion, desire, and volition to bodily awareness, embodied action, and social activity, including linguistic activity."[70] Attempting to chronicle events in the life of a black [male] body and how the body's consciousness is structured and how the *other's* consciousness is structured based on interaction with the black male body is nothing short of marvelous. But what does this analysis provide to a range of black folks who experience consciousness of their bodies outside of Johnson's rather tight, rather gendered, rather heteronormative framework?

A more interesting way to evaluate Johnson's essay is by doing an *agential analysis*. An agential analysis is where we analyze an agent or agents in the act of examining their agency, having their agency challenged by another, or in the act of reclaiming their agency. There are certainly times when an agent can be engaged in all three. To do an agential analysis of Johnson's essay complicates it more than a phenomenological analysis because an agential analysis provides us with an opportunity to investigate the implications of a body whose agency has been placed in jeopardy, where these implications stretch beyond consciousness of a lived experience. Agential analysis foregrounds the material reality of what it means to be without agency or what it means to have one's agency challenged by another. A second more critical insight that an agential analysis offers is that it uncovers the way that, although Johnson purports to ground consciousness in the body, thereby addressing the Cartesian mind/body problem so heavily critiqued by feminist, race, and feminist-race scholars, a measure of (might we even say longing for?) the transcendental male rational subject (agent) remains quite palpable in Johnson's text. The question remains, does Johnson's essay express a desire for black men to have *access to* and be able to fully participate in transcendental male agency, or is his essay a repudiation of it?

In his analysis of the Enlightenment and the invention of whiteness, Joe Kincheloe reminds us that the "transcendental, white, male, rational, subject … operated at the recesses of power while concurrently giving every indication that he had escaped the confines of time and space."[71] new note For Kincheloe, the white male subject pulls off the stunning feat of influencing history by directly interacting with the world through his physical body, while at the same time giving the appearance that he was pure mind and therefore above and superior to the concerns of the physical. Returning to the question mentioned above, reading Johnson, there is a distinct feeling of anger and pronounced resentment in his text. This anger and resentment come about because Johnson (or is it better to say Johnson's narrator?) strongly desires to be mind, that is, to live in the pure space of consciousness and thought, and be like the white male transcendental subject influencing the world yet distinctly apart from it. Yet, Johnson (Johnson's narrator) is continually and by his accounts violently pulled (kicking and screaming) back into his body. It is on these experiences of being pulled back into his body that he bases his phenomenology. Consider, for example, Johnson's narrative about walking in Manhattan, wrapped up in his thoughts about "Boolean expansions." Johnson goes on to say that because he is thirsty, he went into a bar full of white people, and is "seen." Johnson feels their eyes on his body and all of a sudden his world is "epidermalized."[72]

One way to think about this event is as we might call *being interrupted by race*. When one is interrupted by race, one is usually made conscious of the fact of one's blackness by, for example, being the only black person in room, or being followed by mall security. What Johnson explains here is certainly akin to what happens when one is interrupted by race but I would like to suggest that Johnson's experience (an interpretation of it) is less about bodily entrapment, being violently pulled back into his body, or his being "epidermalized" and more about being denied the privilege of pure thought and/or pure rationality that is so oftentimes afforded to white men without them even asking for it.

Further, it is quite curious that Johnson would use thinking about Boolean expansions as an example of a time when he was interrupted by race, as a time when he could be rudely reminded that he was black. "Boolean expansion," whose purpose is "to expand or develop a function involving any number of logical symbols" seems an odd choice to occupy one's mind while walking down Broadway in "platform shoes." We might even say there is a certain absurdity to the entire endeavor, were it not for the need to unpack Johnson's misreading of this particular thought experience. Johnson claims that his "subjectivity is turned inside out like a shirtcuff … so it is not I who make a meaning for myself, but it is the meaning that was already there, pre-existing for me …"[73] This may be true, but what seems more to the point is that Johnson is frustrated at his inability to engage in pure thought *and* be seen as having *the capacity* to engage in pure thought without being reminded of his blackness. For black men like Johnson in "A Phenomenology of the Black Body," Fanon in "The Fact of Blackness," and even George Yancy in *Black Bodies, White Gazes*, there is no repudiation of rationality as such. In fact, when reading these black male scholars, one finds a repudiation of white men's insistence that blacks should not be allowed to dissociate from their bodies, not be allowed to become pure mind—something it seems that they all long for.

An agential analysis of Johnson's essay complicates Johnson in a way that perhaps he did not intend, because it suggests that in analyzing how white society works to deny black men agency, black men in turn place black women's agency under erasure because their experiences come to define all black folk's search for agency. In this essay, Johnson is unable to strike a balance between the agency of black men, black women, and non-normative black folks, because when he talks about the "black body," the body he is referring to throughout his essay is gendered male in the most normative way possible.

A close reading of the beginning of "A Phenomenology of the Black Body" troubles the water of gender perhaps a bit more than Johnson may have intended. He starts the essay with what he calls a "bawdy black folktale,"[74] whose takeaway line, I suppose, is that black men really do have larger penises than white men. Paraphrasing this tale, two white farmers place a bet on which one of them has the larger penis. Willis, a black man is also invited (none too gently) to join the bet as well. The black man wins the bet—winning in terms of size and money—adding that he won with a flaccid rather than erect penis. About this humorous tale, Johnson correctly states:

> [W]e may lose sight of the fact that *his* triumph is based on cultural assumptions that lock him into the body, and to echo W. E. B. Du Bois, create in his life a "double consciousness" in need of resolution.[75]

What needs to be resolved for Willis, and presumably all black men, is, first, how they see themselves and how they are seen by society; second, how black male sexuality is revered and demonized. After making these clarifying remarks, Johnson goes on to explain that his essay will attempt to deal with the "ambiguity of his situation and describe the constraints upon both Willis and his white competitors."[76]

What are these constraints? Maybe one constraint is that a large penis size in all their minds (Willis and the two farmers) confers a certain power, so the larger the penis, the more power one has. Interesting, perhaps but this analysis is complicated by how power is measured. If it is in terms of virility, then Willis wins; but if power is seen as the ability to influence, measured in terms of the social, or in wealth, Willis becomes the clear loser. Since Willis was compelled to be a part of this silly game, what would have happened if Willis's penis was the smallest? Johnson's framing of this incident in terms of "constraints" on Willis takes us back to agency—the chief concern of this discussion. Put simply, Willis is not seen as an agent while his white competitors are; this positioning of Willis as without agency places his life in jeopardy. Though the white men are awed by the size of Willis's penis, this fact inscribes Willis as unnatural, as hyper-sexual, as a beast rather than a man.

Recall earlier in this chapter three markers of agency were identified: choice, rationality, and recognition. It is clear from Johnson's essay that, given the way white patriarchal society is structured, neither Johnson, Willis, or black men in general have a choice to be otherwise or to say how they will or will not be seen in society. The articulation of the fight for black men to be seen as individuals and to self-define is in no way problematic. In fact, if Johnson had merely signaled in his text that he was speaking and theorizing the experience of black men, his essay would have taken on more significant meaning. Since he did not do this, black feminist scholars must challenge Johnson's use of the black male body to signify the experience of the black body. Thus, how the black male body is objectified by white society in Johnson's essay comes to frame the way we are supposed to see all black bodies. There are several examples of the privileging of black male bodies peppered throughout Johnson's essay. These instances point to the raw maleness of the piece, including references to Eldridge Cleaver's *Soul on Ice*, which is rife with sexist language, to his example of walking down the street in platform shoes, or his explanation of what happens when he enters a white bar where he famously write: "I am seen."[77] A conventional way to read Johnson expression that he is "seen" is to argue that he means that he is brought back into his body. His blackness or what he calls "epidermalization" establishes the tension that exists between the black male and the white male body. Citing Fanon: "Yet, Fanon is correct. 'For not only must the black man be black; he must be black in relation to the white man.'"[78] To offer a different interpretation of this experience—which also connects to Willis's story—I would argue that Johnson's concern is not simply that he is constantly "epidermalized" by white society but that in these moments his agency, along with his ability to access traditional white male power, is called into question. In this way, Johnson's phenomenology of the black body reads very similar to Du Bois' double consciousness.

From this perspective, being subsumed into the experiences of black men creates its own form of double consciousness for black women. Double consciousness occurs when the often-positive image that one has of oneself competes with the often-negative image that the *other* has of you. For Du Bois, blacks suffer from double consciousness because white society has a negative image of blacks while blacks (especially those who are educated) see themselves and their role in society in stark contradiction. In Du Bois' estimation, it is only the dogged determination of the black man that keeps his two souls (two psyches) from being severed in half. Because it seems to address issues related to racism and marginalization in a concrete and applicable way, Du Bois' idea of double conscious has influenced the work of several black male scholars including Charles Johnson, Henry Louis Gates, and Paul Gilroy.

Black women scholars have also been influenced by Du Bois' double consciousness. Indeed, we can see similarity, for example, between double consciousness and Patricia Hill Collins outsider-within concept, where Hill Collins makes the case that black women have two unique consciousnesses: one that emerges when they are in a white context and another that emerges when they are in a black context. We might we also use double consciousness to explain what happens when black women's consciousness is erased by the experiences of black men because "for the good of the race," they are asked to suppress their experiences as women. In this way, double consciousness can also be used to explain the twoness of black women: the warring consciousness fighting to be whole. Double consciousness just seems to fit for so many things. Like "interlocking systems of oppression" or "outsider-within," Du Bois' double consciousness is an all-purpose theory; as such, it will not provide us with a new way of analyzing black women's agency. If we are going to address the issue of black women and agency in a more unique way and one that speaks to black women's present condition, then we will have to walk other paths.

Notes

1 Stephan Fuchs, "Agency (and Intention)," in George Ritzer, ed., *Blackwell Encyclopedia of Sociology* (Oxford: Blackwell Publishing, 2007). Available at: www.blackwellreference.com/subscriber/tocnode?id=g9781405124331_chunk_g97814051243317_ss1–24 (accessed May 18, 2011).
2 Ibid.
3 Cillian McBride, "Introduction," in Cillian McBride, *Recognition* (Cambridge: Polity, 2013).
4 Ibid.
5 Charles Taylor and Amy Gutmann, eds., *Multiculturalism: Examining the Politics of Recognition* (Princeton, NJ: Princeton University Press, 1994), p. 25.
6 Ibid., p. 25.
7 Ibid., p. 26.
8 Fuchs, "Agency (and Intention)."
9 Ibid.
10 Susan Heckman, "Reconstituting the Subject: Feminism, Modernism, and Postmodernism," *Hypatia* 6(2) (1991): 45.
11 Rosemarie Tong, *Feminist Thought: A More Comprehensive Introduction* (Boulder, CO: Westview Press, 2009), p. 11.
12 Ibid., p. 11.
13 Ibid., pp. 11–12.
14 Heckman, "Reconstituting the Subject."
15 Ibid., p. 45.
16 Ibid.
17 Ibid., p. 45.
18 Ibid., p. 48.
19 Ibid., p. 49.
20 The Combahee River Collective, "A Black Feminist Statement," in Stanlie M. James, Francis Smith Foster, and Beverly Guy-Sheftall, eds., *Still Brave: The Evolution of*

Black Women's Studies (New York: The Feminist Press, City University of NY, 2009), pp. 3–4.

21 Ibid., p. 5.

22 Dorothy Roberts, *Killing the Black Body* (New York: Vintage, 1998), p. 31.

23 Ibid., p. 31.

24 To put this another way, Hill Collins observes: "A recognition of this connection between experience and consciousness that shapes the everyday lives of African-American women often pervades the works of Black women activists and scholars." See Patricia Hill Collin's seminal text, *Black Feminist Thought: Knowledge, Consciousness, and the Politics of Empowerment* (New York: Routledge, 2000), p. 24.

25 Katie Geneva Cannon, "Slave Ideology and Biblical Interpretation," in Jacqueline Bobo and Cynthia Hudley, eds., *The Black Studies Reader* (New York: Routledge, 2004), p. 415.

26 Saul Bellow, "Papuans and Zulus," *The New York Times*, March 10, 1994.

27 Thomas Jefferson, *Notes on the State of Virginia* (London: John Stockdale, 1786).

28 Michael Knox Beran, *Jefferson's Demons: Portrait of a Restless Mind* (New York: Free Press, 2003), p. 52.

29 Henry Louis Gate Jr., "Mister Jefferson and the Trials of Phillis Wheatley"; paper presented to the National Endowment for the Humanities during the 2002 Jefferson Lecture. Available at: https://www.neh.gov/about/awards/jefferson-lecture/henry-louis-gates-jr-lecture

30 Preface, in Phillis Wheatley's *Poems on Various Subjects, Religious and Moral* (New York: AMS Press, 1976 [1773]).

31 James *et al.*, *Still Brave*, p. xiii.

32 Gloria T. Hull, Patricia Bell Scott, Barbara Smith, eds., *All the Women Are White, All the Blacks Are Men, But Some of Us Are Brave* (New York: Feminist Press, 1982).

33 Miri Song, "Who's at the Bottom? Examining Claims about Racial Hierarchy," *Ethnic and Racial Studies*, 27(6) (2004): 860.

34 It can certainly be argued that given their historical relationship to white supremacy, racism, and colonization, Native Americans have suffered equally with Blacks Americans.

35 Song, "Who's at the Bottom?," pp. 861–862.

36 Tim Wise, *White Like Me: Reflections on Race from a Privileged Son*, 3rd rev. edn. (Berkeley, CA: Soft Skull Press, 2011); Peggy MacIntosh, "White Privilege: Unpacking the Invisible Knapsack," *Peace and Freedom Magazine*, July/August, (1989): 10–12,

37 Betty Friedan, *The Feminine Mystique* (New York: W.W. Norton, 1997).

38 Thank you to Kirsten T. Edwards for this astute analysis.

39 Daryl Cumber Dance, *Shuckin' and Jivin': Folklore from Contemporary Black Americans* (Bloomington, IN: Indiana University Press, 1978), p. 101. As folklore, this story was transmitted verbally from generation to generation.

40 Ibid., p. 102.

41 Shawn J. Parry-Giles, *Hillary Clinton in the News: Gender and Authenticity in American Politics* (Urbana, IL: Illinois University Press, 2014), p. 136.

42 Charles Mills, *The Racial Contract* (Ithaca, NY: Cornell University Press, 1997), p. 16.

43 Manning Marable, "Grounding with my Sisters," in Beverley Guy-Sheftall, ed., *Traps African American Men on Gender and Sexuality* (Bloomington, IN: Indiana University Press, 2001), p. 119.

44 Ibid., p. 125.

45 George Yancy, Black Bodies, White Gazes: The Continuing Significance of Race (Lanham, MD: Rowman & Littlefield, 2008).

46 Ibid., p. 1.

47 Ibid., p. 2.

48　Ibid., p. 2.
49　Mills, *Racial Contract*, p. 2.
50　Yancy, *Black Bodies*, p. 4.
51　Ibid.
52　Ibid.
53　Ibid.
54　Ibid.
55　I am indebted to a group of disability rights advocates for this idea of "pivoting." While attending the Civil Liberties and Public Policies annual conference in 2015, a group of activists talked about always having to turn to face others. One of the activists challenged this turning and demanded that the audience (we) "pivot this way." It was a powerful moment that has influenced my thoughts about marginalized groups demanding to be faced.
56　Several black women scholars have pointed out the distinctiveness of black women's experiences, including Patricia Hill-Collins, Patricia Bell Scott, and bell hooks.
57　Ann duCille, "The Occult of True Black Womanhood: Critical Demeanor and Black Feminist Studies," *Signs: Journal of Women in Culture and Society* 19(3) (1994): 621.
58　Ibid., p. 626.
59　Michelle Wallace, "A Black Feminist Search for Sisterhood," in Hull *et al.*, eds., *All the Women Are White*, p. 6.
60　See Julia T. Wood, "Feminist Standpoint Theory," in *Encyclopedia of Communication Theory* (Thousand Oaks, CA: SAGE, 2009), pp. 397–399.
61　Hill Collins, *Black Feminist Thought*, p. 201.
62　Patricia Hill Collins, "Intersecting Oppressions." Available at: www.sagepub.com/sites/default/files/upm-binaries/13299_Chapter_16_Web_Byte_Patricia_Hill_Collins.pdf
63　D. Berman, L. L. Martin, and L. J. Kajfez, "County Home Rule: Does Where You Stand Depend on Where You Sit?" *State & Local Government Review*, 17(2) (Spring, 1985): 232.
64　Combahee River Collective, "A Black Feminist Statement," in Hull *et al.*, eds., *All the Women Are White*, p. 13.
65　Ibid., pp. 13–14.
66　W. E. B. Du Bois, *The Souls of Black Folks* (New York: W.W. Norton, 1999), p. 11.
67　Combahee River Collective, "A Black Feminist Statement."
68　I am dealing with Johnson's essay, "A Phenomenology of the Black Body" in its original form published in 1976. Charles Johnson, "A Phenomenology of the Black Body," in Beverly Guy-Sheftall, ed., *Traps: African American Men on Gender and Sexuality* (Bloomington, IN: Indiana University Press, 2001).
69　I believe that this is the intended reading.
70　*Stanford Encyclopedia*, "Phenomenology" (Stanford, CA: Stanford University Press).
71　Joe L. Kincheloe, "The Struggle to Define and Reinvent Whiteness: A Pedagogical Analysis," *College English*, 26(3) (1999): 162–194.
72　Johnson, "A Phenomenology of the Black Body," p. 229.
73　Ibid., p. 229.
74　I searched but was unable to find this tale recorded anywhere.
75　Johnson, "A Phenomenology of the Black Body," p. 223. Emphasis added.
76　Ibid., p. 223.
77　Ibid., p. 606, 2001 edn.
78　Ibid., p. 606.

2 Historicizing Agency in the Black Feminist Tradition

A Phenomenology of the Black Female Body

Agency and Pain

How do you quantify pain? Oftentimes when you visit the doctor for an ailment, your doctor may ask you to rate the pain on a scale from 1–10 (with 10 being the highest). Treatment may depend on where one falls on the scale, with the most aggressive treatments reserved for the greatest amount of pain. Wouldn't it be interesting to use a scale to measure black pain? So, one black person may say to another "On a scale of 1–10, how much pain are you in today?" Is black pain even quantifiable? Would it be necessary to divide the pain into categories like *psychological*, *physical*, *emotional*, *spiritual*, etc. to calculate or measure it? Thinking about how to measure black pain is an interesting way to approach thinking about agency, since it seems that for black people in general the road to agency has been arduous, painful, and at times difficult to measure because the struggle is literally off the chart.

In an attempt to make black pain palpable and to show the difficulties of enacting agency in a system bent on denying black people's humanity, John W. Blassingame's (1977) book. *Slave Testimony* provides an unprecedented look at the lives of formerly enslaved black people spoken, many times, in their own voices.[1] Mr. Johnson and Mr. Curry, two of the people interviewed by Blassingame, narrate extremely compelling narratives. Though there are numerous moments in both accounts that trouble the soul, I would like to cite one account from Mr. Johnson's narrative and two from James Curry's that best illustrate the denial of black women's agency and the pain and violence that accompanied this denial.

Speaking in front of the Massachusetts Anti-Slavery Society on January 26, 1837, Mr. Johnson recounts the brutal events of a dinner party attended by his then enslaver. As Mr. Johnson recalls, during dinner, a young female slave, "happened to spill a little gravy on the gown of her mistress." As told by Mr. Johnson, to punish this transgression, the master of this young woman, "took his carving-knife, dragged her out to the wood pile, and cut her head off: den wash his hands, come in and finish his dinner like nothing happened![2]

An account given by James Curry, a former slave from North Carolina, also conveys instances of female slaves being terrorized and subjected to unimaginable violence for seemingly minor infractions. Though many illustrations from his narrative stand out, there are two instances in particular that are rather striking in their inhumanity and brutality. The first situation involves a little girl who was severely beaten by Curry's mistress, while the second is about Curry's own mother. In the former, Curry explains that his then mistress discovered that one of her combs, worth about "twenty-five to thirty-seven and a half cents"[3] had been broken. Suspecting that a girl—of about 9 or 10 years old—had broken the comb, Curry's mistress:

> Took her [the little girl] in the morning, before sunrise, into a room, and calling me to wait upon her, had all the doors shut. She tied her hands, and then took her frock up over her head, and gathered it up in her left hand, and with her right commenced *beating her naked body* with bunches of willow twigs. She would beat her until her arm was tired, and then thrash her on the floor, and stamp on her with her foot, and kick her, and choke her to stop her screams.[4]

Curry recounts that the mistress beat the little girl so badly that it left her (the mistress) "so lame that one of her daughters was obliged to undress her."[5] Not only did the child never fully recover from this vicious assault, she died two to three years later due to inflammation in one of her legs caused by the beating.[6]

In his second account, Curry relates the horrible way that his then master's daughter treated his (Curry's) own mother, who had raised the girl after her mother's death. Being unhappy due to "some trifle about the dinner," the girl came into the kitchen and "struck" Curry's mother. In a clear act of reflexive resistance and self-defense, Curry's mother: "pushed her [the master's daughter] away, and she fell on the floor."[7] The girl told her father when he came home that night and "he [Curry's then master] beat her [Curry's mother] fifteen or twenty strokes, and then called his daughter and told her to take her satisfaction of her, and she did beat her until she was satisfied."[8]

Curry goes on to discuss how he felt about watching his mother being beaten by the child she had raised but also about his inability to help his own mother because he knew that if he intervened physically or verbally, he too might be punished, or worse yet, killed.

As interlocutors, Mr. Johnson and James Curry are in a position of authority, they are tellers of the tale. Indeed, black men tell most of the narratives archived by Blassingame in *Slave Testimony* but also historically, black men have been the voice of the slave experience. This is attributed to a host of reasons, including that black women, especially if they had children, were less likely to escape, as well as black men having more access to public discourse, because of their gender. This is not to say that either Mr. Johnson or Mr. James Curry do not supply us with valuable information and important first-hand accounts of the horrors of enslavement, or that they themselves were not traumatized by witnessing these acts of violence which they could do nothing to prevent. Rather, it is to suggest that black women's subjective position is sadly lacking. Why is the subjective position essential? In order to address this question, we must consider the subject–object binary. Connected to our discussion in Chapter 1, to speak as a subject is to speak from the first person position—to speak as an "I" rather than a "they." Thus, the subject has within herself the ability to construct or frame her world. The subject also has the ability to interpret experiences that occur both internally and externally. When black women lack subjectivity, they find themselves in a constant state of being defined, or they become the object others use to interpret their own experiences. In the case of Mr. Curry, for example, though the violence is perpetrated against black women's bodies, he uses their pain to understand his own experience. We never hear the black women's first-hand accounts of the violence committed against them, and Curry (at least in the way that the narrative is communicated) does not seem to ever offer speculation about how the women felt about their treatment. We never know how the violence shapes the black women in the narrative.

This lack of black women's subjective position presents other challenges as well. For example, since Mr. Johnson and Mr. Curry are the tellers of the tales, it is no wonder that we see the incidents framed through their eyes. We are naturally empathetic toward the victims of all three tales, yet we must also be careful that we do not over-center the feelings or the experience of the speakers. Doing so, perhaps, allows an opening for the patriarchal gaze to enter. So that the reader focuses not so much on the pain endured by the women (and the little girl) mentioned in the narratives, rather, we might be tempted to focus on the pain Mr. Curry and Mr. Johnson felt because they were not able to "protect" the women in their lives and surroundings. To do so leads us directly into discussions of emasculation that historically permeates black critical theory. By centering the voices of Mr. Johnson and Mr. Curry, we also run the risk of further entrenching patriarchal gender difference between black men and women ,so that one reason to end enslavement is so that black men and women will be able to assume their natural gendered roles (black man as protector and black woman as helpmate).

Thus, a conscious effort has to be made to shift our gaze away from, for example, how Mr. Johnson and James Curry felt like non-agents based on their inability to protect their women, and the lack of recognition given by white society to their position as men; and we should focus on, if we can, how the black women's bodies became literal battlegrounds over which agency—for all the actors, including the victimizers—was asserted and/or denied. In shifting our gaze to the black women in the narrative, we can certainly concentrate on the physical brutality of enslavement, of which we are for the most part aware. But perhaps even more importantly we can witness agential brutality as well; in other words, we can assess the toll that slavery took on black women's agency. Typically, when we speak about slavery, we see it in terms of physical or socio-cultural death that enslaved Africans experienced. Physical death marked the end point of slavery's brutality while the social death that enslaved Africans experienced had to do with their being severed from their society and families of origin. In this way, their original communal lives were disrupted. Although enslaved Africans formed other socio-cultural communities, their original ties were cut. On the other hand, cultural death refers to the way that enslaved Africans lost their languages and traditions. To speak of *agential death* is to consider the way that enslavement also brutalized the enslaved person's ability to choose otherwise. Everything related to slavery—chains, forced reproduction, whippings, children taken away from parents and sold—was designed to communicate to enslaved people that they were not agents, nor could they ever achieve agency. We should be careful here that we do not confuse this discussion with psychological torture (which enslaved Africans also endured). To experience agential death or brutality is not simply to *think* that one may or may not do something, it is to have one's very freedom of choice greatly reduced or absolutely nullified.

Beginning with Mr. Johnson's account of the slave woman, whose head was cut off because she spilled a "little gravy," to the little girl who was whipped for *supposedly* stealing a comb, and ending with the savage beating of Curry's mother, we see that none of these black women had agential resistance in the eyes of their violators—they could not choose to be treated otherwise—nor perhaps do they have agential resistance in the eyes of black men as well (a far more complex analysis). In all three cases, when it concerns their agency, black women stand at the edge of the annihilation.

Agency and Ontology

In his book, *Black Skin, White Mask*, Frantz Fanon explains what is at stake for the disembodied and disempowered black subject. To be a black man means to be perpetually "locked in this suffocating reification,"[9] it is to lose the power of self-definition. To say that none of the black women mentioned in Mr. Johnson and Mr. Curry's narratives had "ontological resistance" means that they were not seen as being able to resist how they were viewed by the whites who controlled them and saw them as property, or, for that matter, the black interlocutors who saw them as extensions of themselves. The groundwork for denying black women's "ontological resistance" was laid long before Mr. Johnson and Mr. Curry's narratives were ever told. Early in American history, there was a conscious and concerted effort to *thingify* black women's bodies in two important ways—first, in terms of their labor, and, second, via their sexuality. Paradoxically, before slavery was formally institutionalized and before black women's bodies were overlaid with negative signification or "locked in this suffocating reification," colonial America saw the entrance of thousands of white indentured servants to its shores, many of whom were women and children. Giddings explains the dire situation that these indentured servants encountered:

> They came on overcrowded ships, were hoisted onto auction blocks where they were stripped, examined, and sold without regard to the separation of families. They were thought to be contented with their lot, lazy, and immoral. Female servants were sexually exploited by masters.[10]

This positioning of white women and children sounds frighteningly similar to the way the black women and children were treated during slave auctions. Certainly, throughout the early part of America's colonial history, there was, at a time, little difference between black and white servants. Perhaps what is more surprising is that in some cases blacks on occasion received better treatment than their white counterparts. According to Giddings:

> During the first years of the African presence in North America, Blacks had higher status than other servants, because the circumstances of their seizure put them under the protection of international law.[11]

What happened between colonial America and the great enslavement that changed the status of blacks, particularly black women, in the social order? When did blacks lose their agency? When did they lose their "place in the moral universe?"[12] In answer to this question, Giddings explains that the "need for labor—more profitable labor" precipitated the denigration of black people and the elevation of white people.[13] The need for labor certainly propelled the growth of Colonial America, but as a consequence "some," Giddings explains, "would have to be exploited more than others." Thus, blacks served the purpose of exploitable other based on their "increasing numbers" and the place they held in the European imagination. So, if the English are on the one hand "civilized, Christian, rational, sexually controlled," then "Blacks [could] be victimized by the White impulse to affirm, through Black degradation … the instinctual forces they had within themselves."[14]

It was not long after this that white colonists began to focus not only on blacks (and whites) as groups with profound difference, but to firmly distinguish between men and women as well as establishing a gender as well as a racial hierarchy that ultimately placed black women at the bottom. Giddings writes: "Black women … [were] described by English slave traders as 'hot constitution'd ladies,' possessed of a 'lascivious temper,' who had an inclination for White men …"[15] Beyond being portrayed in such hyper-sexual terms, Giddings also explains that black women's bodies were also subjugated by the creation of laws that made it a crime for white man to have sexual intercourse with black women, made slavery dependent on the race of the mother rather than the father, and distinguished labor fit for white women and black women. Giddings provides the following example:

> In 1629, Virginia administrators had designated "tithable persons" as all those that "worke in the ground of what qualitie or condition soever." In 1643, however, tithable persons included all adult men in addition to *Black* women …. How the new division of labor reflected upon women of African descent became clear in a 1656 tract written by Virginia's John Hammond. Servant women, he wrote, were to be used in a domestic capacity, rather than the field. "ey some wenches … that are nasty and beastly and not fit to be so employed are put in the ground.[16]

From here, Giddings' analysis focuses on John Hammond's description of black women as "nasty and beastly," yet for our purposes it seems crucial to interrogate Hammond's statement that black women (we can presume) should be "put in the ground." First, Hammond's statement conjures images of death as "put in the ground" can easily be read in terms of killing black women's bodies. Second, his statement perfectly illustrates the lack of agency black women have historically had. There is no sense that black women have a choice in where and how to labor, they are "put" somewhere like a field horse. A Marxian analysis might (rightfully so) argue that Hammond also advocates for the exploitation of white women's labor as well. Yet, this does not belie the point that black women's labor is super-exploited for no other reason but because they are black. If anything, it calls further attention to the hierarchy of labor, labor's relationship to skin color, and how people develop a sense of social worth based on the type of labor they do.

Third, black women were reduced to irrational (or lower beings) certainly not on par with white men or women. What makes black women in this sense different from black men who themselves are straining under the weight of crushing racism is that there is a gender component. Whereas white female servants were given domestic duties, black women were treated no different than men. On this we might tongue in cheek say, well, at least, there is gender parity in this situation. Yet, to do so would be to miss the varying paths taken by white women, black women, and black men. On the one hand, the white female body becomes the standard but also *the* female body that matters. And, mattering is important *if* it affords some protection against rape and other forms of social violence. Mattering means that white women produced legitimate heirs that would not be enslaved. Mattering also meant that as a white woman you would be spared backbreaking, physical labor. Speaking to the issue of mattering in a broader context, bell hooks makes two clear points concerning women who did not matter (women who are "put in the ground"), first, that "the black female slave was not as valued as the black male slave," and second, we oftentimes incorrectly associate slavery with the emasculation of black men. hooks writes:

> Sexist historians and sociologists have provided the American public with a perspective on slavery in which the most cruel and de-humanizing impact of slavery on the lives of black people was that black men were stripped of their masculinity, which then they argue resulted in the dissolution and overall disruption of any black familial structure.[17]

hooks counters that black men certainly lost their freedom but this did not mean that they lost all benefits associated with their "masculinity"[18] or *mattering* because they are men. These benefits included not being asked to do what might be considered women's work. Things like cooking, cleaning and child care were preformed by black women, who, unlike men, also had additional duties—like fieldwork—as well. hooks further explains what occurred during enslavement:

While black men were not forced to assume a role colonial American society regarded as "feminine," black women were forced to assume a "masculine" role. Black women labored in the fields alongside black men, but few men labored as domestics alongside black women in the white household. Thus it would be much more accurate for scholars to examine the dynamics of slavery in light of the masculinization of the black female and not the de-masculinization of the black male.[19]

Although we should be critical of all forms of gender characterizations, we cannot be dismissive of the claim that such characterizations—mattering—can have a direct impact on one's life. It meant (and continues to mean) something that black women were made masculine in terms of their labor and how they were punished since "female slaves were beaten as harshly as male slaves," but not in terms of the privileges associated with masculinity since "only a male slave could rise to the position of driver or overseer."[20] hooks reminds us that "any white woman forced by circumstances to work in the fields was regarded as unworthy of the title 'woman.'"[21] Mattering or not mattering also has a moral component which we can witness in the way that enslaved black women's genitalia were commodified sexually *and* via public experimentation.

Agency, Enslavement, and Reproductive Technologies

Because the cult of domesticity is well-covered terrain, gender scholars understand and frequently reference the public and private pressures white women faced to maintain their status as women. One such pressure being the call for women to be pure and modest, ostensibly meaning that women were expected to remain virgins until marriage. Being impure meant being, "A member of some lower order. A 'fallen woman' was a 'fallen angel,' unworthy of the celestial company of her sex."[22]

Although all women were in one way or another cast in the drama of the cult of domesticity—they were either protagonist (white unsullied women) or foil (mainly women of color)—the protection offered by the cult of domesticity was not evenly applied. The unevenness shows itself in the access and control white male society had to and over black women's vaginas, not only sexually but scientifically as well.

As I have discussed in my work on race and reproduction,[23] one way that scholars of reproductive history (black and white) are challenging the history of reproductive technologies and the ideologies that support them is by making visible the brutality that accompanied the creation of fields like gynecology, which developed in part via experimentation on black women's sexual organs. In her essay, "Mastering the Female Pelvis: Race and the Tools of Reproduction," Terri Kapsalis argues that the medical community (past and present) pays homage to men like Dr. J. Marion Sims due to his efforts to cure "vesico-vaginal fistulas" which are "small tears that form between the vagina and urinary tract or bladder that cause urine to leak uncontrollably."[24] Valorized by the medical community, Dr. J. Marion Sims is "remembered as the Father of American Gynecology, Father of Modern Gynecology, and Architect of the Vagina."[25] Complicating Sims' legacy, Kapsalis's essay explains that although Sims was certainly a thoughtful and gifted physician, he would never have been so successful if he had not have unfettered access to enslaved black women's bodies to experiment on. Such access allowed Dr. Sims to work on and perfect his technique to cure vesico-vaginal fistulas. Like other whites of the time, Dr. Sims held beliefs about black women's bodies that were harmful and reductive, seeing them as "inherently more durable than white women."[26] Typically, Sims did not use any form of anesthesia on his black patients, although it was readily available. "However," as explained by Jeffrey S. Sartin, Sims "found that upper-class white women could not tolerate surgery without ether."[27] Disturbing still, Sims operated on enslaved black women in full view of audiences who attended the surgeries, literally in his "backyard hospital."[28] Writing about an enslaved woman called "Lucy," Kapsalis notes: "And as if the pain of unanesthetized vaginal surgery were not traumatic enough, after this first operation, Lucy nearly died from infection due to a sponge Sims had left in her urethra and bladder."[29] In his eyes, black women's pain and privacy were inconsequential. And, as long as science was advanced, their suffering simply did not matter. Lucy did not have a choice on whether to be operated on. She did not have a choice of whether the operation would take place in public. From Dr. Sims' perspective, "Lucy" had no agential or ontological resistance. She was powerless.

Based on the work of Kapsalis and others, black (and white) women scholars are challenging how medical history is—and in some cases continues to be—dehistoricized and de-racialized in the USA. What such challenges ostensibly look like is either rewriting medical texts so that they reflect the abuse of black women's bodies and give voice to women like Lucy by acknowledging their suffering; *or* by presenting a counter-curriculum in the form of essays, articles, and books like those written by Dorothy Roberts[30] and Khiara M. Bridges[31] that take up issues related to race and reproduction. Black women designing a curriculum that pushes back against the decontextualized history and immoral practices of men like J. Marion Sims is a part of black women's justice work. Such a curriculum re-narrates the history of gynecology, re-humanizes the enslaved black women who had no choice whether they would participate in the gynecological experiments of men like Sims, and, most importantly, presents a counter-ideology to the prevailing toxic medical ideology that posits black women as exploitable other, and continues to impact black women's reproductive freedom and agency today.

Charles Mills is another scholar who is doing justice-oriented work related to the socio-political position of blacks (and whites) in society.[32] Using contract theory, Mills skillfully examines how enslaved Africans (and other non-white people) were not a part of the moral universe because they were seen as "inferior," or that they did not *matter* in the way that whites did and do. Like Mills, I also am interested in how blacks (especially women) are left outside of the moral imagination of the West and therefore denied the rights of citizens and those benefits afforded to those that matter—e.g. the right not to be experimented on, the ability to resist being "put in the ground," privacy, and access to things like anesthesia. In addition, I am interested in scaling Mills' analysis of the racial contract to include the issue of agency. Doing so provides us with the possibility of unpacking in another way certain qualities that black people seem to lack (in the estimation of whites) that offer essential protection against violence. Based on our earlier discussion (see Chapter 1), there are three clear markers of agency: the ability to choose, rationality, and recognition. In the narratives cited at the beginning of this chapter (those of Mr. Johnson and Mr. Curry) and Lucy's story, all the black women and the little girl mentioned in this chapter are missing two of the three markers of agency—the ability to choose *not* to be harmed, and being *recognized* as actors. When one is dispossessed, in particular, of these critical markers, all that is left is the potential for violence and pain. In making this claim, we can trace how the assault on black women's agency, the denial of their citizenship, and their exclusion from the moral universe persist after their physical enslavement ends.

Black Women and Agency Post Enslavement

Perhaps the best example of black women struggling for agency post enslavement is shown in the often-referenced struggle for women's suffrage. The Women's Suffrage Movement coincided with the Abolitionist Movement and later with the Black Male Suffrage Movement. Though feminist men like Frederick Douglass supported women's suffrage, Douglass was also very pragmatic when it came to voting rights. As explained by Beverly Guy-Sheftall in *Words of Fire*:

> At the proceedings of the ERA meeting in New York in 1869, the famous debate between Frederick Douglass and white feminists occurred during which he argued for the greater urgency of race over gender. He believed it was the Negro's hour, and women's rights could wait since linking women suffrage to negro suffrage as this point would seriously reduce the chances of securing the ballot for black men, and for black (males), Douglass reiterated, the ballot was urgent.[33]

Douglass was indeed correct; support for black male suffrage would have been sidelined if it were connected to women getting the right to vote. Claiming the right to their rage, white women activists during this time were justifiably upset and perhaps even felt betrayed by the likes of Douglass. Consequently, it is unsurprising that a split occurred between white suffragists and those, like Douglass, who argued for black male suffrage before women's suffrage, again for pragmatic reasons. Sadly (unsurprisingly), during this tension, both racism and sexism surfaced from groups who had up till then seen themselves as allies. One of the leaders in the women's suffrage movement, the revered Elizabeth Cady Stanton, vehemently wrote in the newspaper, *The Revolution*:

> While the dominant party have with one hand lifted up TWO MILLION
> BLACK MEN and crowned them with honor and dignity with the other they
> have dethroned FIFTEEN MILLION WHITE WOMEN—their own mothers
> and sisters, their own wives and daughters—and cast them under the heel of
> the lowest orders of manhood.[34]

Stanton, it seems, let her anger and her privilege flow into her words as she
expresses her ire with black men receiving the vote before not "women" per
se but before "FIFTEEN MILLION WHITE WOMEN." Her views may be at
first difficult to reconcile since she and so many others had not only fought
for women's suffrage but many were also critical in the abolition movement.
How should we understand her early activism to end enslavement with her
racism? As former allies, how do Douglass and Stanton end up on such con-
tentious sides of this issue? And, more critically, where are the voices of
black women?

The first question is perhaps the easiest to address. Douglass and Stanton
end up on different sides of this issue because they see the situation in terms of
their own interest. As a white woman, Stanton and other white women abolitionists saw themselves as superior based on their whiteness and proximity to
white supremacy. Since they are legitimate "mothers, sisters, and daughters"
to white men, they argue that they should receive some benefit from their proximity to the white power structure. It would not be in their interest to advocate
black men receiving the vote first, since black men might be placed ahead of
them in society. On the contrary, although Douglass understands what President Obama referred to as the "fierce urgency of now," Douglass and other
black people (both men and women) also understood that, given the role of
patriarchy in society, it would be far easier a fight for black men to get the vote
first—based on their position as men. White male-dominated society had
already faced one challenge to how society had been structured. namely vis-à-
vis slavery, white male-dominated society was not at that time equipped to
face a challenge to patriarchy as well. Black women like Francis Harper were
also pragmatic when it came to voting, Harper writes, "If the nation could
handle only one question, she would not have the black women put a single
straw in the way."[35]

Since white women and black men were for the most part concerned for the
own in-group and interests (black men perhaps more concerned for black women
than white women were). we might rightly ask, where are black women's voices
during this troubled time? By and large, black women emerged from enslavement and into the debate about suffrage *conflicted*. bell hooks speaks to the
internal conflict black women felt when she writes that:

> To support women's suffrage would imply that they were allying them-
> selves with white women activists who had publicly revealed their racism,
> but to support black male suffrage was to endorse a patriarchal social order
> that would grant them no political voice.[36]

hooks further explains this double bind that black women found themselves in: "At the first annual meeting of the ERA in 1867, Sojourner Truth addressed women's rights again, but worried that the freedom of black men was getting more attention than black women's liberation."[37] The conflict and "worry" that black women experienced, due to who should be first, led to a struggle between speaking and silence where speaking out might meant standing against your black brothers while remaining silent would mean standing in the way of your own interest. The tension between talking back and silence especially in issues related to race and gender is, I think, a particular characteristic of black women in society. bell hooks' idea of talking back is informative. For hooks, talking back means, "speaking as an equal to an authority figure … daring to disagree … having an opinion."[38] Although hooks first refers to talking back in the way that a child talks back to an adult (a major infraction in the black community), talking back is also an assertion of agency since:

> Moving from silence into speech is for the oppressed, the colonized, the exploited, and those who stand and struggle side by side, a gesture of defiance that heals, that makes new life and new growth possible. It is that act of speech, of "talking back," that is no mere gesture of empty words, that is the expression of our movement from object to subject—the liberated voice.[39]

In talking back, black women can position themselves as liberated actors who are empowered and self-constituting. Since black feminists see their position as resisting not only gender oppression but also racial and class oppression, acting or talking back, not just to white, male, patriarchal society but also to white women and black men benefit black women as a group.

More Problems Along the Way

As previously mentioned, black feminist theorists have long stressed that black women struggle from their distinctive, embodied position as black and as women. As has been shown, articulating this standpoint has caused historical tension between black women and white women and, conversely, between black women and black men. Of the two, the uneasiness along gender lines is the most difficult to reconcile especially when black male patriarchal authority enacts violence on a par with white racism. When, for example, noted black male scholars harshly criticized black women's writers like Zora Neale Hurston, Toni Morrison, Alice Walker, and more popular fiction writes like Sapphire and Terry Macmillan—some of the pre-eminent names in American and Black American literature— we must ask why. At one point or another, all of these black women writers have had their work challenged and even maligned (and, in the case of Hurston, completely silenced for a time) for the "crime" of: painting black men in a bad light, being trendy and therefore not serious literature, having under-developed or simplistic characters, as well as being critiqued for *seeing* black women's experiences—outside of black male experiences—as something that is complexly embedded and something worth writing about. In "Toward a Black Feminist Criticism," Barbara Smith calls Darwin Tuner's evaluation of Zora Neale Hurston "near assassination of a great Black woman writer."[40]

Meanwhile, others like Ishmael Reed also offer scathing critique of black women writers. In an interview, Reed famously stated that he would sell more books if he was a "young female Afro American writer" who populated his books with "ghetto women" characters.[41]

Such signification does not come from nowhere; rather, it is rooted in an understanding of black women's place in society as well as black women's supposed (in)ability to resist damning external classification. Barbara Smith aptly states of Reed:

> Neither Reed nor his white male interviewer has the slightest compunction about attacking Black women in print. They need not fear widespread public denunciation since Reed's statement is in perfect agreement with the values of a society that hates Black people, women, and Black women.[42]

That Reed (and the interviewer) can sit in the community of patriarchy and feel empowered to blame *the lack of Reed's sales* on the popularity of black women's literature speaks to the deep and historical struggle for black women's agency both in and outside of the black community.

Reed and others fail to see how African American women writers view black women's relationship to the black community, how they view and write about black women's bodies, but more critically they fail to comprehend the complexity of black women's literature and how black women live and thrive in communities of their own making. As disturbing and insulting as Reed's comments are, we must not fail to see them as nothing less than a part of the continuum of black women's subjugation (physical, reproductive, spiritual, academic, etc.) at the hands of *others*. This claim can be supported vis-à-vis an analysis of the current debate surrounding abortion and the way this debate attempts to overlay signification on black women's bodies.

Agency, Black Wombs, Continued Control

No one should be surprised by the claim that wombs have always been contested political sites. For example, historian Tina Campt analyzes how the German nation state and its self-conceptualization were challenged when many white, German women bore mixed raced children, fathered by African colonial troops during the occupation of Germany after the World War I. Since "racial mixture is the ultimate test of racial difference,"[43] and a perceived threat to the purity of German identity, many children born of these interracial sexual transgressions were later sterilized—which by the way was illegal under "existing laws."[44] Through Campt's analysis, we can see how the vulnerability of German identity turned out to be "apparent through the [white] female body as a vehicle, conduit, or site of entry for potential pollution/contamination."[45] It is no wonder that white women's wombs became one focal point of state control during the Third Reich.

I begin with this example of the Third Reich's effort to control white German women's reproductive capacities for a couple of reasons. First, from a historical point of view, corrosive and patriarchal Nazi ideology and the history of eugenics intersect in significant ways with the politics of black women's agency and reproduction in the United States. During enslavement, the wombs of black women were seen as bearers for the plantation—the valued machine creating generation after generation of bonded labor—and thus subject to control by the state. After enslavement, black women's reproductive capacity came under the control of the state in a different way, however; it came to be regarded primarily as a threat to American identity and arguably continues to be regarded as such to this day. To use Campt's language, black wombs post enslavement are recast as "a vehicle, conduit, or site of entry for potential pollution/contamination" of the white nation state. Second, the Third Reich is a common example of a rigid system of social control. Campt argues that when you "combine" an "essentialist" understanding of race together with "a discourse of racial endangerment," you have "a powerful tool [for] political mobilization, with often unpredictable results"[46]

How does the dangerous combination of essentialism and a discourse of endangerment play itself out in the rhetoric of both the pro- and anti-choice movements in the USA, and how does this impact black women's agency? Those of us who design black feminist curriculum can use ideological criticism, for instance, to make sense of the way in which the black womb is framed in discourses related to abortion and choice, as well as ways to resist such framing. To pursue this issue, it is important to investigate how opposite sides of the abortion debate employ a discourse of endangerment—whether it concerns the endangerment of reproductive freedom, racial endangerment, community endangerment, or the endangerment of life—to mobilize political support for their ideologies. I am interested in the role of black women within this rhetorical strategy through various rhetorical artifacts from both the pro- and anti-choice movements, such as billboards, websites, documentaries, public demonstrations, etc. To analyze these artifacts, this next section employ the theoretical framework of ideological or ideographic criticism, because as Foss writes: "When rhetorical critics are interested in rhetoric primarily for what it suggests about beliefs and values, their focus is on the ideology manifest in an artifact."[47] This framework helps expose how the artifacts used by both pro- and anti-choice movements attempt to "condition" the audience, not merely to adopt a set of "beliefs and behavior, but a vocabulary of concepts that function as guides, warrants, reasons, or excuses for behavior and belief."[48] Though the two sides of the abortion debate differ in their overt political views, they turn out to share an *implicit* ideology about black women's agency and black wombs. This ideology prevents the voices of black women from being heard and valued in a debate that is nonetheless *focused* on black women's bodies.

One result of these "struggles—social and political—[that] take place over which meanings and ideologies will predominate,"[49] is that black women can experience, for lack of better terminology, an *existential hysterectomy*. That is to say that even though their wombs are capable of reproduction, they are rendered womb-less through a hegemonic rhetoric of control that erases *their* own voices about *their* bodies and *their* reproduction. Hortense Spillers identifies a similar phenomenon when she describes the enslaved mother as both "mother" and "mother-dispossessed."[50] The slave is a mother, yet she is denied the right to her offspring. Likewise, in the rhetoric espoused by the pro- and anti-choice movements, the wombs of black women become contested sites—and black women become dispossessed of their reproductive rights as well as their reproductive capacity.

Teaching about Black Women's Reproduction in the USA

When students are taught about the history of black enslavement in America, they may encounter narratives that frame enslavement as a "trade" (an exchange of black men, women, and children for money, goods, or services). Or they may be taught that enslavement was a *peculiar* institution in which good, but complicated, patriots like Thomas Jefferson and George Washington participated because *that's how things were back then*. Some students may be shown the darker aspects of enslavement—whippings, dissolution of families, dehumanization of people based on the specious idea of race. More problematic interpretations of enslavement occur when teachers/professors uncritically present enslavement as a narrative of patriarchy denied, where black men are unable to participate in patriarchal power, thus leading to a continued struggle for black men to be seen as "men" in a society that has emasculated them. What if one approach to teaching students about slavery pivoted from each of these issues to focus on the reproductive control exerted by white society over black women's lives? To do so broadens the dialogue, centers black women's experiences, and makes evident how black women living in the USA have historically and continually experienced controls and restrictions not only on their physical labor but also on their reproductive labor.

Although more needs to be written about black women's reproductive capacity in the years following emancipation. It would be short-sighted to assume that a society fixated on black women's wombs for nearly 200 years would all of a sudden lose interest in them once black women are no longer legal chattel. Indeed, black women's reproductive capacities continued to be a site where both discipline and control were exercised. Post emancipation, black women's wombs were no longer a productive resource to be exploited but instead came to be viewed as a threat to white, Anglo-Saxon society. To analyze this claim, we must take a step back to the formation of the idea of *race* in America. In his seminal text, *Race: The History of an Idea in America*, Thomas F. Gossett does a remarkable job of tracing the formation of the difficult concept of race and racial formation in the USA and England.[51] He writes, "When the English colonists first landed in this country, they immediately encountered one race 'problem' in the Indians. In a few years they imported another when, in 1619, the first boat-load of Negro slaves arrived."[52] Race has been a "problem"— primarily because of the hierarchy and ideology it imposes—in American society ever since Europeans came to these shores, and it did not cease to be so after blacks were freed from bondage. When it was no longer *legal* to exploit black women's reproductive capacity post emancipation, there was a fear that black [problem] women (as well as other non-white or not quite white[53] women) might one day out-produce white Anglo-Saxon women. Dorothy Roberts provides us with an example of this fear, writing that in texts like:

> *Racial Hygiene* Thurman B. Rice [for example] warned that "the colored races are pressing the white race most urgently and this pressure may be expressed to increase." The twentieth-century eugenicists were not content to rely on evolutionary forces to eliminate biological inferiors, they proposed instead government programs that would reduce Black birthrate.[54]

This fear of being "pressed" prompted a discourse of racial endangerment that led to new measures to control black women and their reproductive capacity. Two ways that we can analyze this new imagining of the black womb rooted in the *fear* of overproduction is through Patricia Hill Collins' controlling images and the rise of the eugenics and birth control movements, as cited by Roberts, in the mid-nineteenth century.[55]

In *Black Feminist Thought*, Patricia Hill Collins articulates four categories of controlling images that post enslavement function didactically in white society, instructing whites how to treat the black female body, they are: the mammy, the jezebel, the matriarch, and the welfare mother. In brief, the mammy figure functioned in the white imagination as "the faithful, obedient domestic servant."[56] The matriarch, "symbolizes the 'bad' black mothers." Matriarchs are "overly aggressive, unfeminine women" who "emasculate their lovers and husbands."[57] The breeder woman image which developed "during slavery ... portrayed Black women as more suitable for having children than white women."[58] Post enslavement, the breeder image changed into the third controlling image—the welfare mother or (queen) whose fertility is seen as "unnecessary and even dangerous to the values of the country ..."[59] The final controlling image is that of the jezebel (or hoochie) who is typically seen as "sexually aggressive ... Jezebel's function was to regulate all Black women to the category of sexually aggressive women, thus providing a powerful rationale for the widespread sexual assault by white men typically reported by Black slave women."[60]

Of these four controlling images articulated by Hill Collins, the welfare mother is the most pertinent to our discussion about black women, reproduction and agency since, again, she represents the updated version of the "breeder image" from slavery.[61] This image is used to justify society's imposition "into black women's decisions about fertility."[62] Whereas the breeder woman was valuable through her reproductive labor, the welfare mother is a drain on society's resources. She is typically described as idly sitting around, waiting for her welfare check, and "passing on her bad values to her offspring."[63] This is clearly what rancher and self-proclaimed patriot Cliven Bundy referred to when he told a reporter "one more thing that he knows about the Negro":

> They didn't have nothing for their young girls to do. And because they were basically on government subsidy, so now what do they do ... they abort their young children, they put their young men in jail, because they never learned how to pick cotton.[64]

Bundy's statement contains a complicated confluence of the issue of freedom and fertility. Young black women who have "nothing" to do, get three things according to Bundy—they get pregnant, they get government assistance, and they get abortions. In Bundy's reasoning, the black female body post enslavement has lost its sense of purpose. While enslaved, the black female body had clear direction and was directed—it was a body that labored in the field and labored bearing children. But after enslavement, the black female body has lost its use to society and has become a burden. Although Cliven Bundy's remarks are a convergence of racism, anti-choice, Antebellum apologia, sexism, and victim shaming, it may come as a surprise to find that a similar image of the breeder woman appears in the founding of the birth control movement in this country, a movement dedicated to freeing (mainly white) women from the confines of childbirth. The birth control movement, likewise, represents black women's reproduction as harmful to society, a position that directly threatens black women's agency.

A Vital Service for Whom?

Margaret Sanger, founder of the American Birth Control League, which later became the Planned Parenthood Federation of America, is rightfully celebrated by the pro-choice movement for her efforts to bring birth control and choice to "women." She is also justly praised by some women because her "early activism"—in a way—was "pro-woman" and because she was "vehemently feminist."[65] Sanger, to her credit, believed that unwanted pregnancy could potentially hurt women by leading to unsafe abortions. Women would be more fulfilled, she argued, if they were able to choose to become or not to become pregnant, thereby "liberating women's sexual pleasure from the confines of maternity, marriage, and Victorian morality."[66] For Sanger, birth control was about agency and freedom, she states: "No woman can call herself free who does not own and control her own body. No woman can call herself free until she can choose consciously whether she will or will not be a mother."[67]

Nevertheless, Dorothy Roberts argues that what was described as an option—birth control—for white women of means became a "method of sound social policy" to control the fertility for poor women.[68] Through Sanger's example, we can see how "birth control can be used to achieve coercive reproductive policies as well as liberation" for some women.[69] Whereas white women of means were liberated by birth control, poor women and black and brown women were sterilized by the thousands in this country, simply because their wombs were seen as destructive to society because they could not produce good stock. As stated by David Starr Jordan (a former president of Stanford University): "Poverty, dirt, and crime ... are due to poor human material ... it is not the strength of the strong but the weakness of the weak which engenders exploitation and tyranny."[70] It was the desire to protect good American stock (i.e. of Puritan descent) which fueled the eugenics ideology of the pro-choice movement.

After World War I, Dorothy Roberts argues that Sanger shifted her argument away from reproductive choice to eugenics and mass sterilization. In Sanger's reasoning, birth control became a way of stopping procreation and as such could "serve the national interest"[71] because "the multiplication of the unfit posed a threat to the political stability of the nation as well." After all, Sanger exclaims, "these people can vote."[72] Sanger's beliefs, like those of several other key thinkers in the eugenics movement (Dalton, Starr etc.), hinged upon concerns about birthrate. Those in the movement argued that smart, well-off people have too few children while the unintelligent poor have too many. Sanger goes on to say, in words that are full of patriotism and Christian piety, that "On its negative side it shows us that we are paying for and even submitting to the dictates of an ever-increasing, unceasingly spawning class of human beings who never should have been born at all."[73] The diseased black, brown and/or poor woman is a precursor to the welfare mother who breeds children, who should have never been born.

To address the birthrate "problem" in the 1990s, government officials eventually encouraged many black, brown, and poor women to use Norplant (a birth control device implanted in a woman's arm). Although Norplant was very effective at controlling fertility,[74] it also had terrible side-effects, one of which is "excessive bleeding."[75] Despite the severe discomfort many women experienced, policymakers saw Norplant as a means of effective "domestic population control."[76] While the US federal government "slashed" programs designed to help the poor during the 1990s, it increased Medicaid funding for Norplant. Roberts writes that "By 1994, states had already spent 34 million on Norplant related benefits,"[77] and at least half of those using Norplant were on Medicaid. Not only did local governments make Norplant more easily available, 13 states turned directly to "measures to implant poor women with Norplant,"[78] many of these measures involved offering women some financial incentive or required Norplant "as a condition of receiving benefits."[79]

Here we have identified three distinct stages in the history of black women's reproduction in the USA: (1) the commodified black womb under enslavement; (2) the diseased black womb that should be sterilized during the early twentieth century; and (3) the welfare womb that must be controlled through contraception in the latter half of the twentieth century. One aspect that unites all three of these eras is a language of liberation combined with a tactic of coercion. Through an ideological analysis of the pro- and anti-choice movements we can see that the *theme* of liberation informs the implicit and explicit messaging of these movement. Coercion underlies the rhetoric about black women's wombs yesterday, today, and probably tomorrow.

Rhetoric of Black Endangerment

2010 was a jarring year for black women's agency and reproductive freedom. To the horror of many black activists and scholars, the anti-choice group, Heroic Media, installed billboards in Austin, Texas, with the message: "The Most Dangerous Place for Black People is in the Womb." Since then, similar billboards have found their way to major cities across the country funded by organizations like toomanyaborted.com and MissouriLife.org, with messages that read "Black Children Are An Endangered Species." Though the billboards and other digital content associated with them are certainly meant to shock viewers, something far more insidious is also occurring. On the milder side ("milder" here is used ironically), such billboards engage in shaming black women for exercising the fundamental right to privacy, articulated by Roe. On the more extreme side, the billboards liken the black female body to a death chamber and mark (by its wording) all black girls and women as actual or potential murderers of black children. Literally, to be inside the space of a black womb is depicted as being more dangerous than in the South Side of Chicago during a shoot-out, *or* inside of a super-max prison, *or* fighting in Afghanistan, *or* ghettoized in poor public schools, *or* walking in Sanford, FL, with a hoodie, *or* walking in the middle of the street in Ferguson, *or* asking for help—while black—after you've been in a car accident.

Picking up on the mantra of black death, the organization LEARN—which stands for Life Education and Resource Network—operates the website "Black Genocide." Its goal is to bring more African Americans into the anti-choice movement and to inform the black community that Planned Parenthood engages in "eugenics and genocide" *specifically* against black people. They write:

> Blacks make up 12% of the population, but 35% of the abortions in America. Are we being targeted? Isn't that genocide? ...Margaret Sanger... said, "Colored people are like human weeds and are to be exterminated." Is her vision being fulfilled today?[80]

Although this quote is attributed to Sanger, its source is unverifiable. It seems to be misquoted or completely fabricated by LEARN and others in the anti-choice movement. Unlike Heroic Media, LEARN's rhetoric plays on the fear of racial endangerment at the hands of a segment of white society that is bent on limiting the black population. Yet, like Heroic Media, LEARN not only attacks Planned Parenthood they also name black women as *accomplices* in the *genocide* of black people. Black women are ultimately responsible for the loss, they claim, of "16 million" black lives. By some estimates, these numbers may be close to the number of black lives lost en route to the Americas during the so-called Transatlantic Slave Trade. What a heavy, unethical, and corrosive burden to lie on black women.

In addition to Heroic Media and LEARN, the group Priests for Life organizes the "Pro-Life Freedom Ride" to mirror the freedom rides that helped end segregation in the South. During one of the rides in 2011, the group planned a stop at the grave of Martin Luther King Jr., where they held a rally and carried signs that read: "Abortion"—not heart disease or illness related to poor health care or anything else— "Abortion is the #1 killer of Blacks in America." Priests for Life and their supporters believe that the struggle to end abortion, not mass incarceration, income inequality, or marriage equality (which has finally been won)—is the great civil rights struggle of our time. Perhaps one of the most inflammatory comments made by Alveda King—head of African American outreach and a niece of Dr. Martin Luther King Jr.—is:

> Today, the little baby in the womb appears to his or her mother very much like a little slave. He or she cannot decide whether he or she will live or die … He or she is just like a slave at mercy of slave owners.[81]

The Pro-Choice Response

In an effort to counter these attacks, in February 2012, Planned Parenthood began showing Carol McDonald's documentary *A Vital Service: African American Stories of Reproductive Health Care.* Based on narratives from black women, it portrays Planned Parenthood as a friend and supporter of the black community by showing women who have received reproductive services through Planned Parenthood. The documentary is set up as a series of narratives where mostly black women tell stories about their positive interactions with the organization. Like LEARN and Priest for Life, Planned Parenthood also relies on statistics and information designed to educate the black community on issues related specifically to black women's reproduction. So, for example, Planned Parenthood wants black people to know that they provide breast examinations, which are:

> especially important for African-American women for whom the disease presents a particular challenge. Among women diagnosed with breast cancer, African-American women are most likely to die from the disease— they are 40 percent more likely to die of breast cancer than white women.[82]

Additionally, Planned Parenthood wants the black community to know that:

> Planned Parenthood health centers have provided health care in the United States for almost 100 years and know that a disproportionate number of African-American women face multiple barriers to accessing quality, affordable health care, which leads to higher rates of both unintended pregnancy and abortion.[83]

On its surface, we may see Planned Parenthood's claims as supportive of black women, their overall health, and their reproductive choices. Nevertheless,

Planned Parenthood's language is paternalistic. Rather than using a language of partnership working with black women, they talk about how they work *for* the black community. And they do not discuss the ways that black women and black people have been crusaders for their own health care. Finally, Planned Parenthood does a very poor job of acknowledging its connection to the eugenics movement. By not acknowledging its paternalistic language and problematic history, is Planned Parenthood following a pattern of coercive action that is not entirely dissimilar from that of the anti choice movement? In any case, there are strong ideological claims on both sides, and these claims are rooted in a hegemonic belief about black women's reproductive capacity.

The Ideological Battle

Although ideological criticism has origins in structuralism, semiotics, Cultural Studies, and Marxism, Sonja Foss notes all of these movements are "rooted in some basic notions about ideologies and how they function."[84] What is noteworthy here is that the "notion that multiple ideologies—multiple patterns of belief—exist in any culture and have the potential to be manifest in rhetorical artifacts."[85] Although there is space for a multiplicity of belief within any given culture, what typically happens is that one ideology gets "privileged over others in [our] culture."[86] Though they stand on opposite sides, I would argue that the pro- and anti-choice movements share a similar ideology about black wombs. That ideology is predicated on a historical and socially dominant belief that black women and their wombs need to be controlled because ultimately black women are not capable of making rational decisions about their reproduction. Foss explains perfectly how one ideology can emerge from groups seemingly on different sides of the political spectrum, writing that: "a particular ideology becomes hegemonic as a result of a process in which a variety of groups forge an accord with one another or tacitly give their consent that perspective will be allowed to dominate."[87] Due to the predominance of the shared ideology that supports the pro- and anti-choice movements, black women's voices and perspectives are repressed or simply ignored. This hegemonic bind "constitutes a kind of social control, a means of symbolic coercion or a form of domination of the more powerful groups over the ideologies of those with less power."[88]

Thus, when engaging in a black feminist critique of the harmful ideology of a white and patriarchal society, the question is not "how do we resist?" because black women have always resisted, but rather "*how do we make the other listen?*" So, for example, soon after the offensive billboards appeared in 2010, Sistersong and Trust Black Women released a joint statement responding directly to the Heroic Media and other organizations over the billboards:

> Yesterday, racist billboards went up in Soho attacking black women and our human rights by claiming "the most dangerous place for an African American child is in the womb." SisterSong, a coalition of 80 women of color and Indigenous women's organizations, denounces this cynical attempt to use

race during Black History Month as an excuse to assault women's rights. Black women are not the pawns of these white people who erect such billboards. We find them offensive, racist, sexist and—most of all—disrespectful of our decision making, our 400-year history of raising and caring for black children, and our human right to make health care choices for ourselves.[89]

The group goes on to provide "talking points" that black women may use to refute the allegations of black genocide. In spite of the efforts of both groups to push back, the assaults continue. Putting a finer point on the issue, Foss writes: "When an ideology becomes hegemonic through a process of accord and consent, it accumulates 'the symbolic power to map or classify the world for others.'"[90]

Phenomenology, Dissent, and Colorblindness

This short but sobering analysis of the power of an ideology that has negatively framed black women's agency for over 200 years should remind us that there is no magic bullet, no single thing that will prevent the continued misreading of black women's bodies simply because the ideology that posits black women and their wombs as destructive and in need of control (in one form or another) is sown into the very tapestry of the American psyche. Yet, there is a lesson to be learned here as well, and that lesson is that black women can and should use their bodies as points of reference and inquiry (since, it seems everyone else does). Charles Johnson's "Phenomenology of the Black Body" is an example of a black scholar centering the black body and using it in order to makes visible the strain the black male body is under vis-à-vis white supremacist society. Likewise, George Yancy's "elevator effect" also does an excellent job laying bare the psychological cost of engaging the world while embodied as a black man. Given the high profile deaths of black men and boys, Johnson and Yancy powerfully expose the forces aligned against black male existence.

The problem, if we can term it as such, with Johnson, Yancy and even theorists like Fanon, is that their critiques have carried the day, meaning that their analyses in a way have come to define the totality of the black experience. The next section offers a discussion of phenomenology and a more general discussion on the means used by society to reject lived experience. Finally, I propose a phenomenology of the black female body that, rather than deflecting attention away from black women's bodies in particular, centers attention squarely on them as well as providing another point of reference from which to explain black experiences in a US context.

The lure of phenomenology is that it offers the chance not merely to think about experiences but to thoroughly participate with them. In this way, phenomenology is, for lack of a better term, corporal—it "capture[s] life as it is lived."[91] Phenomenology offers the possibility of actually touching the body of the living agent as a particular site of inquiry, thus the agent becomes a source of knowledge and explanation. For race, gender and other liberation-minded scholars, phenomenology is particularly attractive because it validates the careful attention these orientations pay to experience as a valid, objective, and even quantifiable source of knowledge. This is a critical point, since questions like "how do you know?" have been used to silence or even cast doubt on, for example, racist experiences that people of color face on a daily basis. It is interesting (and sometimes frustrating) that when racist episodes occur,[92] they invite a range of responses including:

> *Shock:* "Oh, my goodness, I cannot believe something like this could happen."
> *Confirmation*: "I told you so!"
> *Deflection*: "How do you know it was racists? Since I was raised to be color-blind[93] and believe society to be colorblind as well I cannot believe this could happen in this day and age. There must be another reason for such an event to take place."

Of these responses, I would suggest that the third one actually poses the most danger, especially to people of color, because it denies their lived experience. Moreover, the denial of experience is attached to making the person who *actually* experienced the event feel as though that by claiming to be the victim of a racist attack, they are being illogical. The danger here is that person who *did not* experience the event is in a better position to understand and judge what really happened.

In the book *Racial Formation in the United States*, Michael Omi provides a critical and apt discussion of what the term "colorblind" means in a US context: "Race thinking," ... no longer significantly informs our perceptions, shapes attitudes, and influences our individual, collective, and institutional practices.[94]

On the whole, Race scholars are quick to refute colorblind ideology arguing, for example, that those who operate from a position of "colorblind" deny the racial experience of people of color as well as their own racial experiences; that those who support and advocate for a colorblind society fail to acknowledge how race continues to shape everyone's life; that those who claim "colorblind" as a legitimate philosophical and social location are acting in bad faith and are thus willfully ignorant in their denial of what is actually occurring in society, etc.

To say that society is "colorblind" is to take a firm ideological position on the place of race in society. When, for example, a white person deploys the rhetoric of colorblindness, this should *not* be taken as a purely aspirational stance. In other words, this should not be misconstrued as the white person saying that society is moving toward being colorblind. Rather, it is to say that "large swaths of society *are* colorblind" and those who *see* race are acting in bad faith or contrary to social and legal norms and perhaps even purposely misinterpreting their experiences for their own gain. The notion of colorblindness hinders people of color because it deflects attention away from the dominant white society that claims to be "colorblind." Consider, for example, the following hypothetical scenario:

You are in a class and a black male student talks about how when he walks on campus he feels hyper-visible. People often ask him if he plays on the basketball or football team. The night before, campus police stopped him for the third time that semester. All they told him was that he was stopped because he looked "suspicious." A young white female student responds by saying she could not believe how this could happen in this day and age. She wants to know if the young man was walking at night and what he was wearing; she relates that there have been burglaries on campus recently; she mentions that she has lots of black friends; she states that she is sure that the police were just doing their job and didn't mean to hurt his feelings, and like most people she is colorblind—she just doesn't see color and doesn't understand how anyone could use their race as a way to explain something bad that happened to them.

This hypothetical scenario illustrates how a colorblind ideology can hinder people of color as well as white people. In this hypothetical scenario, "colorblind" becomes a tool to deflect attention away from patterns of discrimination, harassment and racist micro/macro-aggression that people of color experience every day at the hands of white society—I call this *death by a thousand racist cuts*. Rather than dealing with the harassing and demoralizing behavior for *what it is*, "colorblindness" is deployed as an appeal to see things "rationally" and "neutrally" (hence the questions about behavior and time of day and saying the police were just "doing their job"). She is in effect saying, "Young black man, your color had nothing to do with you being stopped."

Second, colorblindness is used as a shield protecting and excusing the behavior of whites. So in our hypothetical scenario the subtext can be read as follows: *the police are here to protect and serve, but they would never stop a person for simply being black. Instead of incorrectly seeing this as a racial incident, the young black male should see this as minor inconvenience and since he is presumably innocent, he has nothing to worry about.* Of course, this is small comfort to the young man who is doing nothing *but* walking on campus where he is a student while black and male.

Finally, colorblindness provides a way *not* to take race-based discrimination seriously. If race does not exist in a colorblind society, racism must not exist either. Consequently, to follow the logic of being "colorblind," non-white people who claim discrimination based on race are either misconstruing the situation (i.e. not seeing things clearly or rationally), accusing whites of racism where none is present, or focusing too much on race. "Colorblind" in this sense is not an invitation to conversation; rather, it is a way of silencing and closing off dialogue. It is a way of making others feel paranoid and irrational.

"Colorblind" as a Radical and Transformative Politic

"Colorblind" does not have to be a tool to deflect attention away from a racial event; it does not have to mean blindness to the lived experience of non-white people, nor does it have to mean "that the way to solve racial problems from this point on, is to act in a race-neutral manner." The rhetoric of "colorblind" can also be an attempt to tap into the most profound feelings and desires of this nation. There is positive potential in the term "colorblind," but it must be used appropriately and thoughtfully. Alluding to the Declaration of Independence during his second inaugural address, President Barack Obama stated, "We, the people, declare today that the most evident of truths—that all of us are created equal—is the star that guides us still." What these words express is that we are not yet a nation basking in the light of equality. Rather, we are following the light toward equality, but we have to walk through the muck and mire of inequality to get there. It is still an unattained goal. In order to achieve a color-blind society, white people in particular need to rethink how they use the term. This second sense of the term stands more in line with the principles expressed by the Declaration of Independence. This is to use "colorblind" as an aspirational principle, as when President Obama alludes to "colorblind" as the "star that guides us still." To use "colorblind" in this way is to free it from its current status as a societal falsehood (claiming that we are a "colorblind" nation); it transforms "colorblind" into an aspiration—a moving toward (we are striving to become a "colorblind nation"). To see "colorblind" in this way opens up the potential for a radical and transformative racial politics.

With this second sense of the term in mind, let's revisit the hypothetical scenario in which the young black man relates his experiences and the young white woman's response. Instead of asking the young man what he was wearing, talking about police doing their job, and her black friends, she might instead respond in the following way:

> I'm sorry this happened to you. As a white woman, I grew up my whole life hearing that society is colorblind. And as much as I want to believe this that society does not see race, your story and your experiences make me realize that we are not colorblind, but I hope we are working toward it. I am not trying to be offensive by my use of the term colorblind. Being colorblind does not mean that I don't see our nation's problematic racial history and how deeply it impacts us today. It means that I believe one's skin color should have no bearing on how one is treated in society. I hope we can work together to make this a reality. I know that this will be impossible if we continue to question the lived experiences of others.

Deploying the term "color-blind" in this way invites conversation, creates the space for a transformative racial politics to emerge, one that values and acknowledges the lived experiences of others, rather than being hell-bent on rejecting them. The final section of this chapter provides a companion story to the one above from my own personal experience. My aim is to present and subsequently analyze a phenomenology of the black female body.

Phenomenology of the Black Female Body

> There are police cars everywhere. I am confused and frightened. Their lights are flashing around me. I've seen these light before. The color red and blue is seared into my brain its distorts my vision … I've seen red and blue lights at night tearing up and tearing through my neighborhood. I've seen them flash over black bodies lying in the street as the officers (men and dogs) try to keep the crowds at bay. I've seen black and brown bodies bathed in red and blue light as they are led away to the inside of cop cars and jails. This time the light show is for me. I am the star, bathed in their glory. They flash around me, blind me, penetrate my body like x-rays. I am stripped in red and blue with black skin peeping through at the margins. My mind retains its ability to comprehend. This is not a story put together by another me. It is but one story of many …[95]

One reason why race scholars are drawn to phenomenology is because it provides an anchoring validation for our experiences. Because phenomenology provides the opportunity to explain things as they appear, lived experiences become important, definable, and marks a vital point for explaining things. Moreover, once experiences are collected and compared, this provides theorists opportunities to show patterns in social behavior or corroborating information, thereby strengthening claims of, for example, racism or sexism. More personally, from a black feminist perspective, phenomenology allows the possibility to see the ways in which the black women's experiences diverge from that of black males. One of these way includes black women's interaction with state violence perpetrated by police. Although black women are killed by police violence or die while in state custody,[96] their numbers do not rival those of black men. One need only visit databases like *The Counted* to see that black and Latino males make up those disproportionately killed by police. Additionally, "young black men were nine times more likely than other Americans to be killed by police officers in 2015."[97] With the availability of smartphone videos showing the murder of black men like Eric Garner and the aftermath of Philando Castille's shooting, it is really not hard to understand how the tragic deaths of black men come to define and concretize the recent Black Lives Matter (BLM) Movement.

A question we might ask at this moment is "Do black women also experience everyday racism differently from black men?" Given the research in the area of standpoint theory and gendered racism, the answer to this question is yes. Gendered racism is another way to explain how race and sex work together to negatively impact the lives of black women, while at the same time highlighting black women's unique interaction with racial as well as gender violence. For example, black women experienced a particular form of gendered violence during enslavement that included rape and other forms of sexual corrosion and the work of Dawn M. Szymanski and Jioni A. Lewis[98] explores how black women cope with stress brought by gendered racism.

It is important to read the work of Frantz Fanon, Charles Johnson, and George Yancy in terms of an analysis of gendered racism to see whether or not they specifically acknowledge that this is what they are doing. One marker that seems constant in their analysis –linking their various testimonies—is that they all are returned to bodies disjointed, fragmented, and without a community of other black men (or black women), who loving put them back together. It seems as though black men, as expressed by Fanon, Johnson, and Yancy, are responsible for their own healing, if, in fact, they heal at all. The overwhelming sense one gets from reading each of these accounts is justifiable anger; justifiable anger at specific perpetrators, justifiable anger at the social order, and justifiable anger about their treatment by a society dominated by vicious white racism. What readers of such accounts often miss is the desperate individualism expressed by the black male interlocutors. Take, for example, Fanon's description of events while riding a train in Lyon. Fanon is accosted by a young white child who relates to his mother his fear of seeing a black person. Fanon explains:

> "Look! A Negro!" It was a passing sting. I attempted a smile. "Look! A Negro!" Absolutely. I was beginning to enjoy myself. "Look! A Negro!" The circle was gradually getting smaller. I was really enjoying myself. "Maman, look, a Negro; I'm scared!" Scared! Scared! Now they were beginning to be scared of me. I wanted to kill myself laughing, but laughter had become out of question.[99]

Fanon's response to this incident is to seek refuge outside of his body, he "transported" himself "on that particular day far, very far" away "and gave [himself] up as an object." Fanon's frustration is palpable. All Fanon wants is "to be a man, and nothing but a man."[100] The phrase, "to be nothing but a man" is a particular black male utterance. It signifies black male desire to be seen as individuals who want to be taken as individuals rather than have their identity bound up in a group affiliation or with other black men who may interface differently with the world. The call to individuality or individuation is, for some black men, a matter of life and death. Because, as shown by Fanon, to be black and male in society means to carry the weight and consequences of negative and potentially deadly stereotypes. Notice how quickly the little boy on the train moves from "Look! A Negro!" to fear and ultimately to the "Negro" preparing to harm him and others:

> the Negro is trembling with cold, the cold chills the bones, the lovely little boy is trembling because he thinks the Negro is trembling with rage, the little white boy runs to his mother's arms: "*Maman*, the Negro's going to eat me."[101]

As the little white boy's mother attempts to wrest control of the situation instead of focusing on her child's rude behavior, she instead keeps the white gaze focused on Fanon, "Look how handsome that Negro is." Fanon, unable to contain himself any longer, lashes out saying, "The handsome nigger says fuck you."[102]

> The summer before entering college I attended a six-week bridge program. I discovered a lot about myself during that time. I could tell that college was going to be difficult for me. Nevertheless, I walked in with some advantages including a Catholic school education, siblings who had attended college and served as strong examples, smartness and curiosity, and natural leadership abilities. Although I had all this going for me, I had to learn how to become a student. Though my immigrant parents believed in education, they did not understand how things worked in this country. But, learning how to become a college student ended up being the least of my worries, more importantly I had to learn to understand my black girl body in the predominately white context of my Catholic university literally in the middle of nowhere.[103]

Johnson's reaction to being what he calls "epidermalized" is similar to Fanon, as he too hopes to escape the tyranny of group identification. Johnson explains his encounter with a white male professor whom he "knows well."[104] The professor "glances up quickly, yet does not acknowledge that he knows" him.[105] Now there may be several reasons that this professor did not recognize Johnson, including maybe the professor has bad vision and thus had a difficult time seeing him; maybe Johnson caught his professor thinking about something very deep and his professor needs time to switch his brain from the task of absorbed thought to that of verbal communication. By Johnson's account, the professor sees Johnson's body as a fixed object among many other fixed objects. Johnson writes, "he sees me as he sees the fire extinguisher to my left, that chair outside the door."[106]

After being recognized by his professor, Johnson and he shake hands and Johnson has a moment of awareness as he see his black hand against this professor's white hand—this is the moment that Johnson is returned to himself as "'stained,' as thought I were an object for myself and no longer a subject. In fact, the stain of the black body seems figuratively to darken consciousness itself, to overshadow my existence as a subject."[107] Like Fanon, Johnson desires to stand as an subject not being "over-determined from without"[108]—in the singular—rather than an object among other objects.

> Although I attended predominately white schools since I was in the sixth grade, I was always embedded in a critical black community that I (thankfully) went home to every night. I lived in my black community, attended my family's black church, listened to hip-hop, R&B, and soul, went to the shop to get my hair done, and dated black guys. I may have rolled with white people during the day but my soul was black, my context was black, my pride was black. Walking down the street in my neighborhood, I was a dark-skin honey. Thickness meant something, since no one had a problem with big thighs, and butts. Me and my friends were fine! Dudes called us

shorty and although there was a never-ending barrage of street harassment, there was also real appreciation of black girl beauty. At my pretty much damn near white college, thin was in. I'm not sure if any black or Latina girl ever felt pretty. It was weird. Once we hit campus, all compliments stopped, except at night when white boys found many of us alluring.[109]

Similar to Fanon and Johnson, Yancy also describes being returned to his body, deformed and disoriented by the racism he encounters. For Yancy, it is the clicking sound of car doors being locked as he walks down the street. One reaction he has is to open the car door and yell, "Surprise! You've just been carjacked by your worst nightmare, now get out of the fucking car!" What all these encounters have in common is the hyper-masculine frame that structures their response. So one way to resist the white gaze is through direct and physical confrontation. Racism makes them want to holler, but it also makes them want to kick whiteness ass. The sheer gendered physicality of their response is extraordinary as is the way that they fail to reach out to a community of black men. The fact of (male) blackness has very little to do with the fact of (female) blackness or black women's lived experience with whiteness.

Home from my bridge program and feeling all kinds of good about myself, I met up with a white guy whom I had been kicking it with since my sophomore year in high school. He was one of those cool white dudes who had flavor and a certain amount of juiciness about him. We went to the park. He parked his car, real close on the curb—not on the grass but pretty near it so others could get around his car. Walking to the lake and talking like young people do, I was crazy, taken by his dark hair, and pretty blue eyes that were ringed in black. Walking to the car hand-in-hand we stopped for a quick kiss by the car door. We then got in and, oh shit, cop cars out of nowhere. Three of them all around us. We were blocked in. My heart started to pound. I'm thinking about what the fuck we could have done. There must be some mistake, because I know we didn't do shit but look at the lake, walk hand-in-hand, and steal a kiss.

They separated us, taking me to the car parked directly behind us. My vision is blurry. I can feel the cop's hand on my back as he guides me towards his car. I am in a fucking cop car. I am nineteen. I am afraid. My parents would be ashamed. I'm confused. "What's your name?" one of the cops asked me. "My name is Maria del Guadalupe Morris," I replied. "What?" asked the cop, I say again, "My name is Maria del Guadalupe Morris." I get it, in your eyes, my name does not match my embodiment. Michelle, Tyneshia, La'Seah, all good dark skin, black girl names. But, "del Guadalupe?" Something is not right with me. Talking to another police as if I weren't there "Where is she from?" "Is she black"? I see your eyes trying to understand how this dark-skinned black girl, with hair like that can have such a name.

I can hear you. I hear you trying to understand me, why not ask the one person here who can answer the question definitively? But, that's too logical. So I sit and wait for you to remember that I can talk. Looking out the window, trying to recapture the feeling of love and happiness but that feeling is gone.[110]

Lisa Collins explains a similar event when during a graduate class she and a white male friend were asked to "stand in the front of [their] class on representation and race in popular culture." Lisa Collins represented black women while her friend, Nathan, represented white men. Collins writes:

> They chose to focus on Nathan. "Tall," "thin," and "smart looking" were the comments that I heard. Next the professor asked about me. I tasted my own dread and began to detest the professor and all of the eyes on me....[111]

In that instance Collins describes mentally leaving her body in order to avoid her colleagues' scrutiny. Like Fanon, Collins too wants to escape the signification heaped on her by white society. Unlike Fanon, Johnson, or Yancy, the reader does not get a sense of anger from Collins' account. She does not lash out at, verbally assault her audience, or dream of committing a violent act. What one does get is a sense of dread at being visible in such a degrading way and utter detachment. In a move reminiscent of Pecola Breedlove in Morrison's *The Bluest Eye*, Collins' spirit flies away to a place where the eyes of her white audiences cannot follow her.

One of the police officers calls me back, "Hey, where are you from?" "Are you here legally?" "Yes," I answer. "I was born here. My parents are from Costa Rica. I'm from the south side." Warning bells, I'm sure, since the south side conjures up all that's bad with Syracuse with those no good black people robbing and killing the shit out of each other every damn day. The ghetto of all the ghettoes in your world. And, though I'm bothered by the cops' lack of imagining my community as a place where people live, and their inability to wrap their mind around the Afro Latina nation, I am far more disturbed by their eyes as they wander over my body. I don't know what is coming next. Am I going to be arrested? What's going on with my friend, you know the white guy in the other car, the one who I've loved since 10th grade? I want to be near him.

When you *finally* remember that I'm there and to a degree capable of answering questions, you open your mouth and shatter my world. "So," you ask, "how do you know this guy? What's his name? How long have you known him? Did you meet him tonight? What were you doing in the park past hours (never mind that we were there past hours because you decided to stop us). There has been "activity" in this area. How do you know him, again?"

My mind is reeling from your questioning; I am shrinking from your gaze. "I've known him for a long time. My brother introduced us. His name is_____." What kind of activity? Like Frisbee or football? What's activity, is it a thing that people are doing? I'm confused and not sure. This is all I can manage. I begin to cry. Not that I think my tears will pacify you, because I'm not dumb enough to believe that anyone gives a shit when black girls cry.[112]

Black women's tears have no weight, they don't shut down conversation, nor do they elicit pity. It does not seem that tears stopped too many enslavers from separating black women from their children. Tears didn't seem to prevent black women from getting raped. Tears didn't stop lynching. What good were tears when, as explained by Dorothy Roberts. a group of slave women were in the field when a storm hit? The women dug a trench for their babies to lie in while they worked the fields. The storm was so fast and so violent it drowned the babies before anyone could save them. Tears did not prevent a little black girl from having her head pushed into the ground and a white cop kneeling on her back. And, tears did not save Sandra Bland [say her name] from being pulled over for an illegal lane change, having her head slammed to the ground, and dying in her jail cell. Who but other black women care for black women's tears?

I still cry for my girl self. If my tears had words that you would listen to, they would tell you that he (the guy sitting a police car away) was my first real love. Like the kind you cry about when he doesn't call or when you know that he likes you and another girl, and it feels like he shattered the sun. My tears say that although I am a girl in full bloom moving away from home to go to college that I'd give anything to marry him, all he has to do is reach out his hand. He used to pick me up from school and work. This cop could never know how I felt so cool dating a guy in college when I was in high school. How bold as hell I felt because he was this pretty, delicious white boy that white girls just loved, and how I had a look that said "Yeah, I pulled one of your finest, I guess ya'll ain't all that fly!" He doesn't realize that every year for the past 3 years we've gone to midnight mass together and watched as they brought the light of the world into the Cathedral I made my first communion in. He doesn't know, doesn't care, can't imagine ...[113]

The lived experience of black women in a white supremacist patriarchal society is rooted in a lack of protection. Time and again black women are summarily told that our bodies do not warrant protection or respect. The black female body is layered with too much negative signification about its blackness and its femaleness. Later in her essay, Lisa Collins shows how abolitionists were problematically able to reclaim the black male body and use it as an appeal against slavery. As Collins shows, abolitionists could not reclaim the black female body, because black women's bodies were connected to sexuality and sexual desire and thus made inappropriate symbols of "freedom."[114] The fact of female blackness is that, in the white imagination, black women's bodies are always already dirty and debased—and there is no way to deny this charge.

Even when I'm crying, my brain is working. I wonder why he asks such strange and intrusive questions ... shit, all we did was steal a kiss and get into a car on a lovely day. But in a heart beat I understand. The word comes in Spanish and English—prostituta, prostitute. And, then I get it that in your eyes, I am a prostitute, a whore, a call-girl, a night-walker, a hooker. What else could I be? Why else would I be sitting with a pretty white boy, in his pretty car, in a pretty park so close to sundown? My heart is shattered, in that moment I fragment, literally fall to pieces. When you finally run us through your system, find nothing, and send us on our way without even a ticket, my night is ruined. I cannot even look at my love. I am confused by his whiteness and the inability to compartmentalize, to differentiate his whiteness from the whiteness of the police. He, I suspect, feels the same way. I know what questions you asked him. They are the same ones you asked me, with the difference being I am the one who is shamed. He takes me home. I see him one more time after that. It is over. I can't look at him without feeling an acute sense of my being. I cannot look at him without the accusation of being a black whore stuck in my head.[115]

Notes

1 John W. Blassingame, *Slave Testimony: Two Centuries of Letters, Speeches, Interviews, and Autobiographies* (Baton Rouge. LA: Louisiana State University Press, 1977).
2 Ibid., p. 126.
3 Ibid., p. 131.
4 Ibid., p. 131. Emphasis added.
5 Ibid., p. 131.
6 Ibid., p. 131.
7 Ibid., p. 132.
8 Ibid., p. 133.
9 Frantz Fanon, *Black Skin, White Mask* (New York: Grove Press, 1967), p. 89.
10 Paula Giddings, *When and Where I Enter* (New York: Bantam Books, 1985), p. 34.
11 Ibid., p. 35.
12 Katie Geneva Cannon, "Slave Ideology and Biblical Interpretation," in Jacqueline Bobo and Cynthia Hudley, eds., *The Black Studies Reader* (New York: Routledge, 2004).
13 Giddings, When and Where I Enter, p. 35.
14 Ibid., p. 35.
15 Ibid., p. 35.
16 Ibid., pp. 36–37.
17 bell hooks, *Ain't I a Woman: Black Women and Feminism* (Boston: South End Press, 1981), p. 20.
18 Ibid., p. 21.
19 Ibid., p. 22.
20 Ibid., p. 23.
21 Ibid., p. 22.
22 Barbara Welter, "The Cult of True Womanhood: 1820–1860," *American Quarterly* 18(2) (Summer 1966): 151–174.
23 See Maria del Guadalupe Davidson, "Black Women's Bodies, Ideology, and the Rhetoric of the Pro- and Anti-Choice Movements in the US," *Gender and Education* (September 13, 2016).

24 Terri Kapsalis, "Mastering the Female Pelvis: Race and the Tools of Reproduction," in T. Kapsalis, *Public Privates: Performing Gynecology from Both Ends of the Speculum* (Durham, NC: Duke University Press, 2002), p. 263.

25 Ibid., p. 263.

26 Ibid., p. 273.

27 Jeffery S. Sartin, "J. Marion Sims, the Father of Gynecology: Hero or Villain?" *Southern Medical Journal*, 97(5) (2004). Available at: www.medscape.com/view article/479892_3 (accessed July 21, 2016).

28 Kapsalis, "Mastering the Female Pelvis," p. 269.

29 Ibid., p. 273.

30 See Dorothy Roberts, Killing the Black Body: Race, Reproduction, and the Meaning of Liberty (New York: Vintage Books, 1997).

31 See Khiara M. Bridges, *Reproducing Race: An Ethnography of Pregnancy as a Site of Racialization* (Berkeley, CA: University of California Press, 2011).

32 Charles Mills, *The Racial Contract* (Ithaca, NY: Cornell University Press, 1997).

33 Beverly Guy-Sheftall, Words of Fire: An Anthology of African-American Feminist Thought (New York: New Press, 1995), p. 5.

34 Cited in Giddings, *When and Where I Enter*, p. 66.

35 Cited in Giddings, p. 68.

36 bell hooks, *Ain't I a Woman: Black Women and Feminism* (Boston, MA: South End Press, 1981), p. 3.

37 Ibid., p. 5.

38 bell hooks, *Talking Back: Thinking Feminist, Thinking Black* (Boston: South End Press, 1989), p. 5.

39 Ibid., p. 9.

40 Barbara Smith, "Toward a Black Feminist Criticism," in Winston Napier, ed., *African American Literary Theory* (New York: New York University Press, 2000), p. 136.

41 Ibid., p. 136.

42 Ibid.

43 Tina Campt, *Other Germans* (Ann Arbor, MI: University of Michigan Press, 2004), p. 32.

44 Ibid., p. 64.

45 Ibid., p. 41.

46 Ibid., p. 38.

47 Sonja Foss, *Rhetorical Criticism* (Long Grove, IL: Waveland Press, 1996), p. 291.

48 Ibid., p. 294.

49 Ibid., p. 294.

50 Cited in Stephanie Li, "Motherhood as Resistance in Harriet Jacobs's *Incidents in the Life of a Slave Girl*," *Legacy*, 23(1) (2006): 14.

51 Thomas F. Gossett, *Race: The History of an Idea in America* (New York: Oxford University Press, 1997).

52 Ibid., p. 3.

53 I take the phrase "not quite white" from Matt Wray's book, *Not Quite White: White Trash and the Boundaries of Whiteness* (Durham, NC: Duke University Press, 2006).

54 Dorothy Roberts, Killing the Black Body: Race, Reproduction, and the Meaning of Liberty (New York: Vintage Books, 1999), p. 57.

55 We should, by the way, also closely consider the historical significance of the creation of eugenics as a social scientific movement with the publication of Francis Galton's *Hereditary Genius* (1869) and the full emancipation of all black people in America (1865). Here I am referring to June 19, 1865 (also known as Juneteenth). This is the date when slaves in Texas were notified of their freedom—some two years after the Emancipation Proclamation.

56 Patricia Hill Collins, Black Feminist Thought: Knowledge, Consciousness, and the Politics of Empowerment (New York: Routledge, 2000), p. 71.
57 Ibid., p. 74.
58 Ibid., p. 76.
59 Ibid.
60 Ibid., p. 77.
61 Ibid., p. 76.
62 Ibid., p. 78.
63 Ibid., p. 79.
64 Cliven Bundy was hailed a hero by some for defying the Bureau of Land Management in 2014. For more information, see Adam Nagourney, "A Defiant Rancher Savors the Audience That Rallied to His Side," *The New York Times*, April 23, 2014.
65 Roberts, Killing the Black Body, p. 57.
66 Ibid.
67 Ibid.
68 Ibid., p. 58.
69 Ibid.
70 Cited in ibid., p. 159.
71 Ibid., p. 72.
72 Ibid., p. 73.
73 Ibid., p. 74.
74 Ibid., p. 105.
75 Ibid., p. 122.
76 Ibid., p. 104.
77 Ibid., p. 108.
78 Ibid., p. 109.
79 Ibid.
80 "Planned Parenthood," available at: www.blackgenocide.org/planned.html (accessed August 27, 2015).
81 "Pro-Life Freedom Rides Inspired by Historic US Civil Rights Events," available at: www.priestsforlife.org/africanAmerican/blog/index.php/pro-life-freedom-rides-inspired-by-historic-us-civil-rights-eventswww (accessed August 27, 2015).
82 "Our Issues," available at: www.plannedparenthoodaction.org/get-involved/pp-black-community/our-issues/ (accessed August 27, 2015).
83 "Our Issues," available at: www.plannedparenthoodaction.org/get-involved/pp-black-community/our-issues/ (accessed August 27, 2015).
84 Foss, Rhetorical Criticism, p. 294.
85 Ibid.
86 Ibid.
87 Ibid.
88 Ibid.
89 "New Racist Anti-Choice Billboards Show Up in NYC," available at: http://feministing.com/2011/02/24/new-racist-anti-choice-billboards-show-up-in-nyc/ (accessed August 27, 2015).
90 Foss, Rhetorical Criticism, p. 295.
91 Dermot Moran, *Introduction to Phenomenology* (London: Routledge, 2000), p. 5.
92 For more discussion on this issue and colorblindness, see my article "Deflection from the (Real) Issues," in *The American Mosaic: The African American Experience* (New York: ABC-CLIO, 2006). Available at: http://africanAmerican2.abc-clio.com/
93 I have chosen to use "colorblind" (without the hyphen) because this is the way that it frequently appears in literature about race.
94 Michael Omi and Howard Winant, *Racial Formation in the United States* (New York: Routledge, 2015), p. 2.

95 The extracts that follow are from the author's personal experiences.
96 See the case of Sandra Bland. Sandra Bland was an African American woman who committed suicide in prison after a traffic stop. Debbie Nathan's article, "What Happened to Sandra Bland" is very thoughtful: www.thenation.com/article/what-happened-to-sandra-bland/
97 *The Counted*, "Young Black Men Killed by US Police at Highest Rate in Year of 1,134 Death," available at: www.theguardian.com/us-news/2015/dec/31/the-counted-police-killings-2015-young-black-men
98 See Dawn M. Szymanski, and Jioni A. Lewis, "Gendered Racism, Coping, Identity Centrality, and African American College Women's Psychological Distress.," *Psychology of Women Quarterly*, 40(2) (2015): 229–243. doi:10.1177/0361684315616113.
99 Frantz Fanon, *Black Skin, White Mask* (New York: Grove Press, 1967), p. 91.
100 Ibid., p. 92.
101 Ibid., p. 93.
102 Ibid., p. 94.
103 Author's personal experience.
104 Johnson, "Phenomenology," p. 227.
105 Ibid., p. 227.
106 Ibid., p. 227.
107 Ibid., p. 227.
108 Ibid., p. 228.
109 Author's personal experience.
110 Author's personal experience.
111 Lisa Collins, "Economies of Flesh: Respecting the Black Female Body in Art," in Kimberly Wallace-Sanders, ed., *Skin Deep, Spirit Strong: The Black Female Body in American Culture* (Ann Arbor, MI: University of Michigan Press, 2002), p. 99.
112 Author's personal experience.
113 Author's personal experience.
114 Collins, "Economies of Flesh," p. 102.
115 Author's personal experience.

3 Worrying the Feminist Line

Although feminism uses the language of "waves" to discuss various iterations and concerns of radical women doing gender work, the term "waves" does not provide enough language or conceptual space, it seems, to address the changing nature of society and women's place within it. In addition, the metaphor of waves does not allow for the gradual gradations of change or even points of intersection between various generations of feminism. This is not to say that we have not seen large theoretical or attention shifts from one generation to another. What it does suggest is that there are concerns related to race, equality, access, education, etc. that remain central to feminist struggle over time. These central themes or core struggles may get lost when we use "waves" as a metaphor for feminist movement.

To put a finer point on this issue, if we date the first wave of feminism as beginning about 1835 and culminating in 1920 with women gaining the right to vote,[1] the second wave as beginning in the 1960s and reaching its zenith during the 1990s, and the third wave of feminism beginning in the 1990s and stretching to the present (which itself is debatable), we have left a lot of history and change open to discussion. What was happening in the interim or the period between when a feminist wave formed, when it crested, and when a new feminist wave began? Did gender activism cease? Linda Nicholson addresses these very issues in "Feminism in 'Waves': Useful Metaphor or Not?" As she explains, thinking about feminism in term of waves is functional especially when we get to the "second wave" because "it reminded people that the then current women's rights and women's liberation movements had a venerable past—that these movements were not historical aberrations but were part of a long tradition of activism."[2] The wave metaphor also provides a useful conceptual and pedagogical framework when presenting US women's history. Like other fields of thought, it is beneficial, at times, to parse women's history and activism into manageable sections or tie periods together thematically or temporally. In this way, the metaphor of waves of feminism show a continuity of feminist thought even in the midst of societal change.

Nevertheless, Linda Nicholson draws the conclusion that the wave metaphor has "outlived its usefulness" principally because there is a sense "that underlying certain historical differences, there is one phenomenon, *feminism*, that unites gender activism in the history of the United States, and that like a wave, peaks at certain times and recedes at others."[3] As Nicholson also notes, not only is the use of the term problematic and unhelpful in explaining women's historical, social, and political movement, but our use of the term "feminism" is also inadequate in describing all forms of "gender activism in the United States,"[4] particularly since "feminism" as a conceptual and activist framework is a fairly new way to describe women's resistance to patriarchy and other forms of oppression. As noted by Nicholson, "those active in [the suffrage] movement did not use the term [feminism]"[5] to describe their work and attitude about societal reorganization. And at various times, women of color have asked, *"What does it mean to be a feminist?"* particularly since feminism has excluded women of color and their concerns and at times, feminism as a movement has itself been overtly and covertly racist. In addition, using "waves" as a metaphor to sum up the totality of women's (of all races) historical activism simply does not suffice because far too much emphasis is placed on an essentialist understanding of not only feminism but of women's history, while at the same time negating individual communal concerns. This is particularly true when we think of the intergenerational transmission of values among black women, for example, and their concerns around issues like gender, sex and work. Feminism, simply put, is a slippery term which many eschew using.

I introduce this discussion about the waves of feminism and the slippery nature of the term "feminism" for a few reasons. First, to complicate how we discuss women's activism historically. White women, black women, and other women of color have taken different paths in their activism—sometimes their interests aligned (e.g. all women have an interest in fighting against patriarchy); while at other times their interests diverged and created rifts (e.g. the Sandy Springs meeting where black women were intentionally excluded) that we may still be trying to heal. Second, black women's activism cannot be so neatly organized by using the wave metaphor, since much of black women's activism and concerns is inextricably linked to the fight for racial, class, and gender justice as these things are bound to the intergenerational transmission of values and concerns.

Systems of Oppression and Intersectionality

Summed up by Kimberlé Crenshaw in her development of the term *intersectionality* and by Patricia Hill Collins in the critical black feminist analysis she coined as *interlocking systems of oppression*, there is a continuity (some might even say sameness or permanence) about black women's struggle that spans black women's interactions with the West. Intersectionality, now a popular framework in fields like Women's Studies, was developed by law professor, Kimberlé Crenshaw: "to illustrate that many of the experience Black women face are not subsumed within the traditional boundaries of race or gender discrimination as these boundaries are currently understood ..."[6]

In that same vein, Patricia Hill Collins argues that because black women embody racial and gender difference and are oftentimes poor as well, analysis of black women's lived experiences must look at the totality of their experiences with multiple forms of discrimination while at the same time seeing how racial, gender, and class discrimination merge together and become hegemonic. Reading Crenshaw's and Hill Collins' theories through the wide and long lens of history, we can say that there has never been a time in black women's lived experiences in America where they did not have to contend with the intersectional nature of their existence or the interlocking oppressions of race and gender.

Now it is certainly true that class, at various times, has functioned as a point of distinction and group separation with black women of higher classes being able to access structural privilege (attending college or opportunities to travel outside the USA). Yet, though this is the case, middle-class and wealthy black women have nevertheless had to endure racial and gender discrimination despite their access to various resources. So, for example, a friend of former Secretary of State Condoleezza Rice related a situation where she was shopping in a high end store—this is while she was merely the provost at Stanford—Secretary Rice reportedly asked to see a pair of earrings, but instead of showing her a nice pair, the clerk showed her "costume jewelry." Coit Blacker, a fellow Stanford professor, relates that: "Rice asked to see something nicer, prompting the clerk to whisper some sass under her breath." Blacker goes on to explain Rice's response:

> "Let's get one thing straight," he recalls her saying. "You are behind the counter because you have to work for minimum wage. I'm on this side asking to see the good jewelry because I make considerably more."[7]

This account summarized from Glenn Kessler's biography of Rice, *The Confidante: Condoleezza Rice and the Creation of the Bush Legacy*, offers us an interesting point of analysis. Here we have an upper-class, well-educated black woman being offered "sass" for wanting to look at a pair of expensive earrings and a white sales clerk's reluctance to grant the request. One way to read this is as race trumping class, so even if Rice is flashing symbols of class (being well dressed, mannerism, mode of communication, hair in order) what the clerk notices is her blackness. The fact of Dr. Rice's blackness, we can assume, leads to the clerk's distrust and apprehension. The fact of Dr. Rice's blackness also shows a stain and unworthiness—how can those black hands receive something so precious as these earrings? It is an awful phenomenon when things (a pair of earrings) have more value, credibility, and are deemed more precious than a black woman's hand. It is also interesting to note that Rice received a lot of criticism for this interaction in the press with headlines like "When Condi Went Nuclear" and on blog posts like *Jezebel*'s "Condi Rice Doesn't Care About Poor People."[8] Rice's actions are criticized because she was performing upper-class privilege with a black woman's attitude—"I know this poor ass heifer did not just try to give me a cheap pair of earrings!" What seems obvious to any black woman who shops is that Dr. Rice is engaging in an act of "checking." One way that black women assert their agency is through "checking others" or letting them know "what is *or* is not going to happen."

Though this may sound similar to bell hooks' idea of "talking back" where the "oppressed, the colonized, the exploited and those who stand and struggle side by side" assert their subjectivity through the act of speaking back to an authority,[9] it nevertheless is different. When a black woman (in our case) engages in the act of "checking," she is engaging in an act of silencing, putting someone in their place (which is outside of her space) and letting them know that she is *not* the one to harass or belittle. The act of "checking" someone or "checking that shit right now" is always in response to a real or intuitively sensed attack on a black woman's agency. When Dr. Rice engaged in the act of "checking" the clerk who did not show her the earrings she asked for and had the cheek to offer her "sass," that clerk got "checked," that is Dr. Rice silenced her with a verbal assault only a black woman whose agency is being threatened can level. Bringing us back to the point of class, what this instance finally shows is that even if one wears the trapping of class (fine clothing and jewelry), one's class may not necessarily trump one's skin color. In such cases, "checking" is certainly in order.

Although Crenshaw's and Collins' analyses are correct and expertly show the strain of living in America while embodied as black and as a women, I find it necessary to make the observation that at the core of both analyses—intersectionality and interlocking systems of oppression—indeed at the core of black feminist activism in the USA, is the *struggle for agency*. Agency—the right to act and be seen as an actor—is not *a* foundational principle in black feminist thought, it is *the* foundational principle in black feminist thought. Agency is the underpinning of the support structure for black feminist critical theory. This is important since to frame black feminist thought around the central theme of agency (or as supported by the concept of agency)—rather than on voice or identity being foundational—makes black women's demand for agency one of the oldest and most enduring philosophical positions expressed in the USA. Black women's articulation of agency occurs in print some two years *before* the *Declaration of Independence* which famously asserts:

> We hold these truths to be self-evident, that all men are created equal, that they are endowed by their Creator with certain unalienable Rights, that among these are Life, Liberty and the pursuit of Happiness.

Prior to those words being seen in print, in 1774, Phillis Wheatley, writing to Reverend Samson Occum states: "for in every human Breast, God has implanted a Principle, which we call Love of Freedom; it is impatient of Oppression, and pants for Deliverance."[10] In this declaration, Wheatley is clearly referring to the innate desire of people to be free from oppression, to self-determine rather than being determined by another—the basic desire for agency. Speaking of those who refuse to see the agency and humanity of enslaved Africans, Wheatley goes on:

I desire not for their Hurt, but to convince them of the strange Absurdity of their Conduct whose Words and Actions are so diametrically, opposite. How well the Cry for Liberty, and the reverse Disposition for the exercise of oppressive Power over others agree, –humbly think it does not require the Penetration of a Philosopher to determine.[11]

In this passage, Wheatley provides a genteelly stated but pointed critique of those who talk about freedom yet oppress others, calling their actions "diametrically opposite" to their beliefs. We should see Wheatley's analysis of the paradox of living in America at that time as one in a long line of protestations about the lack of America's founding ideals. Her analysis is rooted in her understanding that human desire for agency and oppression is antithetical to human nature and American ideals. This is the foundation of black women's theory that has spanned the ages and forms the core of what we can refer to as traditional black feminist thought.

Traditional Black Feminism and Agency

Some might wonder why I have added the term "traditional" to black feminism, since we might argue that, as a theoretical framework and a set practice, black feminism, like deconstruction or postcolonial theory, represents a critical interpretation of things like racism, patriarchy, and classism. Black feminism, again like postcolonialism and deconstruction, also represents an established radical resistance to commonplace narratives that posit some as "other" or inferior. In other words, black feminism exists to "talk back" and assert black women as tellers of their own stories. Though this is certainly true, black feminism is not merely a theoretical framework, it is theory in action, meaning that black feminism is a body of knowledge that is created by black women living in different social and historical contexts in the here and now. *Traditional black feminist* is a term I use to describe women of African descent, living in the USA, who belong to a particular generation or who work from a particular world view. These are black women scholars and activists following Ida B. Wells who work out of a decidedly and reflectively black feminist position. They not only act(ed) as black feminists, they call(ed) themselves black feminists because the work they did reflect(ed) their political stance. In this sense, black women like Anna Julia Cooper and Ida B. Wells were not black feminists but, as Joy James argues, they were black feminist foremothers or black feminist prototypes.[12]

In the Introduction to *Words of Fire*, Beverly Guy-Sheftall does a magnificent job of tracing the trajectory of black women's struggle and the development of the black feminist tradition from proto-black feminists like Maria Stewart who "admonished black women in particular to break free from stifling gender definitions and reach their fullest potential by pursuing formal education and careers;"[13] to scholars like Paula Giddings and Alice Walker. As argued by Guy-Sheftall, it was during the Civil Rights and Black Power Movements that "black feminist struggle came to the forefront in a more sustained manner and among a larger group."[14] Women in both the Civil Rights and Black Power Movements were doing their fair share (and some have argued more then their share) of the work to support both movements, yet they faced discrimination based solely on their status as women. It was out of this frustration and awareness that *traditional black feminism* was born.

Traditional black feminist concerns are articulated most concretely by the women of the Combahee River Collective. Guy-Sheftall explains that the Combahee River Collective took its name from "Harriet Tubman's 'military campaign' in South Carolina (1863), which freed nearly 800 slaves."[15] The document produced by this group of bold and daring women forms what can be called the first clear articulation of traditional black feminist thought. The member of the Combahee River Collective and other black radical women who were engaged in the Civil Rights and Black Power Movements felt that it was necessary to articulate a black feminist thought because black women's concerns were not taken seriously. Moreover, they noted that black women were particularly vulnerable to racist, sexist, heterosexist, classist oppression because they are black and women. The Combahee River Collective also highlighted the voices and concerns of black lesbians, arguing forcefully that "sexual politics under patriarchy is as pervasive in black women's lives as the politics of class and race."[16] Although there are many different articulations of black feminism, there are core features that demarcate traditional black feminist thought. Here again, Guy-Sheftall's work is illuminating as she provides certain "premises" in black feminist thought that remain "constant." Guy-Sheftall frames the argument in the following way:

1   Black women's "oppression" is specific and their lives are impacted by "race," "gender," and class.
2   Based on this multivariate and layered oppression, the solutions to black women's issues will be "different" from those of their gender ally (white women) and their racial ally (black men).
3   Black women cannot fight for racial equality without also fighting for gender equality. Both "struggles" are co-existent.
4   The struggle to end racism while simultaneously working to address "other isms" is not inconsistent or at odds with them.
5   Black women's freedom movement is based on their "lived experiences."[17]

These "premises" remain constant in traditional black feminist thought because they are articulated in the traditional black feminists' demand for black women's agency. Though not explicitly stated, agency is the core of black feminism and black women's collective action. The right to be seen as an actor, the right to resistance, the right to be seen as rational are embedded in the "premises" thoughtfully articulated by Guy-Sheftall. Whether or not it is explicitly stated, black feminist theory emphasizes the importance of agency.[18] In black feminist theory, then, the call for agency—to act like an agent and to be perceived as an agent—is a call to be more than a thing and to gain the power of resistance to the agency of others.

Anita Hill and the Struggle for Agency

The call for agency post the Black Power Movement and well into the so-called feminist movement became urgent with Anita Hill. Many young black women (or white women for that matter) may not have heard of Anita Hill and, if they have, it may be difficult to explain to them how critical Anita Hill's story is to black feminism. This is not to say that Anita Hill's story was not important to white feminists nor is it to be dismissive of the way that Anita Hill's story galvanized activism around sexual harassment in the workplace. What it does suggest and even highlight is that Anita Hill's story is the story of a black woman. Thus, we must be very careful about turning her story into a universal narrative about what happens to women in the workplace since doing so negates Anita Hill's position as a black woman in the workplace. Her story is as much about gender as it is about race, and moreover it is about how race and gender met in the body of Anita Hill and therefore made her public shaming and victim blaming more palatable for the American spectator.

In 1991, George Bush nominated Clarence Thomas to the Supreme Court. At the time Thomas was a federal judge serving on the United States Court of Appeals for the District of Columbia. If confirmed, Thomas would be the second black man to serve on the highest court in the land. A controversial figure from the beginning, Thomas was slated to replace one of the greatest civil rights icons of all time, Thurgood Marshall. Many black leaders feared that Thomas would not be strong when it came to civil rights, while many of those in the pro-choice community feared that he would probably work to overturn *Roe v Wade*,[19] Additionally, many in the legal community questioned whether Thomas had the "experience"[20] to fulfill the role of Supreme Court Justice since he had only served two years on the federal bench. During Thomas's confirmation hearing, Anita Hill—then a law professor at the University of Oklahoma—testified in front of the Senate Judiciary Committee that during several interactions Thomas had made inappropriate comments that were sexual in nature when she worked for him years before at the Equal Employment Opportunity Commission.

Thus began what Katherine M. Marion appropriately describes as a "detailed televised interrogation of Anita Hill by an all-white, all male Senate Judiciary Committee …"[21] While certainly it is true that the three days of testimony that Anita Hill endured "galvanized a groundswell of feminist activism"[22] and ushered in what some refer to as the third wave of feminism, articulated by Alice Walker's daughter, Rebecca, who wrote "Let this dismissal of a woman's experience move you to anger. Turn that outrage into political power. I am a postfeminist. I am a Third Wave." What it also did was galvanize black women across the country who, a month after Hill's examination, printed a full-page statement in *The New York Times* entitled, "African American Women in Defense of Ourselves." The obvious analysis here is that the Thomas hearings provided yet another moment in history where racial and gender discrimination met in the body of black women. The women who penned and signed the letter make it abundantly clear that what happened to Anita Hill is but a point (albeit very public one) on the historical timeline of black women's oppression in the USA. They wrote, "This country, which has a long legacy of racism and sexism, has never taken the sexual abuse of Black women seriously. Throughout U.S. history Black women have been sexually stereotyped as immoral, insatiable, perverse ..."[23] Yet, we might also see this black feminist protestation as an act of "checking" where black women put (in this case) the media, the Bush administration, and black men in particular, who certainly saw the racism of the Thomas hearing but were curiously blind to the sexism. The black women who bravely spoke out in "African American Women in Defense of Ourselves" using the collective "we" are asserting agency not only for themselves but also for Anita Hill. "African American Women in Defense of Ourselves" is but one example of black women publicly asserting agency for themselves and the black community. In many ways, it is reminiscent of one of the famous Ida B. Wells' editorials about lynching black men for supposedly raping white women. "In May 1892," Wells wrote:

> Eight Negroes lynched since last issue of the *Free Speech*. Three were charged with killing white men and five with raping white women. Nobody in this section believes the old thread-bare lie that Negro men assault white women. If Southern white men are not careful they will over-reach themselves and a conclusion will be reached which will be very damaging to the moral reputation of their women.[24]

Wells' anti-lynching campaign is an assertion of black agency as we have described, as she posits her rhetoric in the form of resistance to black people being determined. We can also see agency here in the form of bodily determination where blacks should have a say in what is done or not done to their bodies—the power to resist external definition. The Anita Hill case and the letter in support of her and all black women are, for lack of a better term, par for the course. Demanding agency is what traditional black feminists have done from Wheatley, to Wells, to Hill. Yet, with the rise of the so-called third wave of feminism, the way that black women define agency and the attention they pay to it have changed.

The Changing Nature of Agency

In 1994, Lisa Marie Hogeland published the essay "Fear of Feminism" where she discusses young women's anxiety about identifying as feminists. Hogeland argues that in order to address the concerns young women have with feminism, we must differentiate between "gender consciousness" and "feminist consciousness." According to Hogeland, "Gender consciousness takes two forms: awareness of women's vulnerability and celebration of women's difference." On the other hand, feminist consciousness is rooted in politics. Hogeland writes, "Feminism politicizes gender consciousness, inserts it into a systematic analysis of histories and structures of domination and privilege."[25] Because of the formidable forces aligned against feminism—patriarchy, white supremacy, capitalism, violence against women and children—young women (and not only young women) have every reason to fear "reprisal" for declaring oneself a feminist.[26] Young women may also fear feminism because they have "fears both of lesbians and of being named a lesbian by association."[27] Hogeland also argues that young women are also engaged in the process of identity formation, asking poignantly about the forces and people who construct their lives. For so many young women, she asserts, "intimate relationships become the testing grounds for identity" and though not inherently bad, feminism or identifying as a feminist may seem limiting especially when it comes to heterosexual relationships."[28]

Hogeland's analysis of the fear of feminism opens a critical space for discussing the difference between traditional black feminists and young black women today on the question of agency. Like Hogeland, we too might ask what do young black women today fear about a traditional black feminist approach to agency? One apprehension could be that whereas traditional black feminists saw agency as liberation and as a necessary condition for black women being *seen* in the world as equal to all others, young black women see agency as it is articulated by traditional black feminists as constraining and beholden to a politics of respectability that limits their ways of being a black woman in the world. The significant change for young black women is that their association with the second sex and the second race no longer hinders them, indeed many see this association as no longer valid or at the point of being completely overcome. This is not to say that racial and gender categories no longer exist, nor is it to say that patriarchy, capitalism, and white supremacy have been completely defeated. What it does suggest is that these categories are, first, no longer large enough to contain the fluid and multitudinous nature of black women's identity; second, that the categories are not as rigid and hegemonic as they were in the past; and finally that these categories have been weakened and made less important by a generation whose mission is to defy all signification.

Young black women do seem to face a different terrain than the one faced by older black women. On the social level, there has been visible, tangible, and real progress made. Although traditional black feminists' arguments about agency remain an important and critical tool with which black women can challenge racism and patriarchy, it would be unwise for traditional black feminists not to pay attention to how black women, particularly young black women, perceive themselves and their agency today. The first substantial challenge to traditional feminists' notion of agency came from third-wave feminists who challenged their mothers' feminism, and in doing so began to reframe the dialogue surrounding agency within feminist thought. Chiefly, third-wave feminists argue against rigid notions of gender and some reject the label of feminist altogether. It is not that they do not appreciate the struggles faced by the preceding generation; rather, it is that those third-wave feminists want to have a space to define themselves and their own concerns. Diane Elam sums up the tension succinctly:

The problem manifests itself when senior feminists insist that junior feminists be good daughters, defending the same kind of feminism their mothers advocated. Daughters are not allowed to invent new ways of thinking and doing feminism for themselves; feminists' politics should take the same shape that it has always assumed.[29]

Just as third-wave feminists found themselves at odds with second-wave feminists because they wanted to expand the definition of feminism, young women today (shall we call them a fourth wave?), though perhaps still concerned with issues related to enlarging/altering the definition of feminism, more to the point they are *playing* with the notion of agency in a way that has not been seen before.[30]

This discussion is further complicated by the fact that many young black women today potentially glimpse only half of the story—that is, many young women of the current generation see themselves as agents but not as being dispossessed of their agency, whether socially, politically, economically, or culturally—and this, perhaps, is the crux of the disagreement that traditional black feminists have with the new generation. Clearly, the current generation's limited point of view is at least in some measure a product of the commodification of contemporary culture—we live in the age of slogans such as "do you" and "I'm in it for me" and "it's all about me." These perceptions are reinforced by many of the black women in contemporary music and television, for instance, Beyoncé, Rihanna, and the women on the hit shows *Basketball Wives*, *Single Ladies*, and *Love and Hip Hop, Atlanta*, who in some cases present a brash, hyper-sexualized and no-holds-barred interpretation of black femininity today. Agency is clearly marketed to young women as something that can be purchased or as something that they already possess. It is also clear that young women can point to many examples of black women who exercise power in more traditional areas of society, including Michelle Obama, Condi Rice, Ruth J. Simmons,[31] and the many other successful black women in industry and academia. Young black women thus have visible proof of black women who are influential in white and predominately masculine areas of society. Given this, we might rightly ask, why shouldn't we expect young black women to view the world as their oyster?

A problem, then, that calls for exploration concerns how their perception of black female agency should be evaluated. Perhaps their perceptions are accurate and simply a sign that the ambitions of black feminists have now been achieved by this younger generation—dare I use the phrase, "Joshua Generation"?[32] If this is the case, then it would point to the need for traditional black feminists to acknowledge that success and to shift their focus to issues that are more germane to black women today. Or, if this is not the case, then it would point to the need for traditional black feminists to reach the younger generation and to help this generation to appreciate how their *apparent* gains in agency play into the continued dispossession of black women. Put simply, the question is this: is the present generation of young black women experiencing the realization of black feminist efforts from the past or is it deceived about its own agency?

As a tentative rejoinder to the question posed above, perhaps black women of the younger generations—the so-called Generation X and the Millennial Generation—do not feel the call to agency to be as powerful as their foremothers did; they do not perceive the issue of agency, as it is expressed by previous generations, as an issue that concerns them any longer. This lack of attention to agency echoes one of the main criticisms of the current generation of feminists generally, namely, the criticism that third-wave feminism lacks a cause. First-wave feminists rallied around the establishment of voting rights for women, while second-wave feminists rallied around concerns related to equality in the public sphere.

Clearly, in both cases, their causes were directly linked to issues of agency. First- and second-wave feminists issued calls for rights that were typically seen as male rights; they sought to position themselves as actors and demanded to be perceived as actors. Should we be concerned that the groups that stand to gain from those earlier struggles for agency—third-wave feminists (many of whom are mothers), the current Millennial Generation of feminists (we hope) who walk among us today, and the generations (what will we call these sisters?) to come—do not identify with the issue of agency as their foremothers did? Or should we just accept that the lived-experiences of the current generation are radically different from previous generations? Leslie Heywood and Jennifer Drake provide insight into Generation X and the Millennials, arguing that these generations are different from previous ones based on their awareness of and interaction with multiculturalism and "globalization."[33] In this respect, Haywood and Drake indicate that the lived-experience of younger women is indeed radically different from previous generations. With globalization, competing social rituals, the intensification of multiculturalism, the normalization of alternative sexualities, and so forth, the present-day generations of women have a large amount to process. Since this is the case, it stands to reason that their thoughts about agency would differ from that of their mothers and they might not be regarded in terms of black and white.

What Constitutes Agency?: Two Rival Interpretations

Beyoncé's song "Who Runs the World (Girls)" provides a perfect way to illustrate how traditional feminists and women of the younger generation interpret agency differently. While browsing the web on this topic, one may come across lively debates over "Bey," her song "Who Runs the World (Girls)" and the accompanying video, and the song's potential resources for feminism. Traditional black feminists who view the video will see yet another woman exposing her body parts to the camera and singing shallow, some might even say nonsensical, lyrics like:

> Some of them men think they freak this like we do/But no they don't/Make your cheques come at they neck, /Disrespect us no they won't.

With lyrics like this and the video that accompanies it showing Beyoncé and an array of female dancers dressed in tight-fitting, seductive clothing while confronting a group of heavily armed men, Demetria Lucas, the former relationship editor for *Essence* and creative genius behind the blog *abelleinbrooklyn*, is prompted to comment that:

> A mind is a terrible thing to waste and so is a perfectly good video that doesn't match the song. Despite the declarations in the lyrics (and the unrelated hotness of the video), it's a still a man's world, and it will always be as long as women think their vaginas are where their power lies.[34]

Lucas's comment that "it's a man's world, and it will always be as long as women think their vaginas are where their power lies" perfectly illustrates the tension between traditional black feminists and younger women today. On the one hand, the video for Beyoncé's song "Who Runs the World (Girls)" views like a twice-told tale where women seemingly devoid of power use the only weapon they believe they possess over male authority and brutality and that is their "vaginas." Not unlike Aristophanes' comedic play *Lysistrata*, where Athenian women withhold sex from their menfolk in order to end the Peloponnesian War (all kinds of problematic), the women in Beyoncé's video seem to say that women's sexual power is greater than any gun or tank. From a traditional black feminist perspective, this rings like a preposterous and dangerous claim.

In contrast to the traditional black feminist response, Arielle Loren adopts an opposite point of view in her *Clutch Magazine* article, "Is Beyoncé the Contemporary Face of Feminism?" (May 20, 2011). Loren observes:

> Not only are most women tired of the hardcore oppression and patriarchy rhetoric, but also they're ready to embrace their bodies and sexuality in a public way ... 20-something-year-old women are ready to showcase the multidimensionality of womanhood ... without having an identity crisis.[35]

Lauren's words are "checking" *par excellence*. She fires several shots at traditional black feminists, including the claim that young women don't call themselves feminists even if they "share [feminism's] core ideologies." She goes on to note that the term equality has taken on a new meaning for young women though she does not clearly state what this new meaning is. Third, young women are tired of all the "oppression and patriarchy rhetoric," because it gets in the way of *them being them*. Traditional notions of feminism, overt focus on oppression and patriarchy impede young women, who desire fluidity of expression and being. From Loren's perspective, Beyoncé represents a new woman who has it all—career, family, power, and crazy sex appeal. Lauren goes on to accuse traditional feminists who are critical of Beyoncé of displaying a "disconnect between theory and real life." She rejects Lucas' commentary on Beyoncé, because it seems to imply that "powerful women cannot bask in their sexuality, femininity, and confidence without jeopardizing their authority" and adds that Lucas is one of many feminists who have been "focused on the 'male gaze' for far too long."

From a traditional black feminist perspective, while Lauren may be correct to state that women command the dance floor when this song is playing at the club and they go to work the next day feeling empowered, Beyoncé's brand of agency may well signify what traditional black feminists mean when they say that young black women today see their agency but they fail to see when their agency is being challenged or jeopardized. This is especially true when we compare, for example, what is suggested by Beyoncé's song "Who Runs the World (Girls)" with the lived experience of girls and women of all hues. As put by the Crunk Feminist Collective: "It is dangerous to make open statements that women run the world, because there is so much evidence [that] women get the shit end of the stick in the world."[36] From being sexually trafficked, to making less than men, who along with kids make up the bulk of those trapped in poverty, to being lashed 10 times for driving, to being one of the missing girls in China, women across the world get the "shit end of the stick." The Crunk Feminist Collective goes on to say that we should be supportive of certain aspects of Beyoncé, especially her amazing dance skills and her skills at creating magnificent lyrics, "But to call her the face of modern day feminism is ahistorical and a slap in the face" to those women of all hues who continue to face unparalleled and unchecked discrimination.

Traditional black feminists (and feminists in general) might be concerned about Beyoncé and her song "Who Runs the World (Girls)" being held up as an emblem of black women's agency, because it may cause young black women to glimpse only half of that story. That is, they may come to see themselves as agents, boldly claiming that they "run this motha," but they may not see the many real instances in which they are dispossessed of their ability to act where instead of running "this motha," they are the ones being run.

Although Lauren argues that young women today do not want to call themselves feminist, Beyoncé has indeed come out and called herself a feminist. She has done this (or alluded to being a feminist) at several points in her career, including in *Harper's Bazaar* where she stated:

> I don't really feel that it's necessary to define it. It's just something that's kind of natural for me, and I feel like ... you know ... it's, like, what I live for ... I need to find a catchy new word for feminism, right? Like Bootylicious.[37]

Most famously during the 2014 MTV video music awards, Beyoncé stood on a stage—a black figure framed in intense white light—with the word FEMINIST blazing behind her. This, for some, was a moment of triumph. Not since Gloria Steinem has feminism had such a pretty face to represent it. This is not said to be flippant. One of the appeals of both Steinem (who is thrilled by Beyoncé taking up feminism) and Beyoncé is that bodily they stand opposite of the bodily myth of the feminist. Both are attractive and both seem to use their attraction for their own means. In this situation we are tempted to ask who is right—is it the traditional feminists who argue for a conventional approach to agency grounded in the subject being conceived of as a rational being with the ability to act; or, are younger women who are better equipped to partition *good* and *bad* and find ambiguity in situations that were unambiguous to earlier generations of feminists? Though provocative, finding an answer to this question is probably less important than discovering what prohibits constructive dialogue from actually taking place between traditional black feminists and younger black women today. To address this issue, in Chapter 4, I would like to suggest that Gadamer's *horizon of understanding* offers a possible resource to bridge the divide between these two rival interpretations of black women's agency.[38]

Notes

1 The 19th Amendment was passed without any kind of racial distinction. It granted all women the right to vote equally. It should, however, be noted that black women, particularly those living in the South, were summarily disenfranchised through state and local laws that prevented them from voting. It was not until the 1960s and the passage of the Voting Rights Act that all black rights to vote came under federal protection.
2 Linda Nicholson, "Feminism in 'Waves': Useful Metaphor or Not?," *New Politics*, XII-4 (48) (2010). Available at: http://newpol.org/content/feminism-waves-useful-metaphor-or-not
3 Ibid., p. 1. Emphasis added.
4 Ibid., p. 2.
5 Ibid.
6 Kimberlé Williams Crenshaw, "Mapping the Margins: Intersectionality, Identity Politics, and Violence Against Women of Color," in Martha Albertson Fineman and Rixanne Mykitiuk, eds., *The Public Nature of Violence* (New York: Routledge, 1994), pp. 93–118.
7 Matt Corley, "Condi Dresses Down Minimum Wage Worker," available at: http://thinkprogress.org/politics/2007/08/29/15812/condi-scoffs-at-minimum-wage-worker/
8 Available at: http://jezebel.com/294675/condi-rice-doesnt-care-about-poor-people
9 bell hooks, *Talking Back: Thinking Feminist, Thinking Black* (Boston: South End Press, 1989), p. 9.
10 Phillis Wheately, "Letter to the Reverend Samson Occum," in Henry Louis Gates and Jennifer Burton, eds., *Call and Response: Key Debates in African American Studies*, (New York: W.W. Norton, 2011), p. 13.
11 Ibid.
12 Joy James is a noted black feminist scholar and professor of Africana Studies at Wiliams College. See Joy James, *Shadowboxing: Representations of Black Feminist Politics* (New York: St. Martin's Press, 1999).
13 Beverley Guy-Sheftall, Words of Fire: An Anthology of African-American Feminist Thought (New York: New Press, 1995), p. 3.
14 Ibid., p. 3.
15 Ibid., p. 15.
16 Ibid., p. 16.
17 Ibid., p. 2.
18 To put this another way, Hill Collins observes: "A recognition of this connection between experience and consciousness that shapes the everyday lives of African-American women often pervades the works of Black women activists and scholars." Patricia Hill Collins, "The Social Construction of Black Feminist Thought," in Beverly Guy-Sheftall, ed., *Words of Fire: An Anthology of African American Feminist Thought* (New York: The New Press, 1995), p. 24.
19 A concern that was not unfounded.

20 This is a loaded term when applied to non-white people and women.

21 Sierra Austin *et al.*, "Anita Hill Roundtable," *Frontiers*, 35(3) (2014): 65.

22 Ibid., p. 65.

23 "African American Women in Defense of Ourselves," in Jacqueline Bobo, ed., *Black Women as Cultural Readers* (New York: Columbia University Press, 1995), p. 42.

24 Cited in Joy James, *Shadowboxing*, p. 50.

25 Lisa Marie Hogeland, "Fear of Feminism: Why Young Women Get the Willies," in Susan M. Shaw and Janet Lee, eds., *Women's Voices/Feminist Visions: Classic and Contemporary Readings* (New York: McGraw-Hill, 2014), p. 656.

26 Ibid., p. 656.

27 Ibid., p. 656.

28 Ibid., p. 656.

29 Diane Elam, "Sisters are Doing it to Themselves," in D. Looser and A Kaplan, eds., *Generations: Academic Feminists in Dialogue* (Minneapolis: University of Minnesota Press, 1997), p. 55.

30 The notion of young black women *playing* with agency is significant because it harkens to another significant instance where foundational principles were challenged—poststructuralism's challenge of the precepts of structuralism. A watershed moment in the history of theory, Derrida's "Structure, Sign, and Play" introduced the rudimentary ideas concomitant with deconstruction and poststructuralism. The post-structural critique of structuralism is useful for our purposes because, like Derrida, this analysis is concerned with questions related to discourse and language and how young black women are shifting what were once fundamental beliefs about black women's agency, This shift—just like the one from structuralism to poststructuralism—should be seen as disruptive.

31 The first black woman President of Brown University.

32 That is, the generation that has made it to the Promised Land of racial and gender equality.

33 Leslie Heywood and Jennifer Drake, "'It's All About the Benjamins': Economic Determinants of Third Wave Feminism in the United States," in *Third Wave Feminism: A Critical Exploration* (New York: Palgrave Macmillan, 2004), p. 16.

34 Demetria L. Lucas, "Sound-Off: Is Beyoncé Sending the Wrong Message?" *Essence*, May 19, 2011. Available at: www.essence.com/2011/05/19/beyonce-who-run-the-world-girls-video-female-empowerment-sound-off

35 Arielle Loren, "Is Beyoncé the Contemporary Face of Feminism?" *Clutch Magazine*, May 20, 2011.

36 The Crunk Feminist Collective is a group of activist scholars who strongly identify with the hip hop generation. They are committed to advancing their "feminist goals, ideas, visions, and dreams in ways that are both personally and professionally beneficial." See mission statement at: www.crunkfeministcollective.com/about/

37 Cited by Dodail Stewart in "Let's Invent a Catchy New Word for Feminism," *Jezebel* 8/4/11.

38 For a complete discussion, see Hans Georg Gadamer, *Truth and Method* (London: Sheed and Ward, 1979), p. 347, where Gadmer explains that conversation as:

> a process of two people understanding each other. Thus it is a characteristic of every true conversation that each opens himself to the other person, truly accepts his point of view as worthy of consideration and gets inside the other to such an extent that he understands not a particular individual, but what he says. The thing that has to be grasped is the objective rightness or otherwise of his opinion, so that they can agree with each other on a subject.

4   Millennials

Black Women Forming and Transforming Agency

Coattails

Highly visible figures like Harvard law-educated Michelle Obama as First Lady, Dr. Melissa Harris Perry and her once influential news program on MSNBC, Loretta Lynch as the first black woman Attorney General, television writer and producer Shonda Rhymes, and Dr. Valerie Jared, the US Ambassador to the United Nations, speak to the enormous strides black women have made in public life. We may not be present in the numbers we desire, but we are visible in ways that (if but a little) counter negative images of black women. It means something for world leaders visiting the United States of America to be greeted by a black woman. It means something to say that the top law enforcement officer in the country is a black woman and that the former chief diplomat, the president's voice to other nations, was in the very recent past a black woman.

Yet, though powerful and agential, these black women are what we would call agents *of a sort*[1] since based on real and perceived societal pressure, though publicly visible and to an extent recognized by others, their agency is never solidified, meaning they are always in danger of having their agency challenged or compromised. Agency for black women is never simply a given. Nevertheless, as individuals who through talent, social and political networks, and sheer luck they are, at times, able to enact *individual* agency on a par and even above their white counterparts. Michelle Obama, Melissa Harris Perry, Loretta Lynch, etc. all have the markers of traditional black female excellence (perhaps some might say exceptionalism). Another way to say this is that they embody the metaphor of the strong black woman. Much has been written about the image of the strong black woman. Dawn Marie Dow shows how black women oftentimes have to "negotiate" the conflicting controlling images of the welfare queen—an image typically used to punish black women for staying home with their children rather than engaging in the external labor force—and the strong black woman. Dow describes the strong black woman as: "represent[ing] extreme female self-reliance, emotional resilience, and moral propriety and was produced by and for African American women in response to negative mainstream images of African American womanhood."[2]

At this point is it productive to juxtapose bell hooks' critique of the *strong black woman* to Dow's definition especially where hooks argues that the strong black woman image hurts rather than helps black women. First, Obama, Lynch, Harris-Perry etc. read as firmly situated in a black cultural context: they all attended elite universities, and they are all committed to a variation on the notion of racial uplift. Variation because it is difficult to accuse any of these women of attempting to reinforce a class distinction in the black community where, for example, upper-class blacks enact whiteness and upper-class privilege, believing, as stated by Kevin Gaines, that upper-class blacks "are responsible for the welfare of the majority of the race."[3] What can be argued is that Michelle Obama, for example, sees herself—and is seen as—a role model for young black women. Michelle Obama literally embodies possibility because she signifies all that black girls can one day be if only … In an open letter to Michelle Obama, the artist Beyoncé sums up how many black women and girls feel about Michelle Obama:

> Michelle is the ultimate example of a truly strong African American woman. She is a caring mother, she's a loving wife, while at the same time, she is the first lady. No matter the pressure, and the stress of being under the microscope, she's humble, loving and sensitive.[4]

Michelle Obama is a traditional black feminist who understands the structure of white supremacist patriarchy. She acts to resist these forces by excelling in white-dominated spaces and embraces the idea that she is a role model to other black women, not only because of her achievement but also because of her ability to overcome obstacles in her way. Traditional black feminists like Viola Davis perfectly capture the frustration of being a black woman in white space who works to overcome obstacles and sees herself as role model for other black women and girls. In her 2015 Emmy speech. Davis states:

> In my mind, I see a line. And over that line, I see green fields and lovely flowers and beautiful white women with their arms stretched out to me, over that line. But I can't seem to get there, no how. I can't seem to get over that line.

Davis's speech is powerful on so many levels, including her ability to connect Harriet Tubman's vision of standing on opposite sides to white women but never being able to cross the line to signal that she is truly equal with them, to Viola Davis's own struggle with being denied access and equality with white women actors because she is a black woman. For this reason (and myriad others), Obama and Davis represent examples of "strong" black women overcoming in the face of overwhelming challenge. In this sense, they are the continuation of the trope of the traditional black feminist struggle for agency—to act and be seen as an actor—in spite of all odds. Their enactment of agency is familiar and clear. There is no ambiguity in terms of the work it takes to be seen as a person in a society bent on denying your agency. For traditional black feminists, the path to agency is narrow and straight.

At this point, one question we might ask is whether traditional black feminists' enactment of agency helps advance black women's agency *as a group* in the ways that we might think or hope for. Another way to ask this is to question whether their (Obama, Davis, Lynch, Harris-Perry) coattails are long enough to pull black women as a group with them? Further, is there a difference between individual and group agency? To pose these questions is to stumble on a danger for younger black women who may see the advancement of a few black and make the intellectual leap to believing that things are better for black women as a group, based on the success of the lucky few. It might be tempting to believe that since white supremacist capitalists' patriarchy lets a few black women in and sees their presence as non-injurious, that makes it easier for other black women to enter the door. This line of thinking leads to personal rather than group action, it leads to understanding one's self for one's self and not in relation to others.

Rampant individualism is, perhaps, a marker of the generation known as millennials. Yet, individualism is also a grounding principle in US social and political thought. For blacks, race has always been the mitigating factor, limiting what they can and cannot do. Yet, a stark difference is that younger blacks are not only buying into the idea of individualism, they potentially see individualism as something that is accessible and enactable. For this reason, young black women (in our case) today may come to see themselves as a Joshua Generation, having made it to the "promised land" of gender and sexual equality. Having seen the real accomplishments of black women, they no longer discern the relevance of their mothers' calls for agency. Referring to younger black women today as part of the Joshua Generation is no mere play on biblical imagery. Joshua is, in fact, an important symbol of persevering beyond struggle and finally making it to the promised land. In the black tradition, Martin Luther King Jr. is the great Moses figure who leads his people through the Civil Rights Movements. King loses his life before his people make it to the other side, leaving Joshua to continue the journey. While some have argued that President Obama cast himself (and is reckoned by others) as a Joshua figure and thus different from the heroes of the Civil Rights Movement (including King), because he shows not only strength in the struggle but what is possible on the side; for younger black women, it is Michelle Obama, Beyoncé, Loretta Lynch, and Melissa Harris Perry, who, because of their race and gender come to represent Joshua—cast in the image of black women.

But there is another change that is at play behind this attitude shift. The younger generations, like third-wave feminists, are much more attuned to and comfortable with ambiguity, meaning that they are more open to situations—be they sexual or political—that would have given older generations pause. This too shapes their perceptions of agency in regard to sexuality, relationships, and the representations of women in media culture. Based on this ability to accept ambiguity, younger generations seem much more open to issues that would have curled a toe or two (in a bad way that is) of earlier feminists who sought to critique the interlocking systems of oppression—race, class, and gender. A perfect example of this can be found in Joan Morgan's work. In her analysis of *trickin* which means "specifically using sex to gain protection, wealth and power," Morgan observes: "power is still divided by gender." Morgan goes on to reason that:

> the one self-inflicted Achilles' heel men have is their tendency to define power partially in terms of sexual conquest. Punanny is the one things women *control* and men have an unlimited desire for. That makes it, even in post-feminist times, one helluva negotiating tool.[5]

Now there are several outright flaws and incorrect assumptions in Morgan's analysis, including the idea that *all* women are in control of their (to be vulgar) "punannies," the reduction of men to mindless beasts who cannot resist "punanny," and the question of whether *pussy power* truly inverts the real power dynamic between men and women. Morgan's analysis highlights the ambiguity the younger generation may find. for example. in sexuality and what constitutes sexual objectification. Morgan also challenges us to rethink women's power and agency in a way that would be uncomfortable for many old school black feminists who typically see a woman relying on her pussy as lacking substantive agency since her power is derived from sex and not, for instance, from voice.

Another example to illustrate this difference between older and younger generations of black women can be taken from Elaine Richardson's study of young black women's reaction to Nelly and the St. Lunatics' song and video "Tip Drill." If we had to date the moment where camps (old and young) stood divided over the issue of agency or that point in time where there was a strong sense that the prevailing narrative of black feminist agency was challenged— "Tip Drill" is the point. This is not to say that hip hop as a musical, artistic, and lived experience was not pushing the boundaries before or that it did not lead us to discuss black women and their place in hip hop music and culture. What "Tip Drill" (the song and video) and the dirty south and bounce music have opened up is a space for its discussion about black women and power with situations that read as exploitative.

Again, the video "Tip Drill" specifically represents a critical point in black feminist thought and how it is perceived as it challenged black feminist understanding about agency. Southern hip hop (or the dirty south) has historically pushed against sexual, gender, and language borders, and some might argue that it has also challenged society's understanding of decency. We see this with the Too Live Crew and their song like "Me So Horny," which uses a highly parodied and stereotypical voice of an Asian woman, as well as their blatant sexual use of women's bodies during their tours and in their videos. In the vein of the Too Live Crew, Nelly's music also pushes the boundaries of decency, while at the same time playing up a new connection between hip hop "and the adult entertainment world—particularly strip clubs and pornography production."[6] This lucrative association between hip hop and pornography is explained further by Margaret Hunter's analysis of 50 Cents' "interactive pornography video ... *Groupie Love*."[7] Playing this interactive video makes 50 Cents' "X-rated life-style" available to viewers. The game's marketing explicitly states:

> You're banging their girls backstage at the concerts and hanging with them on the tour bus ... The viewer will be able to choose which girls to have sex with and where the sex will take place.[8]

Marketing is key. Since the audience for this game is men and the overarching theme of the game is participation in the market economy of hip hop, women's bodies are reduced to commodities; they are products to be consumed. The men who play *Groupie Love* can choose when and where sex will take place, the women, on the other hand, have no choice. They are always available; they are literally programed not to say "no." In this "reality," rape is impossible.

Nelly's "Tip Drill" video is interesting because, like the video game, the male consumer is invited into a hip hop fantasy lifestyle but this time with real women whom we might also see as agents of a sort (to be discussed in more detail later in the chapter). Before explicating Nelly's video, it is important to note that there was push back by younger black women against how he portrayed women. So, for example, at Spelman University in Atlanta, a group of young women challenged Nelly about his video and asked for a campus discussion (which he refused). Echoing a traditional black feminist position, these young women spoke out against what they consider oppressive and dangerous for black women. Despite this pushback, we cannot lose sight of the fact that "Tip Drill" was a commercial success for Nelly and the music industry. It reflects the perfect union of hip hop and soft porn; "Tip Drill" took commodification of black women's bodies to another level. Yet it also presents traditional black feminists with an interesting dilemma which we can articulate in the following way: do we (traditional black feminists) add to the discourse of commodification by positing analysis that see the women in "Tip Drill" as objects lacking agency? And further, by doing so, are we silencing the women by labeling their freely chosen expression as exploitation?

"Tip Drill" the video and "Tip Drill" the song are two very different entities that can function independently of one another. The following address the complexities and messages found in both.

"Tip Drill": The Video

For those who may not be familiar with "Tip Drill" in its visual form, the video begins with Nelly and the St. Lunatics rolling up to a mansion, and the viewers are invited along. The interesting narrative structure and framing of the video position the cameras to make the viewer feel like an absolute part of the action. In this way, the viewer is called in as a participant, and thus is central to the overall production. Upon opening the door to the house, Nelly, his crew, and "you" walk into a stereotyped hyper-masculine sexual fantasy. Setting the stage for what is going to be a wild experience, several women are displayed along an elaborate staircase. As you come in, they are facing the door, but once everyone is inside, the women turn 180 degrees and present their butts to Nelly, his crew, and again "you." Because their backs are turned toward the camera, the women are positioned in a weakened state, first, physically (how can they see if an assault is coming); and, second, in terms of their humanity where because we cannot see their faces, we may be less inclined to behave in an ethical manner toward them. Women of various shades of black and brown wearing next to nothing (tiny bras and thongs), their bodies glistening, are telling you that they are game for pretty much everything; resistance is written nowhere on their bodies. This is a space where rape or other forms of sexual violence cannot happen. It is significant that throughout the video, the males are all completely dressed. This signals to the viewer that it is not the male body that is on display, vulnerable, or available.

As the camera moves from room to room, the viewer is shown women contorting their bodies to the music and we also witness various members of Nelly's crew engaging in symbolic touching of the women. This could be for a host of reasons, including that the video reflects the decorum of the strip club where the women are to be seen and ogled but never touched (at least in public). So, even if a patron pays for a lap dance, the patron receiving the lap dance is not supposed to touch the dancer. Symbolic touching in the video may also represent an invitation for the audience to imagine themselves in, for example, Nelly's place. In this way, Nelly's hands become your hands. Consequently, symbolic touching is used as a means to help the viewer visualize themselves in the actions. Ultimately the video depicts *fantasy* sex and *pretend* penetration—where the point is titillation not release.

Perhaps the two most controversial aspects of the video are, first, the fetishizing of lesbian sex where various women are engaged in, again, symbolic oral and anal sex. Elaine Richardson's work is informative here. Through interviews with teenage black girls, Richardson uncovers how they negotiate images of black women in hip hop. Richardson also explains how the girls are able to subvert Nelly's othering of black women engaging in, for example, "lesbian" sex. Where, for Nelly, such play with sexuality functions to simulate viewers and prove that the party is indeed wild, via the interviews with the young women, Richardson argues that the young girls in the study who watched Nelly's video "strive to reinterpret traditional gender roles."[9] A discussion recorded by Richardson with the young girls shows these bright young people are working well beyond any simplistic imagining of black women. When discussing a scene where two women are engaged in simulated anal sex, the young people offer an interpretation that concludes with the following assessment of the video performers' actions: "BE: That's why I think she got paid though…she was workin like foreal." Where some analysis of the scenes where symbolic lesbian sex is being enacted might see a negative portrayal of women, the young girls brilliantly complicate, reimagine, and reinterpret these images. Causing us to ask *are the women being exploited and othered* or are they as BE states. *getting "paid" because "she was workin like foreal"*? Richardson provides a rejoinder to this question by stating: "...the girls see the video workers as subverting the male rappers' power. The video worker is just that, a worker. She is good at her game, 'workin like foreal.'" In saying this, BE reimagines the video worker (not video vixen or video whore) as a woman engaged in a task related to sexual titillation which ensures her a certain amount of pay. The better she performs or the more realistic she is, the better her tips.

Second, several times in the video Nelly or one of the St. Lunatics is presented throwing large sums of money (fists full) at several women hitting them in the face, breast, vagina, or butt. There are numerous ways such actions can be analyzed. One way is to read these actions through the lens of performance (hinted at in the first example). Multidisciplinary by nature, performance studies "straddles the boundaries of sociology, anthropology, theatre studies, dance, ritual and religious studies, the sociology of the body ..."[10] For Clammer, "performance is essentially the creation, presentation or affirmation of an identity (real or assumed) through action."[11] One question we may then ask is, what aspect of identity (or identities) is being presented or affirmed in "Tip Drill"? As a rhetorician, I must also ask not only how the viewer is situated but how does "Tip Drill" as an artifact make a claim about the identities of black men and women?

To the first question about identity, it seems that Nelly and the St. Lunatics are performing a stereotypical understanding of urban, black male identity. This identity is certainly used by white corporate and media executives for the purpose of profit-making but it is also supported by the black male hip hop establishment who also have a mind to profit-making. It might be going too far to call this a symbiotic relationship because there are clear power imbalances between the mainly white male corporate and media executives and oftentimes young black male artists. Nevertheless, the nature of the relationship between these two groups (and the criticism surrounding this relationship) reads strikingly similar to that of hip hop artist and video worker. In both cases, we might see how the group that appears exploited seem to participate in their own exploitation, while at the same time in some cases resisting that exploitation in subversive ways. What we also see is a hierarchy of exploitation where white, male music executives who embody disembodied reason and wealth sit at the top of the economic hierarchy. The viewer never sees white male music executives. In fact, most consumers of hip hop would be hard pressed to actually name one or any of them or be able to point them out in a crowd of other white males. In the case of this group, their invisibility is their strength. Black male rappers are next in the hierarchy. Black male bodies are, without question, exploited via their blackness and their maleness—in the world of commerce, blackness and maleness are marketable qualities. The marketability of the black male bodies leads not only to commodification but also hyper-visibility. Thus, black men live *exposed* lives. What I would also like to suggest is that black men are not hyper-visible—and marketable—simply in terms of their bodies, but also because of their voices. When engaging the world of hip hop, one should not discount the power of voice. It is the voice of black men that carry hip hop's message. Consequently, not only should we see black men as hyper-visible but also hyper-audible. Their strength (marketability) lies in their ability to sell the narrative (at times a false one) of black experience. In this way, they are reminiscent of griots and although we see black male bodies throughout videos in one way or another, their bodies in some ways are inconsequential.

The identity that we see performed by Nelly and his crew is, on one hand, a thoroughly complex mixture of market forces, manipulated bodies, sound and narrative construction; yet, on the other, it is also one-dimensional, commodified, and controlled. To say this presents us with an opportunity to treat the identity of black men in hip hop videos as dialectical. In so doing, we are allowed to hold their complexity and one-dimensional presentation in tension. Black male identity is complexly shown in the video through their access to material wealth. Though we might argue that black male wealth is funneled through the lens of limited access (e.g. black men can only seemingly attain wealth through the entertainment industry), nevertheless the men in the video can participate in the excess and waste that only wealth can bring. It is clear that Nelly and company are some money earnin', big ballin' brothas. They support this identity through, for example, waste—how many times do we have to see bottles of Cristal (which can cost well over 400 dollars a bottle) poured onto the ground?; but also through the large house they have access to and through their dress and jewelry. Another way to read black male identity as complex and powerful is through the performance of throwing money everywhere, especially at the women in this video. This a very gendered action. The physical throwing of money at the women for some may call to mind the buying of black female slaves for the purpose of sexual exploitation. Throwing money should also be seen as an act of symbolic ejaculation. Since they cannot squirt their semen all over the women because that would be seen as hard core pornography, the greenbacks literally take the place of their ejaculation. The constant spray of money is symbolic of both their wealth and their virility. If you are an old school black feminist, anyway that you look it all indicates complete disregard for the women.

"Tip Drill": The Song

"Tip Drill" is not the most complex and engaging song one might have ever heard. "Tip Drill" repeats itself to the point of potential boredom after a while and is lyrically limp, though in its favor is a popping beat that one can dance to at the club. Yet, behind the beat and simplistic annoying lyrics Nelly and the St. Lunatics are telling a story about black sexuality and gender norms. Therefore, instead of being dismissive of the track (chalking it up to senseless inartistic dribble), it might be best to analyze the importance of what Nelly *is* saying to young black men and women and how this perhaps influences how they see one another and how they see themselves.

First, to clarify our terms, a *tip drill* is a form of symbolic engagement between female strippers and male customers. The job of the female stripper is to get money from the male costumers through dancing and seduction, while the male displays power by exerting control over the woman (especially in front of his boys).[12] One interesting way to analyze the song is in term of call-response. In the black tradition, call-response refers to an interlocutor speaking directly to a crowd, who in return talk back. In talking back, the audience lets the interlocutor know that they hear and are in agreement with what is being said. Talking back also encourages the interlocutor to speak more. "Tip Drill" exhibits this play between interlocutor and audience when, for instance, Nelly or one of the St. Lunatics tells listeners to call "out" (i.e. make visible) any "tip drills" that they see and rewards them for their response.

Nelly and the St. Lunatics are using call-response in a way much like you might hear a preacher use it in a Baptist church when he/she is invoking the Lord and asking churchgoers to support this invocation through response such as "we hear you" and "preach." Both are engaged in participator dialogue. Yet, what is also curious about the song's use of call-response is that throughout the song Nelly and the St. Lunatics are not just calling and responding to one another, they are also speaking to gendered audiences. So, in this first example, Nelly is asking (telling) male listeners/viewers to "call out" tip drills that they see. The power these men have to "call out" women is extraordinary since they in effect may identify any woman as a tip drill. In this second example, however, Nelly is speaking to an audience of women. In his "call," Nelly tells the women that they know why the men are present. To this insinuation he receives no reply. Nelly then "calls" again, this time offering what we might read as a "diss" since he says to the women that he wants to have sex but won't because he's afraid that the condom might "slide" (perhaps exposing him to an STD or unplanned pregnancy). Again, he receives no response. What should we make of the women's silence?

Unfortunately, "Tip Drill" is peppered with lyrics like that are repeated over and over. A curious effect of this repetition especially when the lyrics are directed at the women is that instead of becoming annoyed, there is a sense of anger simmering below the surface. It begins to feel like Nelly is needling the women. At some point in the song, one gets the distinct feeling that the listener *and* even Nelly and his crews are waiting for the women to speak, to either deny or confirm that they are tip drills. Finally, a light-skinned black woman (representing all the women's voices) responds in verse three by saying rather forcefully that Nelly and his crew are the real "tip drills" because they are spending what amounts to a lot of money—buying clothing and cars for the women—and getting nothing but a fantasy in return. The retort is powerful. It is the response of this singular woman who speaks for all black women, and though most of the critical scholarship done on "Tip Drill" focuses on the video and how women are seen as exploitable, in fact, the listener is taken by surprise due to the woman's rather forceful response. She opens her mouth and claims her agency. In turn, the listener is left with the *no response* from Nelly or the St. Lunatics about whether *they* are the actual tip drills. Nelly and the St. Lunatics carry on as if the woman has not uttered a word in her defense. If we analyze the response in light of the way that young black women attempt to assert their agency in a society determined to undermine their attempt, we might yield some interesting results we might also better understand what I'll call the messy middle between traditional black feminists and young black women.

The Messy Middle

In "She was Workin Like Foreal," Elaine Richardson interviewed several young black women to discover how they negotiated negative representations about black women. Richardson showed several hip hop videos and, perhaps no surprise here, the video that elicited the most reaction was "Tip Drill." Richardson found that for the most part, the young women did not find Nelly's song or video to be demeaning to women in the least bit. As "BE" (one of the young women interviewed by Richardson) points out, there are two types of girls: those who strip in order to better themselves and those who just are "tip drills," i.e. have no self-respect (I will say more about this in a moment).[13]

This is a telling example of how these young black women partition *good* and *bad* and find ambiguity—the messy middle—in situations that are unambiguous to traditional black feminists. What is especially interesting about this example is how the young women attempt to wrest positive subjectivity out of a situation that previous generations of feminists would perceive straightforwardly to be degrading. The young women find ambiguity here in several different ways, including seeing the women as just actors, thus divorcing what the women do from who they really are. The most interesting argument that the young women make is that video workers or strippers who use "tip drilling" to "better their situations" are indeed respecting themselves.[14] Tip drilling, in this view, can be justified, if it is used as a way to improve one's life, for example, by paying for college, buying a new car, or paying one's rent. On the other hand, the young women condemned and were deeply concerned about those women who tip drilled simply because they enjoyed it. The implication of this view, as Richardson explains, is that "one deserves no respect and has no self-respect if being a tip drill is the primary sense of self."[15]

Here we see a key difference between the perceptions of agency in young women and those of traditional black feminists. The young women see those women who use "tip drilling" to better their lives as exercising their agency. Indeed, these women are not conceptualized as the objects of male sexual desire, instead they are seen as enterprising women who are capable of separating who they are from what they do (which shows a subversion of the way that double consciousness is usually figured). These women use men and "tip drilling" as the means to achieve their own goals—this also serves in a way to invert the power dynamics between the stripper and the customer—and so, the young women ask, who is the one getting played here? Earlier generations of black feminists, in contrast, would be likely to perceive this situation quite differently. They would interpret it as the explicit objectification of women in order to serve male desire. An old school black feminist would be likely to *call a spade a spade* and would emphasize the wrongness of what is being done, regardless of the reasons for doing it. On such a view, this would include pointing out the fact that women who "tip drill" are allowing their bodies to become objectified and commodified by men, and in so doing, they are also perpetuating negative stereotypes about black women and reinforcing repressive structures that are used to control them. For these reasons, they would point out that the woman, who might believe herself to exert agency in this situation, is really living in self-deception and is in fact under the control of male power structure. So, whereas the younger generation finds ambiguity in the action of the woman who does a "tip drill," preceding generations would not find ambiguity on that level and instead would situate the action within a broader set of power relations. Having established this sharp difference between the two perspectives, must we be resigned to a mere difference of opinion or is there some way to bring these two interpretations closer together? Where is the middle?

One possible middle can be found in Joan Morgan's discussion of hip hop and its relationship to young women today. Morgan argues for a bold feminist response to hip hop that is "brave enough to fuck with the grays" and that "acknowledges the benefits of objectified female sexuality [and] male chauvinism."[16] Drawing on this point, Richardson affirms that women have "the right to express their sexuality in homo- and hetero-erotic ways, both linguistically, rhetorically, lyrically, and physically, to display their bodies as they want, in the dance hall, the club, or wherever they deem appropriate …"[17] While one may agree with Richardson that women have the right to self-expression, is it not a mistake to assume that all forms of self-expression affirm female agency? For example, black women who use *trickin* (by stripping or any other way) to get money from men are free to display their bodies as they want. But, it might be a mistake to categorize this as an affirmation of black female agency, since these women express themselves within the power structure that sexualizes black women's bodies in order to exploit them for male use. Some forms of self-expression, like *trickin*, may well be inappropriate not on moral grounds but on political ones, because they conform to false perceptions of women's position in society and do not disrupt the unequal power dynamics between men and women. Such forms of self-expression, though perfectly within the range of individual rights and the freedom to self-expression (which black feminists affirm), should not be confused with subversive or revolutionary actions, either.

In spite of this disagreement with Morgan and Richardson, they are successful in illustrating the difference between the agency of young black women today and the agency of earlier generations—that is, younger women's greater openness to various kinds of agency, young black women's ability to compartmentalize different aspects of their agency, and having a greater tolerance for the ambiguities in agency. And so, a crucial issue for this study concerns how traditional black feminism can reach out and engage those young women who, perhaps like Morgan, are looking for, "a feminism that would allow them to explore who [they] are as women—not victims."[18]

If we seek to validate Morgan and other young black women and also affirm the traditional black feminism that *got us here*, the dilemma is as follows. On the one hand, if black feminism simply gives up its prior occupations and reaches out to younger black women where they are today, then it risks losing some of the key insights and critical tools that have defined it. On the other hand, if black feminism does not redefine or reconstruct itself at all, then it risks losing touch with those young women or not reaching them at all.

So, in conclusion, I want to propose a possible solution to this dilemma, though it is likely to be almost as controversial as the problem that it is trying to solve. To do this, I want to go back to an important insight from the Radical Feminist movement of the 1960s and 1970s. While I do not agree with all of their views, what intrigues me is their notion of androgyny. Following the Radical Feminists' split into two different groups—the radical-libertarian feminists and the radical-cultural feminists—Tong relates that the radical-libertarian feminists advocated the view that:

> an exclusively feminine gender identity is likely to limit women's develop-ment as full human persons. Thus, they encouraged women to become androgynous persons, that is, persons who embody both (good) masculine and (good) feminine characteristic, or, more controversially, any potpourri of masculine and feminine characteristics, good or bad, that strikes their fancy.[19]

Celebrating the play between masculine and feminine expression, Joree Freeman, whom Tong cites as one of the foremothers of radical libertarian fem-inism, identifies this androgyny in the persona of the "bitch." Freeman writes that:

> a Bitch does not want to limit herself to being a sweet girl with little in the way of power. Instead, she wants to embrace as part of her gender identity those masculine characteristics that permit her to lead life on her own terms.[20]

Freeman's "bitch" has been criticized for being "too masculine," it can also be seen as an affirmation of ambiguity, instead. With the context of hard core hip hop and young black women's play with agency, I think that Freeman's andro-gynous Bitch can provide a good model of how black feminist theory can begin to "fuck with the grays," to borrow Morgan's term, of agency for young black women today.

Tracy Sharpley-Whiting offers valuable insight into how young black women navigate negative images of themselves in her influential text, *Pimps up Ho's Down: Hip Hop's Hold on Young Black Women*. Sharpley-Whiting's book walks the reader through the rough terrain of hip-hop and black women's role within the genre. According to Sharpley-Whiting, black women identify with hip-hop, even though they are identified by hip-hop in ways that some might find problematic. With all the talk of "slapping a bitch," "sexually assaulting women," and reducing women to sexual objects that exist solely to satisfy male desire, it's hard *not* to find the misogyny in hip-hop disturbing and damaging. Instead of dismissing hip-hop altogether, however, Sharpley-Whiting argues that it is necessary to confront it by developing a new gender politics through it:

> It's a provocative cultural commentary that makes a case for hip hop's commercial success as heavily dependent upon young black women. Overexposed young black female flesh, "pimpin," "playin," "sexing," and "checkin" in videos, television, film, rap lyrics, fashion, and on the Internet, is indispensable to the mass-media-engineered appeal of hip hop culture, which is helping to shape a new black gender politics.[21]

The question, then, is whether or not traditional black feminists will have a guiding hand in shaping "a new gender politics" that does not forget the importance of the concept of agency. This can only happen if traditional black feminists are willing to open the door to other expressions of agency and interpretations of it to enter into its discourse. Black feminism needs to engage the question of how black women of this generation, who exist in between hip hop culture and Michelle Obama, can successfully affirm both. They must be willing and open to addressing in a way that creates dialogue definitely unpolitically correct and perhaps impertinent questions posed, for example, by Joan Morgan when she ponders (non-jokingly) questions like: "Can you be a good feminist and admit out loud that there are things you kinda dig about patriarchy?"[22] They need to invite a discussion with different women, those who go to clubs, who wears tight clothes and have long, shiny nails, and who has a gang of her bitches. Or she may be a college student with a high GPA who by day is the president of the student government and at night blogs about all of the guys she slept with, giving us the play by play of where they did it, how good/bad he was, and whether or not it was worth her time.[23] Regardless, the point is that traditional black feminists need to re-conceptualize black female agency. Even if we do not, this younger generation will forge this new gender politics—yet they still need us, perhaps now more than ever.

Gadamerian Hermeneutics and Bridging the Divide Between Competing Claims

Because black women's agency today presents us with complex challenges, the "fixes" must also be complex, unconventional, and even unorthodox. Another step in the direct of creating a new gender politic that expands the concept of agency as it relates to black women's lives is via a discussion of Gadamerian hermeneutics. In this spirit, we should see traditional black feminists' continued advocacy for black women's agency as linked to the pursuit of a society where all members are seen as free and equal. In such a context, traditional black feminists would assert that agency is a critical component of a society built on the foundation of social justice. Rhetoric and communication scholars see the importance of social justice in their scholarship and some like Wander (1996), as cited by Roy and Oluda, have "highlighted the importance of infusing social justice in rhetorical and communication studies."[24]

As cited by Roy and Oluda, others like Frye (1996) "have pointed out the one way to pursue social justice in communication studies is to focus on how 'dominant discourses, social structures, patters of interactions, and the like produce and reproduce injustice.'"[25] Roy and Oluda do an excellent job of highlighting the work of communication scholars who have applied Gadamer's insights to the area of social justice. Like Roy and Oluda, I find Gadamer's hermeneutics appealing because of his emphasis on dialogue: "extends beyond textual analysis, and its application has significant implications for communication research and the study of social justice."[26] Gadamer's discussion of *horizon* and the *fusion of horizons* is also valuable as we attempt to understand, and if possible, bridge the divide between two rival interpretations of black women's agency. Gadamer writes:

> Every finite present has its limitations. We define the concept of "situation" by saying that it represents a standpoint that limits the possibility of vision. Hence essential part of the concept of situation is the concept of "*horizon*." The horizon is the range of vision that includes everything that can be seen from a particular vantage point ... A person who has no horizon is a man who does not see far enough and hence overvalues what is nearest to him. On the other hand, "to have an horizon," means not being limited to what is nearby, but to being able to see beyond it ... [W]orking out of the hermeneutical situation means the achievement of the right horizon of inquiry for the questions evoked by the encounter with tradition.[27]

When Gadamer observes that individuals have a "historically effected consciousness," he means that their experiences, histories, and cultural backgrounds shape their perceptions of the world—it is the totality of these experiences that make up an individual's horizon. And, as such, this also helps us to understand how conflicts can emerge between individuals. Put simply, they are situated along different horizons. Nonetheless, this clash of *horizons* does not set up an impenetrable barrier to human communication and dialogue. On the contrary, its resolution can occur through what Gadamer calls a *fusion of horizons*, where two people can engage in a shared conversation about ideas, concepts, opinions, etc. This does not mean that our biases are no longer there or that our lived experiences are not brought to bear in a conversation. What it does mean is that there exists the potential for both interlocutors' horizons to expand through their interaction, which may lead to the enrichment of both lives.

Gadamer's hermeneutics can easily apply to groups like traditional black feminists and younger black women who have different horizons. The work of scholars like Haywood and Drake and public intellectuals like Rebecca Walker clearly indicate that the lived experiences of younger women are indeed radically different from previous generations. With globalization, competing social rituals, the intensification of multiculturalism, the normalization of alternative sexual lifestyles, and so on, the present-day generations of women have a clearly different *horizon of understanding* than any group of women in history.

In order to bridge this divide, we can take a cue from Stanley Deetz's reading of Gadamer. Neither group should attempt to feel empathetic toward the other since this would suggest: "guessing the inner life of the speaker"[28] or, in our case, group. Rather like Deetz suggests, if a fusing of *horizons* is to take place, traditional black feminists and young black women today must realize that: "understanding fundamentally is a problem of understanding people messages rather than understanding people."[29] Traditional black feminists do not have to understand—where understand should be interpreted as comprehend—young black women today, rather, traditional black feminists should attempt to understand the messages relayed from the various standpoints, experiences, and histories of young black women.

A good example of how we can make this argument more concrete is by discussing how both groups perceive hyper-commodified sexuality. In the case of hyper-commodified sexuality, what is perplexing for traditional black feminists is that when they hear, for example, black women like Joan Morgan articulate the *power* to be found through the hyper-commodified sexualization of one's body. In, for example, Morgan's analysis of *trickin*, which means, "specifically using sex to gain protection, wealth and power," she puts forward the observation that "power is still divided by gender." From this starting point, she goes on to argue that women have to be skilled at using their power in order to get what they want—hence *trickin*.

Working from Stanley Deetz's position, trying to understand the person might amount to asking questions like "Who raised this person to think this way?" Or, it might take the form of accusing the speaker of being "nasty" and having no self-respect. While, on the other hand, working from a position of trying to understand the message articulated by young black women would yield different results. Using this approach to understand the *horizons* of young black women today, traditional black feminists might contend that it is the over-emphasis on the black female body that has contributed to black women's sexual and rhetorical subjugation. And, though traditional black feminists might agree that black women should be free to enact sexuality on their own terms, they would also ask whether it is not an oversimplification and a mistake to assume that all forms of self-expression affirm one's agency. For example, black women who use *trickin* (by stripping or other means) to get money from men are free to display their bodies as they want. But may be incorrect to categorize their actions as an affirmation of black female agency, since these women express themselves within the power structure that sexualizes black women's bodies in order to exploit them for male use. *Trickin* may or may not be wrong on moral grounds as a form of self-expression, but the point is that it may be wrong on political ones. Such an approach leads, in my estimation, to dialogue.

Using Gadamer's model, it is not a matter of understanding the women, rather, an effort needs to be made to understand the message—which I would argue is embodied in the argument that both sides make regarding their respective views of sexuality. Traditional black feminists are impacted by a history that constructed black women as sexually deviant, and they see young black women today who by *trickin* or any other means play into this image of black women's sexuality as reductive, ahistorical, and dangerous for all black women. Conversely, the message of today's younger women is that their *horizon of understanding* is shaped by the commercialization of sexuality and sex—indeed, it is their cultural heritage willed to them in part by a successful feminist movement. These two positions represent the history and prejudices of both sides. But, as Gadamer instructs, our prejudices do not have to limit our understanding nor do they have to "cut [us] off from positive insight."[30] Rather, our prejudices make us "free." Deetz puts it succinctly:

> The creation of more complete understanding necessitates the desire to grasp the tradition, prejudices, of what is said in such a way that it fuses with the hearer's own tradition rather than trying to objectively reconstruct what the other meant.[31]

If we fused these two positions, we might posit a discussion around modern black women's sexuality that respects black women's right to express themselves, yet at the same time acknowledges the way in which some sectors of society view black women's bodies as objects. This view of sexuality might also encourage black women to begin a critical discourse around what sexuality means in the current unfolding of the post-postmodern world. In order to achieve some of the goals presented in this chapter, we may need to destabilize black feminist theory itself.

Notes

1 I use the phrase *of a sort* to described the intactness of their agency—showing how their agency is complicated and unlike white men, for example, can never be taken for granted.
2 Dawn Marie Dow, "Negotiating the Welfare Queen and the Strong Black Woman: African American Middle-Class Mothers' Women and Family Perspectives." *Sociological Perspectives* 58(1) (2006): 36–55.
3 Available at: http://nationalhumanitiescenter.org/tserve/freedom/1865–1917/essays/ racialuplift.htm
4 Beyoncé's words about Michelle Obama were quoted in many places, including the following article from the *International Business Times*: www.ibtimes.co.uk/michelle-obama-under-fire-calling-beyonce-role-model-1519062
5 Joan Morgan, When Chickenheads Come Home to Roost: A Hip-Hop Feminist Breaks it Down (New York: Simon & Schuster, 1999), p. 198.
6 Margaret Hunter, "Shake It, Baby, Shake It: Consumption and the New Gender Relation in Hip-Hop," *Sociological Perspectives*, 54(1) (2011): 15. doi:10.1525/ sop.2011.54.1.15.
7 Ibid., p. 16.

8 Ibid., pp. 16–17.
9 Elaine Richardson, "She Was Workin Like Foreal: Critical Literacy and Discourse Practices of African American Females in the Age of Hip Hop," *Discourse and Society*, 18 (2007): 802.
10 John Clammer, "Performing Ethnicity: Performance, Gender, Body, and Belief in the Construction of Signaling of Identity," *Ethnicity and Race Studies*, 38(13) (2015): 2159–2166.
11 Ibid., p. 2160.
12 Richardson, "She Was Workin Like Foreal," p. 794.
13 Ibid.
14 Ibid., p. 794.
15 Ibid., p. 794.
16 Morgan, When Chickenheads Come Home to Roost.
17 Richardson, "She Was Workin Like Foreal," p. 801.
18 Morgan, When Chickenheads Come Home to Roost, pp. 56–57.
19 Rosemarie Tong, *Feminist Thought: A More Comprehensive Introduction* (Boulder, CO: Westview Press, 2009), 50.
20 Ibid., p. 50.
21 T. Denean Sharpley-Whiting, *Pimps up Ho's Down: Hip Hop's Hold on Young Black Women* (New York: New York University Press, 2007), p. 10.
22 Morgan, When Chickenheads Come Home to Roost, p. 57.
23 See note 15 of the Introduction.
24 Abhik Roy and Bayo Oluda, "Hans-Georg Gadamer's *Praxis*: Implications for Connection and Action in Communication Studies," *Communication, Culture, and Critique*, 2.3 (September 2009): 255–273. doi:10.1111/j.1753-9137.2009.01038.x. P. Wander. "The Ideological Turn in Modern Criticism," *Central States Speech Journal*, 34 (1983): 1–18.
25 Roy and Oluda, p. 257.
26 Ibid., p. 258.
27 Hans Georg Gadamer, *Truth and Method* (London: Sheed and Ward, 1979), p. 259.
28 Stanley Deetz, "Conceptualizing Human Understanding: Gadamer's Hermeneutics and American Communication Studies," *Communication Quarterly*, 26(2) (1978): 18.
29 Ibid., p. 18.
30 Ibid.
31 Ibid.

5 Troubling the Water

Black Feminist Theory and the Hegemony of Thought

What are the implications of unsettling the consistency, stability, and safety that black feminist theory has come to represent? Black feminist theory is at its best when it is being transgressive, destabilizing, and unsafe. This is because black feminist theory is fundamentally an emancipatory project. It is unable to live up to this goal if it is seen as a fixed and immutable theory that is deployed either as a sound bite (e.g. white supremacists' capitalist patriarchy); as a catch word (e.g. intersectionality); as a canned response to incidents that negatively impacts black women's agency (e.g. "my existence is resistance"); or finally, as a clever gimmick such as the Feminist Phone Intervention.[1] The purpose of this chapter, accordingly, is to show that if black feminism is going to live up to its emancipatory potential, it must let go of its scripted, safe, and bounded actuality. Beginning with a brief discussion of black feminism, this chapter will go on to identify one of its current weaknesses: its inability to address non-normative forms of sexual expression. To conclude, I draw on José Estaban Muñoz's articulation of disidentification, which I use to dismantle the current bridge of black feminist thought and replace it with the possibility of constructing multiple types of bridges. It is by restoring the multiplicity, plasticity, and dynamism of black feminist theory that it can reclaim its status as an emancipatory praxis.

Black Feminist Theory, *Different*, and *Different from*

Among the myriad articulations of black feminist theory (1970s–present), the gold standard formulation comes from the exhaustive work of Patricia Hill Collins.[2] Although much of Hill Collins' research is pertinent to this discussion, I would like to focus primarily on *Black Feminist Thought*—her magnum opus. First issued in 1990, *Black Feminist Thought* in many ways came to define the field of black feminism. It calls on readers to think about the multiple and intersecting ways that black women's lives are framed, disciplined, and controlled. Through a process of amalgamation where she expertly synthesizes the ideas of the Combahee River Collective, Barbara Smith, Beverly Guy-Sheftall, Patricia Bell Scott, and other black feminist thinkers, while at the same time advancing her own critical perspective, Hill Collins provides what we should consider to be four of the most important lenses[3] through which black feminist scholars view black women's existence in a US context, namely: (1) interlocking systems of oppression;[4] (2) controlling images;[5] (3) standpoint;[6] and (4) black feminist epistemology.[7] For her part, Hill Collins defines black feminist thought as,

> consist[ing] of specialized knowledge created by African-American women which clarifies a standpoint of and for Black women. In other words, Black feminist thought encompasses theoretical interpretations of Black women's reality by those who live it.[8]

This definition of black feminist thought is deliberate and careful as it walks the fine line of not claiming that "all African-American women generate such thought" or that groups other than black women "do not play a critical role in its production."[9] In this way, Collins' understanding of black feminist theory is both inclusive and exclusive. It is inclusive in asserting that non-black women can also shape black feminist thought; and it is exclusive in distinguishing between *skin folk and kin folk.*[10] By establishing their unique standpoint from other groups—because of their history, interaction with white patriarchal society, etc.—Collins maintains that there is a knowledge specific to their position as black and as women.

It is no stretch to say that black feminist theory was purposely designed to be distinct from feminist theory—which by and large operated without a critical race analysis—and race theory—which functioned without a critical gender lens. This rhetorical turn focusing squarely on the lives of black women is important because black women's liberation has often been subsumed under the liberation struggles of either white women or black men, where the categories of race and gender seem stubbornly solidified. So, in the liberation struggles of white women, black women are claimed as allies because they are women. From this line of reasoning, white feminists assert that it is in the best interest of all women to unite in order to overcome the oppressive force of patriarchy. On the contrary, black men argue for a shared racial history in which black women and black men are allies. Black male theorists thus assert that it is in the best interest of all black people to unite in order to overcome the oppressive force of racism. Time and time again, however, black feminists have advanced the argument that black women cannot disassociate themselves either from their gender or their race since they are impacted by both.

Black feminism is also designed to be different from other forms of theory as well in that, unlike many other forms of theory (postmodernism, poststructuralism, etc.), black feminist theory rooted itself in emancipatory praxis. That is not to say that black feminism is simply an explanatory theory of the conditions that have shaped the lives of black women in the USA for more than 200 years, nor it is meant to merely "talk back" to oppression. Rather, black feminist theory is supposed to name, shame, resist, destabilize, and dismantle the various systems of oppression that impede black women's agency and full participation in society. I would argue that a starting point for black feminist theory is the acknowledgment and embracing of black women as *different from* all others.

Before moving too quickly into a discussion and more importantly challenge of *different from*, I think that it is important to carefully explain the variance between black women as *different*—a designation that has been use to marginalize and suppress black women and their agency—and black women as *different from*—used in historical articulations of black feminism as an instrument of liberation.

Difference *and* Different from

To see black women as *different*—or use language that communicates their difference i.e. welfare queens, angry black woman, jezebel, etc.—is to demarcate black women as marginal, outsiders, and/or non-normative. In such a society, black women are spoken about as the ultimate site of *difference* or as the *othe*r. Black feminist scholars like Ann duCille have written powerfully about black women as *other* perhaps most saliently in her essay, "The Occult of True Black Womanhood" where duCille says: "Within and around the modern academy, racial and gender alterity has become a hot commodity that has claimed black women as its principal signifier ... Why are black women always already Other?"[11] duCille is chiefly concerned about how non-black women academics use black women and their lived experiences to build their own careers. Further, duCille's essay points to the ease non-black women academic find in locating/figuring/styling the black female body as *different* or *other* primarily because the black female body in their minds represents *the* very body of subjugation. In other words, the black female body concretizes or illustrates what real and, even in some cases, utter marginalization looks like. In this way, the black female body helps non-black women scholars move discussions outside of the theoretical realm and into the space of the flesh. Thus, to encounter the black female body using touch, taste, smell—all of your senses—is to literally encounter—for some scholars—society's tangible *other*. Black women personify the intersectional impact that racism, classism, sexism, lack of opportunity has on a *real* body. The saying *the spirit made flesh* offers a way to conceptualize what the black female body has come to mean. Taking a bit of a Levinasian turn, positing black women as the ultimate site of *difference* or as duCille might say "hyperstatic alterity"[12] leaves open the possibility of their erasure and demise—they (black women) are beings that are so *radically different* from the norm (male-white-rational-not poor) that it is almost impossible to comprehend their humanness and thus their right to exist. For Lévinas, it is the face that communicates "you shall not commit murder."[13] For black feminist theorists, the ultimate fear is that black women are perceived as faceless and as such, they are marked for death.

This linguistic position has consequences that extend beyond the conceptual or philosophical level. For example, it means that those who occupy the subject position feel comfortable talking *about* black women and *for* black women. Jacqueline Jones Royster speaks to this phenomenon in her article "When the First Voice You Hear is not Your Own," when she writes,

I have been compelled on too many occasions to count to sit as a well-mannered Other, silently, in a state of tolerance that requires me to be as expressionless as I can manage, while colleagues who occupy a place of entitlement different from my own talk about the history and achievements of people from my ethnic group, or even about their perception of our struggle.[14]

By capitalizing the "O" in "Other," Royster signals that there are *two* others from her perspective: the first is the traditional *O*ther who lacks agency, while the second is the "*other*" who speaks *from* the subject position and as such wields power. In this sense, Royster has been *O*thered by the *o*ther because her story has been claimed or is told for her. To put a finer point on it, Royster is made the object in a narrative about black women where her embodied position *as a black women* should afford her the subject position—and the power that accompanies it—and thus she should be teller of the tale. Royster is bewildered by how easily her position as subject is invalidated by others who lack her positionality and authentic critical authority to speak. In this situation, Royster underscores not only how she is silenced but also how her resistance is constrained. As a way to resist the social and self-alienation, marginality, violence, and "hyperstatic alterity" that accompany *difference*, I would argue that black feminist theory—though they may not articulate it this way—posits the notion of what I call *different from*. The following explains what I mean by *different from* and its importance in black feminist theory.

   Put simply, for black feminist theory to say that black women are *different from* is to acknowledge that black women have a unique socio-historical experience from all others; and these experiences shape the way that black women move through the world. *Different from* emerged as a key concept in black feminism for several reasons. First, by claiming *difference* as a radical point of self- or group liberation, black women resist the act of linguistic *othering* that occurs simply from living in a society based on racial and gender hierarchy. Second, claiming the position *different from* as a critical tool for liberation; where *difference*—

- black *women* are black but not *males*;
- *black* women are women but not *white*;
- black women are *neither* white nor male—

becomes a site of resistance and positive distinction, as opposed to these things being seen as negative traits. Third and relatedly, *different from* adds moral accusatory power to black women's claims for justice. Since black women lack the social location to participate in racial, gender, and typically class oppression, who better to speak truth to such corrosive forces than black women? Finally, since black women can never wholly be members of one of the groups who traditionally wield corrosive social power, they are in effect able to articulate a path to freedom that allows them to embrace the intersecting characters of their identity in a way that affirms their sense of self without harming others, while at the same time challenging society to be more inclusive.[15] This final stance is important because it highlights the fact that black feminist opposition to white supremacist-capitalist-hetero-patriarchy is at the very core of its being structured around resisting inequality in *all* the ways that this hydra impacts black women. Black feminist theory is not interested in black women losing their identity, but it is critically interested in black women being seen as equal with all other identities, as opposed to being labeled as inferior based on characteristics that black women have little or no control over. In this way we can see how *different from* is inextricably bound to the notions of equality, equity, and justice.

Challenging the idea of *difference* while at the same time articulating the standpoint of *different from* have been the very foundations of black feminist theory—historically, this is what black feminism is and this is what black feminism does: black feminism contests violence, black feminism articulates equality. It might then come as a surprise that my work, then, seeks to challenge—call into question—and even destabilize the very foundational principle of *different from* that has shaped black feminist theory from its beginning. I am doing this not to be contrary or provocative, but because at *this* point in the evolution of black feminist theory *different from* is showing limitations in its reach and capacity to express and explain the extended terrain of black women's lived experiences today. The core issue of this discussion has to do with what I see as the present non-inclusiveness of black feminism to take into account young women's concerns about their agency and the way that they are currently pushing and stretching their sexuality; ways that might seem uncomfortable especially for more traditional black feminists. This non-inclusiveness is a theoretical corollary of black feminism's original founding on the notion of *different from*. The key question here is "Can we rethink or reimage *different from* and especially its dependence on the notion of equality so as to make it more inclusive of, for example, sexual expression that trends towards what some might consider deviant or even self-harming?"

Reimagining Different from

Black feminism posits that since black women occupy two (sometimes three or more) marginalized groups, black feminist theorists argue that society treats them as unequal or *Untermenschen*. Thus, as we have seen, much of black feminist theory focuses on achieving equality (sameness) with others or to use the phrase of the Combahee River Collective. black women desire to be seen as "levelly human," not above others or below them, rather, on the same plane. One, perhaps, critical but certainly accurate way to think about "levelly human" is as the plateauing of identity where there is a sense of flattening of both change and growth—i.e. identity construction and challenge have come to a standstill because we are now all the same, i.e. levelly human. There is nothing wrong with working for equality or wanting to be seen as "levelly human" in and of itself, but thinking *only* in terms of being treated equally or the same as one's oppressors does not allow a radical politics to emerge. Nor does it allow in this case black feminist scholars to think through what it really means to be equal to white men, white women, and black men. Does equality mean that black women are afforded the same power to disenfranchise; to enact violence; to discriminate against others; to speak as loudly; or to take up more space? What stand should black women as a group and black feminism as a theory aspire to? Given the current system, what does equality mean? In the end, does over-dependence on the idea of equality mean abandoning the emancipatory philosophy of *different from*? I would answer "yes" since one does not need to be saved from *sameness*.

To bring this discussion together. I would assert that the concept of *different from* and its dependence on the notion of equality are without question important because they have allowed black feminist theory to celebrate and embrace difference while at the same time arguing for equality. Nevertheless, in its present formation it seems to lead towards a leveling of identity, while at the same time it does not pull black women outside of systems of violence and oppression. Indeed, it may even accept the said violence as long as black women are no longer on the receiving end of society's scorn. Now while I hesitate to go that far, what I do believe is that articulating a theory that does not expressly address *what equality looks like* in a given oppressive system is a theory that risks being seen as non-inclusive, non reflective, and ultimately self-serving.

So, the challenge here is to reimagine *different from* so that black feminist theory would not only embrace black women's position as *different*, but more importantly it would challenge equality as the sole goal for liberation. In this way, *different from* continues to be an important tool for black women's liberation and identity formation, but also *different from* potentially points us in the direction of a radical reimagining of society itself. In this new and expanded sense, *different from* suggests that one stands as a non-participant in systems of domination as *different from* those identities that seek equality in access to tools of oppression.

One way to understand why black feminism should consider *embracing* this newly articulated *different from* is vis-à-vis the example of how members of the LGBTQ community embrace oppositional and maligned positions like *queer*, or African American scholars like Luvell Anderson, who convincingly argue for the power in the social position of the *thug* from a black male cultural context. In this way, oppositional stances like *queer*—used as a way to reject gender or sexual norms; and *thug*—used in hip hop and among some black men "as an unapologetic affirmation of their experiences as black men"[16] lose the rhetorical force to injure while gaining the rhetorical force of self-definition because these terms reject the othering accompanied by *difference* while simultaneously claiming to be *different from*. In other words, to be *different from* becomes a starting point for resistance; it also signals that you will never be lured by promises of equality in systems of domination; you will never be complicit in the oppression of another. Second, in claiming the reimagined status of being *different from*, black women are able to articulate and advocate for a theory that reflects the uniqueness of their upward trajectory of their *being-in-the-world*. In this way, they reject the horizontal leveling out that accompanies calls to equality. To this

I would add that from the newly articulated *different from* the concepts of "woman" and "black" are ever evolving; they are vertical, rather than horizontal and in this way encompass multiple planes of black women's being.

A quick word about Hill Collins ... to be clear, there is absolutely nothing wrong with Hill Collins's articulation of black feminist thought or the four lenses she uses to encapsulate black feminism, mentioned earlier, that filter our understanding of what it means to do black feminism and what it means to be a black feminist. Indeed, Hill Collins's definition and the four lenses—if I might be allowed to structure it this way—are a necessary condition in post-1990 discourse surrounding black feminism and black women's resistance to oppression. What *is* problematic is how black feminist theory grounded in *different from* as the vehicle for equality and liberation is currently understood and deployed: as inert and totalizing. Given its longevity and taken-for-grantedness, I find it frustrating that black feminist theory rooted in the narrow frame of *different from* just seems to roll off the tongue of all kinds of people: a hegemonic signifier supporting or refuting things, people, or actions without thought to its appropriateness, its efficacy, its stagnation, or the failure of its reach. Because of this, black feminist theory runs the risk of losing its emancipatory potential. If this catastrophe (and it would be a catastrophe) is to be avoided, we *must* directly confront the issue of what may happen to a revolutionary theory when it trades the creativity of (de)construction and possibility of inducing chaos for a well-worn, stable bridge. Though it may not seem intuitive, the first step is addressing what I see as the current hegemony of black feminist thought.

Playing in the Fold of Hegemony

Because it is among other things "slippery" and "difficult,"[17] hegemony is not a word to be used lightly. For his part, Donaldson (through Gramsci) describes hegemony as,

> the winning and holding of power and the formation (and destruction) of social groups in that process. In this sense, it is importantly about the ways in which the ruling class establishes and maintains its domination. The ability to impose a definition of the situation, to set the terms in which events are understood and issues discussed, to formulate ideals and define morality is an essential part of this process. Hegemony involves persuasion of the greater part of the population, particularly through the media, and the organization of social institutions in ways that appear "natural," "ordinary," "normal." The state, through punishment for non-conformity, is crucially involved in this negotiation and enforcement.[18]

To call something hegemonic, then, is to say that it is totalizing, destructive, and oppressive. The power of the hegemonic rests in its ability to pass itself off as normal and natural. One such *something* that race scholars tend to classify as hegemonic is *whiteness*. Sara Ahmed identifies whiteness "as an ongoing and unfinished history, which orientates bodies in specific directions, affecting how they 'take up' space."[19] Whiteness bestows or denies privileges based primarily on one's racial proximity to it. The power of whiteness rests in its ability to mark others as different, non-normative while it—whiteness—remains unmarked and mostly unnoticed. Additionally, some feminist and masculinity scholars use the phrase *hegemonic masculinity* to describe the "oppressive" relationship that exists between men and women.[20] Hegemonic masculinity locks men into a toxic singular modality or way of being a man in the world—masculine, heterosexual/ normative, seeking (demanding) sexual gratification by women. Those outside of this modality are seen as non-normative, deviant, counter-hegemonic,[21] (e.g. gay men, femmes, queers), and exploitable. As we have seen, black feminist theory is often positioned in opposition to the hegemony of racist and sexist forms of oppression.

But, we should think more broadly about hegemony. Hegemony does not only encompass what is totalizing, destructive, and oppressive but also includes social forces, theoretical responses to a given situation, and ways of moving through the world that are mundane, prescriptive, taken for granted, and *firmly decided*. The idea of being *firmly decided* calls to mind the legal term *stare decisis* which means "to stand by things decided." The purpose of *stare decisis* is to "discourage litigating established precedents." Critics of *stare decisis* rightly assert, "that the doctrine occasionally permits erroneous decisions to continue influencing the law and encumbers the legal system's ability to quickly adapt to change."[22] Does seeing hegemony in these terms expand our use of the word to include not only systems of oppression like whiteness and masculinity but also modes of inquiry like black feminist theory? This is a challenging question since we typically think of black feminist theory as doing counter-hegemonic work. Yet, and herein lies the rub, black feminist scholars tend to use terms like hegemony to describe external systems of oppression but fail to see how terms like hegemony in its expanded form can also be used self-reflexively; in other words, hegemony can also be applied to black feminist theorizing itself. In this way, to call black feminist theory hegemonic is to *play in the fold of hegemony*. Stopping here for a moment, I use the term *fold* to invoke in a very limited way a Deleuzian[23] spirit. Put simply, for Deleuze, the fold represents an opportunity for the subject to encounter its subjectivity; it is a melding of the external and the internal. I have always seen the Deleuzian fold as a place (period, time) for self-reflection and agency—where the subject might think about what is and contemplate the possibility of the "to be." Charles Stivale puts it nicely, writing, "the development of the fold demonstrates that philosophy finds in the fold the expression of a continuous and vital force of being and of becomings."[24]

In turning to Deleuze, I do not intend to provide a systematic overview of Deleuze's work, instead my focus will be on the implications of Deleuze's notion of the fold for black feminism. This choice of focus is not arbitrary because, as Tom Conley observes, the notion of the fold "counts among the most vital and resonate terms in [Deleuze's] copious and varied writings."[25] Importantly, Deleuze develops his notion of the fold as a part of his analysis of power structures. In that analysis, Deleuze raises a question about the power of resistance that should be of central concern to all black feminists. Deleuze writes:

> What remains, then, except an anonymous life that shows up when it clashes with power, argues with it, exchanges "brief and strident words", and then fades back into the night, what Foucault called "the life of infamous men", whom he asked us to admire by virtue of "their misfortune, race or uncertain madness"?[26]

With this question, Deleuze wonders whether marginalized groups, such as black women, can produce any real change in speaking truth to power. What, in other words, is the point of struggling against the proverbial wall of racism, classism, gender discrimination, and economic oppression, if these struggles are destined to fade "back into the night"? This is certainly an understandable reaction on the part of many black women "who are daily beaten down, mentally, physically, and spiritually—women who are powerless to change their condition in life." One mark of their victimization, as hooks notes, is that they "accept their lot in life without visible question, without organized protest, without collective anger or rage."[27] In the face of such a reality, the question shared by both Deleuze and black feminists concerns whether there can be any source for resistance against power structures, and, if so, what those resources are. Deleuze's notion of the fold, I want to suggest, is potentially significant in this regard. Like duCille and other black feminists, Deleuze is not so much concerned with alterity as with subjectivity, especially the becoming of subjects who are unable to self-define, to become themselves, or to create themselves anew due to the pressures of social forces. For this reason, Deleuze's notion of the fold can provide new and valuable resources for addressing questions of black female subjectivity raised by duCille and others.

The French term, *"pli,"* as Conley explains, refers "both to a twist of fabric and to the origins of life, bears a lightness and density that marks many of the philosopher's reflection on questions of *being* and on the nature of *events*."[28] What is thought-provoking about Deleuze's notion of the *fold* is that, like a piece of fabric, it maintains its physical presence but at the same time can create new spaces within its formation of new crevices and pleats. This is why the fold is capable of "bearing almost infinite conceptual force."[29] Through its multiple *foldings*, the subject maintains access to the internal and external aspects of her being. This means that "A person's relation with his or her body becomes both an "archive" and a "diagram," a collection of subjectivations and a mental map charted on the basis of the past and drawn from the events and elements in the ambient world."[30] With this notion of the fold, then, I want to suggest that the folding of the subject provides an interesting model for thinking about the way in which black females can both inherit a historical condition and at the same time create new identities within that condition.

It bears noting that there is not an inside or outside prior to the fold, instead the *fold* creates the inside as well as the outside. The inside and outside of the fold are two sides of a single surface. Conley adds:

Thus the fold allows the body and the soul of the subject to be and to become in the world through "intensions" ... felt about "extensions" in space. Because the inside and outside are conjoined by the point of view of the soul on the world, the apprehension of the condition of possibility of variation allows the subject to think about how it inflects and is inflected by the mental and geographical milieus it occupies.[31]

That said, we need to ask whether there can be an inside of thought for black women who are caught up in systems of power and trapped in the position of other forgotten. Has the internal been forgotten? If so, how can it be recovered? Echoing the insights of Fanon and hooks, duCille seeks a way for black women to escape the external gaze that fixes black women in the static, illusionary, position of the other. This is accomplished through the recovery of a black female identity which is no longer a marker of alterity but is capable of speaking its own name. In this attempt, Deleuze is an important ally, because his notion of the *fold* signifies a way of producing an identity internally.

Like duCille, Deleuze rejects the idea of an ahistorical subjectivity whose identity would escape from the vicissitudes of history and the external world. Instead of being ahistorical and fixed, both thinkers would agree that subjectivity must be achieved, in other words, that there is a struggle for subjectivity. Conley explains that this struggle is a "battle to win the right to have access to difference, variation, and metamorphosis."[32] Similarly, duCille describes the nature of this struggle in terms of the struggle by black women to become the authors of their own text. Through this struggle, they seek to establish a space of their own, as something other than the other. The fact that this is a "struggle" suggests that the formation of positive subjectivity can only occur through resistance to existing systems of power. Subjectivity, according to Deleuze, is in a certain sense defined by its power to resist, because "diffuse centers of power do not exist without points of resistance that are in some way primary."[33]

What type of internal relation to oneself is established by *folds*? In *folding*, one is able to encounter another self, in a different way from the identity imposed by external, marginalizing forces. Deleuze explains the dual nature of this relation to oneself in the following terms:

On the one hand, there is a "relation to oneself" that consciously derives from one's relation with others; on the other, there is equally a "self constitution" that consciously derives from the moral code as a rule for knowledge.[34]

In addition to the various forces that define the subject from the outside, Deleuze acknowledges the "moral code" to know thyself.[35] In this respect, his notion of the fold can be useful to black feminists who seek to counter the commodification and colonization of black women. This operation is at work in duCille's reference to the many women who have preserved counter-histories and counter-memories of black women.

Importantly, Deleuze emphasizes that this counter-history need not be a mere reaction to a prior set of historical conditions. Instead, the relation to oneself has an independent status. As Deleuze explains:

It is as if the relation of the outside folded back to create a doubling, allowed a relation to oneself to emerge, and constitute an inside which is hollowed out and develops its own unique dimension …, the relation to oneself that is self-mastery, "is a power that one brought to bear on oneself *in* the power that one exercised over others"…[36]

Deleuze, like duCille, is interested in establishing a positive notion of difference. Instead of being a product of a relation to something else, positive difference is something like "the right to difference, variation and metamorphosis."[37] This means that the struggle for subjectivity is not just a reaction to a prior situation; instead it is a creative force and a source of change.

Along these lines, Deleuze's *fold* provides a space for black women to create a positive identity from a perspective and position internal to themselves. As Deleuze suggests, it is "a differentiation that leads to a folding, a reflection."[38] *Folding* is thus not merely about resisting the external; it is primarily about creating a "relation to oneself."[39] Since the process of *folding* functions "beneath the codes and rules of knowledge and power," what is also critical is that the *folds* are "apt to unfold and merge with them, but not without new folding being created in the process."[40] It is important to emphasize that Deleuze does not intend the *fold* as a retreat from the external world, since the outside and the inside are not distinct from one another.[41] Rather, while the *fold* provides a safe place for encountering oneself, what is as critical is that black feminist subjectivity also *unfolds*. It is in *unfolding* that she may encounter the world in a newly constructed identity that can resist external constitution—"unfolding means becoming."[42] Now going back to my original point, I believe that *playing in the fold of hegemony* produces the following: it complicates and interrogates that which black feminist critical theorists hold dearest, keeps black feminist critical theory on its toes, opens up the possibility for reconstruction, demands reflexivity, and, finally, allows black feminist theorists to see the ways in which black feminist theory may not be as inclusive[43] as is commonly thought, and finally helps black feminists formulate the "to be."

Dennis Schep provides an example of doing what I call *playing in the fold of hegemony* in his analysis of Judith Butler's seminal concept *performativity* as it relates to gender. To be clear, gender performativity relates to "the idea that a gendered identity is produced only as it is enacted."[44] Thus,

gender is performative, for Butler, because it exists *only* in the acts that constitute it … a gendered identity is produced through specific bodily gestures, practices, declarations, actions, and movements. A gendered identity is thus an effect of doing gender. The theory of gender performativity thus permits Butler to advance an innovative theory of subjectivity.[45]

On Schep's analysis, although Butler's notion of performativity is designed to complicate and disrupt binary notions of gender, the concept of performativity itself becomes hegemonic because it does not account for those whose psyches (in some instances their very lives) require an anchoring in a concept such as gender. Based on Scheps' reading, viewing performativity as hegemonic (limiting) (encumbered) allows us to see how the concept of performativity (like whiteness and masculinity) is taken for granted by theorists while at the same time elevated to the status of being counter-hegemonic even as it performs in hegemonic ways. The claim here is that if gender is *always already* performed and there is no outside of this framing, then the concept of performativity in relation to gender is indeed hegemonic, and as such marginalizes, for example, trans folks (or even heterosexual folks), some of who may require binary gendered anchoring as either male or female. A similar analysis can be applied to black feminist theory.

Black feminist theory exists: (1) to *name* black women's multivariate oppressions; (2) to *explain* black women's multivariate oppressions; and (3) to *resist* black women's multivariate oppressions. Thus, black feminist theory should always be read as action-oriented. Yet despite its revolutionary focus, black feminist theory is limited in terms of whom it includes, what actions it includes, and what expressions of agency it includes. These exclusions are embedded in the very structure of its analysis. Take, for example, the outrage over bell hooks' critique of Beyoncé in "Moving Beyond Pain." There hooks offers a traditional black feminist analysis of Beyoncé's visual album "Lemonade."

It is worth noting that in "Lemonade," Beyoncé takes viewers through a powerful and private tour of her relationship with her husband (hip hop artist Jay Z) and the accusations of infidelity that have plagued the couple for many years. There are many noteworthy things about the video album, including the now famous line "Rachel with the good hair," an appearance by the stunning and powerful Serena Williams, and black women of all hues firmly centered in the video so much so that it, for some, reads like a full imagining of what #blackgirl-magic really is. Perhaps the most discussed scene of the video album is Beyoncé walking down a street in a gorgeous yellow dress with a baseball bat, smashing cars as she goes. bell hooks, among others, took note of this scene in particular. hooks is concerned that Beyoncé turns to violence as a way of addressing the hurt and rage that she feels due to her husband's betrayal. hooks writes:

> Female violence is no more liberatory than male violence. And when violence is made to look sexy and eroticized, as in the *Lemonade* sexy-dress street scene, it does not serve to undercut the prevailing cultural sentiment that it is acceptable to use violence to reinforce domination, especially in relations between men and women. Violence does not create positive change.[46]

Many, especially younger women, have taken issue with hooks' critique, while others are shocked and horrified that bell hooks would attack Beyoncé so publicly simply because she does not conform to traditional black feminist notions of proper behavior. For others, bell hooks' critique of Beyoncé reeks of respectability politics. First discussed by Evelyn Brooks Higginbotham, "respectability politics" refers to the actions taken by those in out-groups (racial, gender, class, etc.) in order to get better treatment from those who belong to the in-groups. These actions might include speaking (or not speaking) in a certain way so if you are a black person skilled in Black American English, you may not use BAE when you are around whites. Or, you may dress a particular way or engage in certain kinds of activities that are prevalent among in-group members.[47]

hooks' response to Beyoncé is an example of the hegemony of black feminist thought that has come to define how black women should act and respond. There is no outside of it, no other way to act or be. This hegemony of thought shows itself clearly in hooks' rejection of Beyoncé's "rage" in the video as an unacceptable representation of "female power" and her biting critique of Beyoncé's use of violence in the video as antithetical to change reads preachy and respectable. Other than Audre Lorde's much celebrated "Uses of Anger" (which today reads as tame compared to what we see in Beyoncé's video), black feminism mostly eschews violence and rage as acceptable responses to injustice. What, I think, young black women are looking for is a black feminism that is more physical, one that it rooted in a politics of the body: a black feminism that is nasty, and deviant, and violent, and sexy, and unapologetic.

Black Feminism, Black Sexual Deviance, and Disidentification

In her article, "Beyond Black and Blue: BDSM, Internet Pornography, and Black Female Sexuality," Ariana Cruz transgresses the established boundaries of discussions of black female sexuality. Delving into the murky, violent, and historically complicated pornography where black women engage in sexual encounters with white men, where there is "racist language, role-playing, and the construction of racists scenes."[48] Citing traditional black feminist scholars like Lorde who reject these forms of sexual expression that "perpetuate patterns of domination and submission," Cruz skillfully argues for a radical rethinking of black women's sexuality via transcending normative sexual borders. Whereas Cruz is looking at the "complexity and diverseness of Black women's sexual practice," I am more interested in disrupting the hegemony of black feminist thought that excludes black women who profess to have "sadomasochistic soul[s],"[49] are performers in hip hop videos where their bodies are commodified, or who, like Beyoncé, embrace violence as part of their black feminism.

Like so many other theories (traditional or conventional?), black feminism puts too much emphasis on redirecting the eyes of the others from black women's bodies. This is based on the long and harrowing history of black women's physical and sexual exploitation during enslavement, medical (including gynecological) experimentation on black women's bodies, and modern-day reproductive technologies that seek to control black women's reproductive capacity. Based on this history of repression, it is really no wonder that black women have been reluctant to focus on their bodies as critical sights of resistance, to embrace violence as form of resistance, or to talk about pleasure associated with commodification and objectification. This is difficult terrain and those black women who venture into these spaces are routinely disciplined. And even as we love Beyoncé for her domination of the news cycle and her celebration of black women of all hues, traditional black feminists cringe at her full sexual embodiment. How do we bridge these two extremes? How do we celebrate Beyoncé and the full bloom of her black womanhood and at the same time take seriously the concerns of traditional black feminists who feel that the focus on the body is a fool's path to freedom?

In his book, *Disidentification: Queers of Color and the Performance of Politics*, José Esteban Muñoz presents the complex and potentially liberatory idea of *disidentification*.[50] On the one hand, to *disidentify* is to resist binary social (external) constructions of the self, while at the same time one is not inclined to construct personal binaries or segments of the self that label the self "good" or bad. "As a practice," Muñoz writes, "disidentification does not dispel those ideological contradictory elements; rather, like a melancholic subject holding on to a lost object, a disidentifying subject works to hold on to this object and invest it with new life." The point is not to expunge what may be considered bad or "harmful" or "contradictory" but to hold these things in tension.[51] Terms such as queer and hybrid are examples used by Muñoz to describe disidentification. For Muñoz as well as theorists like Judith Butler, there is a space of wonder, creativity, and agency that can happen in what I've refer to as the *messy middle* or that area created when binaries collide.

In *Lemonade*, Beyoncé presents the viewer with multiple contradictory images and words that are as problematic as they are pleasurable. In her critique of Beyoncé, bell hooks focuses on the violence of, for example, Beyoncé smashing a car with a baseball bat, but never acknowledges the pleasure the viewer may receive from seeing Beyoncé present herself as the ultimate "eye candy" for the viewer (sexy, violent woman). In this sense how different is she from, say, comic book heroines like Wonder Woman, whose appeal is in her ability to kick your ass in a tight outfit that shows off all her curves? Unlike hooks, Muñoz acknowledges the pleasure viewers might feel from images that challenge our politics. Disidentification allows us to recognize and own the sensations and, yes, pleasures that we feel in situations that our critical frameworks call us to disavow. Muñoz is correct when he argues that it is politically dangerous to do so because it can be argued that we place our theory, perhaps even our liberation, in jeopardy if we find-acknowledge-pleasure in what is simultaneously read as painful and dehumanizing. But *not* to recognize the sometimes twin feelings/sensations that accompany forms of objectification, I think, limits the creative power of our theory by making it denialist, one-dimensional, and even essentialist. Black feminist theory is indeed robust enough to provide salient critiques to conventional questions. Unlike some mainstream feminism,[52] black feminism has not quite found a way make a space for the unconventional, the problematic, the exploitative to exist as a valid and affirmed position within its theoretical structure.

A final word on Beyoncé. So it is one thing to be excited about Beyoncé calling herself a feminist, and influential feminists labeling her *the new face of feminism* while ignoring how she and her husband have talked about other (presumably black) women (calling them bitches) and Beyoncé's over-sexualization of herself. Disidentification provides us with a space to hold these different aspects of Beyoncé in tension so that we avoid the trap of claiming one aspect of her identity over another. It is one thing for women like Beyoncé to call themselves feminists, yet other feminists (black ones) have to reconcile this pronouncement with what reads as the antithesis of black feminism because her sense of self is so tightly wrapped up in her body. Yet, this is precisely what black feminism needs to do, and here I have suggested that the way forward is to incorporate disidentification into black feminist theory. Disidentification allows black feminism to play in the messy middle and signals to young black women that going forward with this thought: "black feminist theory is also their fucking theory to do with whatever they can fucking reimagine." ·

CODA: Random Thoughts

Simon and Garfunkel's song "Bridge Over Troubled Water" (1970) was inspired by a line from the Negro spiritual "Mary Don't You Weep": "I'll be a bridge over deep water if you trust in my name." In the refrain to "Bridge Over Troubled Water," Garfunkel channels gospel music powerfully and sings:

> Like a bridge over troubled water
> I will lay me down
> Like a bridge over troubled water
> I will lay me down

Paying homage to this inspirational and universal song, the likes of Willie Nelson, Johnny Cash, and Jon Bon Jovi have all covered the tune—not simply because the song hints at a spiritual relationship with God— but because the song also evokes the way in which people are there for one another in tough times. But when black feminist icons Roberta Flack (1971) and Aretha Franklin (1972) performed covers of this song, its meaning was expanded. There is something, especially in Franklin's version—with its inclusion of the call-response tradition ubiquitous to the black church—that is so moving and sublime when the song is sung in a black woman's voice. It evokes the history of black women's struggle and sacrifice in which black women's bodies have been bridges that support those in need.

Yet, this image of the bridge has also taken on a more negative connotation, as a metaphor of how black (and brown) women's bodies function as support for "others" who have exploited them. Elsewhere I have written about how black feminist scholar Ann duCille likens black women's bodies to a bridge that men and non-blacks have crossed in order to stake their claims as scholars. In addition, the text *This Bridge Called My Back* bears witness to the struggles and intersectional identities of women of color whose bodies have become battle-grounds in struggles that have been waged by others.[53] Donna Kate Rushin's "The Bridge Poem," which is anthologized in that book, aptly describes the frustration felt by black women who are often called upon to mediate (bridge) the divide between different groups and disparate discourses:

> I will not be the bridge to your womanhood
> Your manhood
> Your human-ness ...
> I'm sick of mediating with your worst self
> On behalf of your better selves ...
> Forget it
> Stretch or drown
> Evolve or die.[54]

Rushin's poem expresses the frustration felt by black women who are over-burdened by the support they are constantly called on to provide for others. It suggests that others turn to black women because black women have mastered the arts of survival. Yet, Rushin powerfully commands others to either "stretch or drown" because black women are just plain old tired of functioning as a means of static support or living in relationships without reciprocity. We might also see Rushin's poem as a repudiation of Stokely Carmichael's inflammatory statement that the "position of women in the movement is prone,"[55] meaning subservient, obedient, and fuckable. Thus, "The Bridge Poem" stands as a strong example of the myriad ways that black women reject or resist being used as support structures.

Black feminist theory *itself* was created to be a bridge. It was not merely a bridge that helped to cross over the troubled waters of racism, sexism, and classism; it was also a bridge that joined black women together, linking them through shared lived experiences and through acts of resistance. From Sojourner Truth's question, "ain't I a woman?" to the Combahee River Collective's "Black Feminist Statement," to Patricia Hill Collins' insight into "interlocking systems of oppression" black feminist theory has always been a solid bridge: constant, stable, and offering black women safe passage through the dangers of living in a white supremacist patriarchal society. But what if we were to trouble these waters once again?

Notes

1 As stated on its Tumblr page, the Feminist Phone Intervention advises women who are receiving unwanted attention to give guys a fake phone number. So when the person dials instead of reaching you they will receive "an automatically-generated quotation from feminist writer bell hooks." The women using the service will be able to "protect [their] privacy while dropping some feminist knowledge when your unwanted 'suitor' calls or texts."

2 This is not to take away from the work of excellent black feminist scholars like Beverly Guy-Sheftall, bell hooks, or Barbara Smith. It is merely an acknowledgment of Hill Collins' dominance and her thoughtful framing of black feminist theory.

3 With the fifth being intersectionality which was first articulated by Kimberlé Crenshaw in "Mapping the Margins." See Kimberlé Williams Crenshaw, "Mapping the Margins: Intersectionality, Identity Politics, and Violence Against Women of Color," in Martha Albertson Fineman, and Rixanne Mykitiuk, eds., *The Public Nature of Violence* (New York: Routledge, 1994).

4 Collins argues that black women are trapped in a matrix of oppressive systems including race, class, and gender all working together to suppress their freedom and oppress their lives.

5 Collins argues that certain tropes or images were developed during enslavement to control black women (the mammy, the matriarch, the bad black mother, and the jezebel). These images are designed to control black women's actions and confine black women's self-articulation.

6 Standpoint is a critical concept in black feminist thought. Hill Collins argues that because they share a racial and gender history that black women in the USA have a shared standpoint, or way of seeing the world which is shaped by their experiences with white supremacy and gender discrimination.

7 Black women have created their own theory knowledge that is not opinion-based but based on their lived experiences.

8 Hill Collins, *Black Feminist Thought*, p. 22.

9 Ibid.

10 This is a term used to describe people who share your race but do not share your politics. An example of skin folk/not kin folks might be someone like Clarence Thomas.

11 Ann duCille, "The Occult of True Black Womanhood: Critical Demeanor and Black Feminist Studies," in Elizabeth Abel, Barbara Christian and Helene Moglen, eds., *Female Subjects in Black and White: Race, Psychoanalysis, Feminism* (Berkeley, CA: University of California Press, 1997), p. 21.

12 Ibid., p. 22.

13 Emmanuel Lévinas and Alphonso Lingis, *Totality and Infinity* (Pittsburgh, PA: Duquesne University Press, 1969).

14 Jacqueline Jones Royster, "When the First Voice Your Hear is Not Your Own," in Cheryl Gunn and Andrea A. Lunsford, eds, *On Rhetoric and Feminism 1973–2000*, (New York: Routledge, 2015), p. 123.

15 This is, perhaps, a difficult sentiment to agree with. But what it suggests is that there is no outside maleness, whiteness, or classism. Positionality matters. At best, one can strive to be constantly aware of one's privilege and how it is being enacted.

16 Abby Ohlheiser, "The Changing Context of Who Gets Called a 'Thug' in America," *The Washington Post*, April 28, 2015.

17 Mike Donaldson, "What is Hegemonic Masculinity?," *Theory & Society*, 22(5) (1993): 643–657.

18 Ibid., p. 645.

19 Sara Ahmed, "A Phenomenology of Whiteness," *Feminist Theory*, 8(2) (1993): 150.

20 Donaldson, "What is Hegemonic Masculinity?" p. 645.

21 Donaldson argues that homosexuality is counter-hegemonic. He writes:

> There are three main reasons why male homosexuality is regarded as counter-hegemonic. Firstly, hostility to homosexuality is seen as fundamental to male heterosexuality; secondly, homosexuality is associated with effeminacy; and thirdly, the form of homosexual pleasure is itself considered subversive.
>
> (ibid., p. 648)

22 See www.law.cornell.edu/wex/stare_decisis

23 Much of this discussion of Deleuze can be found in an earlier publication of mine. Maria del Guadalupe Davidson, "Rethinking Black Feminist Subjectivity: Ann DuCille and Gilles Deleuze," in *Convergences: Black Feminism and Continental Philosophy* (New York: SUNY Press, 2010).

24 Charles J. Stivale, ed., *Gilles Deleuze: Key Concepts* (Montreal: McGill-Queen's University Press, 2005), p. 180.

25 Tom Conley, "Folds and Folding," in Charles J. Stivale, ed., *Gilles Deleuze: Key Concepts* (Montreal: McGill-Queen's University Press, 2005), p. 170.

26 Gilles Deleuze, *Foucault*, trans. Sean Hand (Minneapolis: University of Minnesota Press, 1988), p. 95.
27 bell hooks, *Feminist Theory from Margin to Center* (Boston: South End Press, 2000), p. 1.
28 Conley, "Folds and Folding," p. 170.
29 Ibid., p. 170.
30 Ibid., p. 172.
31 Ibid., p. 178.
32 Ibid., p. 172.
33 Gilles Deleuze, "Foldings, or the Inside of Thought (Subjectivation)," in Michael Kelly, ed., *Critique and Power: Recasting the Foucault/Habermas Debate* (Cambridge, MA: MIT Press, 1994), pp. 315–346.
34 Conley, "Folds and Folding," p. 100.
35 Ibid., p. 100.
36 Deleuze, "Foldings," p. 100.
37 Ibid., p. 106.
38 Ibid., p. 100.
39 Ibid., p. 104.
40 Ibid., p. 105.
41 Ibid., p. 119.
42 Ibid., p. 175.
43 This is a tricky term to use here since inclusive implies an opening to all. I use the term inclusive here to mean inclusive—applicable—in one way or another to the multi-varied experiences of all black women.
44 Maya Lloyd, *Judith Butler* (Cambridge: Polity Press, 2007), p. 48. Dennis Schep, "The Limits of Performativity: A Critique of Hegemony in Gender Theory," *Hypatia*, 27(4) (2011): 864–880.
45 Lloyd, *Judith Butler*, p. 48.
46 bell hooks, blog, May 9, 2016. Available at: www.bellhooksinstitute.com/blog/2016/5/9/moving-beyond-pain
47 A famous example of respectability politics is a story by the poet Amari Baraka, he recalls an experience he had while a college student at Howard University (an HBCU). Apparently, Baraka and a friend were eating watermelon in front of a dorm when an administrator admonished them from eating the watermelon near a busy street where they could be seen by whites.
48 Ariane Cruz, "Beyond Black and Blue: BDSM, Internet Pornography, and Black Female Sexuality," *Feminist Studies*, 41(2) (2015): 410.
49 Ibid., p. 412.
50 José Esteban Muñoz, *Disidentifications: Queers of Color and the Performance of Politics* (Minneapolis: University of Minnesota Press, 1999).
51 Ibid., p. 12.
52 See Lynn S. Chancer, *Reconcilable Differences: Confronting Beauty, Pornography, and the Future of Feminism* (Berkeley, CA: University of California Press, 1998); also Lynn Chancer, "From Pornography to Sadomasochism: Reconciling Feminist Differences," *The ANNALS of the American Academy of Political and Social Science*, 571(1) (2000): 77–88; and Lauren Rosewarne, *Cheating on the Sisterhood* (Santa Barbara, CA: Praeger/ABC-CLIO, 2009), for more discussion on this issue.
53 Cherríe Moraga, and Gloria Anzaldúa, *This Bridge Called My Back: Writings by Radical Women of Color* (New York: Kitchen Table, Women of Color Press, 1983).
54 Ibid.
55 The story goes that Carmichael made this rather inflammatory statement in jest. Nevertheless, it was taken very seriously, especially by women activists who used it to critique the patriarchy of the Black Power Movement.

6 Conclusion

On the Grayness of Gray

This book began with me expressing my apprehension about the direction of black feminism. I wondered whether black feminism resonated with younger black women and if there was a real divide between how young black women and older black women articulate agency. These fears have not gone away, nevertheless, I will use this final chapter to present a broader vision of the future of black feminism which (1) rearticulates the importance of agency in black women's lives; and (2) argues for a wider notion of agency that is big enough to "fuck with the grays" while at the same time holds true to those things, including the seminal concept of agency, that have supported black women in the USA.

The Ambiguity of Gray

The word "gray" offers us many points of analysis and speculation. It can of course signify a color when we situate it on the color wheel, where it seems to be a mixture of black and white. In this way, gray is a middle point, it is what is produced when diametric colors (black and white) converge in equal parts. When we think of gray in these terms, we oftentimes forget that you do not need equal parts of white and black to make gray. There are different grays that can be produced depending on the amount of each color mixed and depending on whether one adds white to black or black to white. All this suggests that gray is a complex and nuanced color—it is never neutral. Another way to define gray is as "having an intermediate and often vaguely defined position, condition, or character," for example, "an ethically gray area."[1] To think about gray in this way calls to mind the uncertainty that the word *gray* invokes especially when dealing with people or situations. Very few of us like to be involved in situations that are murky or situations, where the outcome is unknown for either one or a host of reasons. Similarly, very few people want to be associated with, for example, a colleague they may see as gray. Encounters with people like this leave you wondering whether they like you or, maybe more important, whether you can trust them.

Finally, we can think about what I'll call here the gray theory of race and gender. One way that we might be tempted to conceptualize the gray theory of race and gender is to argue that it is nothing more than a call to accept the fluidity of race and gender. To say that race and gender are fluid, at least within certain fields, is not a radical idea. In critical gender studies and in some areas of critical race studies, scholarly claims to the fluidity of gender and race stem in part from the desire to disrupt binary thinking about each of these categories. In critical gender theory, scholars like Judith Butler, particularly in her book *Gender Trouble*, worry the line on our notion of gendered identities. The cover of her book where there appears to be a little boy wearing a dress disrupts what we know or think we know about gender—"is this a girl with *masculine* features?" or "a boy whose parents made him wear a dress?," or "a boy who likes to wear dresses?" The picture is disturbing precisely because it falls in the grays and challenges our sense of what we believe should be definite. A more recent example of worrying the gender line can be seen with models who disrupt our understanding of gender by modeling the clothing of the gender opposite their own. Ericka Linder is, for example, an excellent example of what it means to transgress traditional gender borders in modeling successfully. And, to the sur- prise of many another model, Casey Leger is the first female identified model to sign an exclusively male modeling contract with the Ford agency. In a *Time* magazine article, Leger offers the following comment:

> I understand signifiers. We're social creatures and we have a physical lan- guage of communicating with each other. But it would be a really beautiful thing if we could all just wear what we wanted, without it meaning something.[2]

Leger's comment that she wishes she could adorn herself how she wanted "without it meaning something"[3] speaks to the insistence of critical gender scholars that we divorce appearance from ways of being and acting.

Another rather insidious way that grayness has factored in our public dis- course on gender is with the troubling case of the black South African athlete, Caster Semenya. A runner of extraordinary talent, Semenya has faced inter- national scrutiny from her fellow athletes, journalists, and Olympic officers over what they see as the grayness of her sex. Semenya is such a dominant runner that her fellow competitors called her a *man*, a term when used to describe women is over-loaded with signification. During the course of her career, Semenya has been barred from competition and subjected to sex tests by track and field offi- cials. The noted cultural anthropologist and bioethicist Dr. Katrina Karkazis, quoted in *The New York Times* article, "Understanding the Controversy Over Caster Semenya," states that Semenya has been overly scrutinized for "being too fast and supposedly too masculine."[4] At issue is Semenya's level of testosterone, which was said by some to be abnormally high. Such high levels, it was argued by her mostly white competitors, gave Semenya an unfair advantage over *real* women, thus they believed that she should not be able to compete with *real* women. There is no science to support such accusations. The white athletes accusing Semenya should perform a careful historical analysis of both white privilege, racism, and gender bias against people who do not fit neatly into binary gender categories because of their gender grayness; they should also be critiqued for their use of maleness as a disqualifying category to exclude black women from competition.

Race scholars may be a bit more reluctant to go as far as critical gender scholars, since race in some regards seems less malleable … more black and white than does gender. How difficult is it, for example, to talk about race in terms of *neutral* or *nonconforming* or *fluid*? Historically, those who have skirted racial lines through acts like passing, claiming multiple racial identities, or relabeling themselves like Tiger Woods, attempted to do with the term *cablinasian* are ridiculed within an inch of their public lives. Beyond being ridiculed for embracing the idea that race is fluid, those who engage in the grayness of race also run the risk of being left without the cover of a community when shit goes down. So, if Tiger Woods is in fact *cablinasian*, should he be surprised when the black community refuses to come to his defense when he encounters whiteness that reads him and treats him like he's black? Race scholars may certainly argue against and resist binary systems that define races in oppositional terms, yet they are not likely to support those who argue against the socio-political realness of race, or see race as a category that one can enter or exit at will. Yet, what is the objective here? We know that race scholars do not want a system where people of color are defined in opposition to white. Nor, I suppose, do they want a world that does not see race or, to put it another way, they do not want to live in a world devoid of race. And, indeed many race scholars see the complexity of living and embracing mixed race identity as a social and political undertaking.

Between these various position is the messy middle, the gray area, a place of ambiguity. I believe that we can respond to the uncertainty in one of two ways: first, resist or ignore the messiness presented to us by grayness of race and gender; or see the gray areas presented by these categories as having a potential for dialectical convergences, out of which we might develop a multiplicity of meanings. Because it lacks materiality and concreteness, very few may want to walk in this space. But, this is precisely the space were a new form of agency is being created, especially by young people and those living on the margins.

Street-Level Theory

"Times they are a changing" and just because theory may not *be there* that doesn't mean that the streets haven't already reached *there.* Young people are fucking with the grays of race and gender all the time. I want to be careful here because I do not want to suggest that young people do not see the everyday impact of race and gender on their lives and how racism and gender discrimination limit their agency. In fact, they do and it is the younger generation (particular those of color), who have led the charge on campuses across the country, as they argue for more inclusive and diverse educational spaces, precisely because they understand that their universities do not see them as bodies that matter. Take, for instance, the incident that rocked the University of Oklahoma in 2015. On March 8, 2015,[5] a video surfaced showing Sigma Alpha Epsilon fraternity members at the University of Oklahoma singing the following racist chant:

> There will never be a n–r SAE
> There will never be a n–r SAE
> You can hang him from a tree, but he'll never sign with me
> There will never be a n–r SAE

Whether those words were sung in jest, without conviction, or in ignorance does not really matter. What does matter is that these white male students were enthusiastically singing that black male bodies can be hanged and brutalized and that there is no way that a black male body would ever be able to "sign with them" because black male bodies are *bodies that don't matter*. The paradox is that on Saturdays young men like them pack college football stadiums all over the country to cheer for these very same bodies that they would never "sign with" and that it would be OK to marginalize or murder. I want to highlight two things about this example: first, a group of mainly black students challenged the behavior and worked hard to ensure that the university moved toward becoming a more just and equitable space. Second, this incident offers an opportunity to compare it to other gray racial incidents that occur on campuses and in society all the time. In order to highlight this, I'd like to juxtapose what has come to be known as the "SAE Incident" against an experience I had several months after this event.[6] I was teaching a class abroad to a mixed group of students, who lived and worked in the country. There were two black men in the class and about four white men. One of the white men talked about what it is like going to a club in a European city and having to compete with the black guys for attention. The white men claimed that if there were black men in the club, no one else "had a chance." I looked at the black men for confirmation and they shook their heads in agreement. I said to the black men, full of indignation: "Wait, you are being objectified and sexualized. Doesn't that bother you?" They looked at me with straight faces and said, "No, it's kind of fun to have all the attention." Question: how can students at the very same university react so differently to events that might be read as shockingly similar, especially since in both cases black male bodies are being othered? This is the grayness and ambiguity of being that I'm talking about.

Further, these young men knew that white women liked them because they were "exotic." And as one of the white guys said, "The more thugged out black guys looked, the more the women wanted to date them." Both instances seem to play into stereotypes about black male bodies and both represent all that race and gender writing is trying to resist. Yet, one event elicits anger, outrage, and calls for diversity; while the other elicits enjoyment. Are we "fucking with the grays" or do we want to say "fuck the grays"? For me, both remain in tension. Discussing this encounter of black male sexualization brings us back to the story that began this book, the one the young black women in my class who told me that this "agency thing was not such a big deal." I think the current story reflect this sentiment as well. It is not necessarily a matter of being able to parse good and bad (racist chant = bad) (objectification in a club = good); rather, it is the ability to be able to see agen*cies* in the gray and *this* (the plurality and the ambiguity) becomes a form of resistance and radical re-articulation of what it means to be an agent. Black women must then acknowledge that these issues become even more salient when looking at black women's historical struggle for agency, and how young black women (sisters of today) interface with their worlds.

Going There

Joan Morgan—to whom this chapter pays homage—is one of the first writers who attempts to make visible the grayness of black women's lives and the tensions associated with finding a feminism that works for younger women, including herself. In her book *When Chichenheads Come Home to Roost*, Joan Morgan declares that she needs a feminism "brave enough to fuck with the grays."[7] Morgan continues:

> Just once, I didn't want to have to talk about "the brothers," "male domination," or "the patriarchy." I wanted a feminism that would allow me to explore who we are as women—not victims. One that claimed the powerful richness and delicious complexities inherent in being black girls now—sistas of the post-Civil Rights, post-feminist, post soul, hip-hop generation.[8]

Morgan's comments point toward what she calls a "fatigue" with focusing on those tried and true tropes of black feminist discourse, tropes that focus on *the struggle* and black women's *otherness* while ignoring the full range of agencies and identities that young black women are embracing and exploring. I too, will admit to a fatigue with traditional black feminist analysis that is akin to the fatigue and even exasperation expressed by Morgan. Nevertheless, most younger black women do not simply need a black feminism that is "brave enough to fuck with the grays," they need a black feminism that is more *expansive, fluid*, and *robust*.

So much of black feminist scholarship was laid down by capable scholars like hooks, Hill Collins, Guy-Sheftall, etc. The scholarship is so well done that the words of these sages are repeated in one form or another in most of the black feminist scholarship that is produced. Themes like "outsider-within," "sexist-capitalist-patriarchy," "intersectionality," "standpoint," "interlocking systems of oppression," etc. are cast and recast over and over in much of our work. As mentioned in a previous chapter, it seems like black feminists (and for that matter women of color feminism), scholarship seems to have taken on a hegemonic quality—where hegemonic means "ruling" or "dominant." I'm not sure if one can use the term "hegemonic" without it being pejorative, but this is certainly what I have attempted to do. Black feminist theory, as it applies to black women's lives, is without question *the* lens through which we critique black women's beings-in-the-world. Foucault said that there is no outside of history, meaning that history as a construct represents an impenetrable barrier so much so, that if one is being honest, there is no way to conceptualize things outside of it. So too, for those of us committed to doing black feminist scholarship, there seems to be no *outside* of black feminist thought. Like Foucault, perhaps, the point is not to seek an outside, rather, we must seek a way to expand the theory so that it can take up new ways of being a black girl/woman in the world. If not, then new ideas cannot be born and we will be forced to confront younger black women's agency using methodology and language that may not be appropriate or wholly applicable to their lived experiences.

Through this reading we might assert that, as it is presently articulated, black feminism is not yet capable of doing what is required to keep young women engaged in black women's critical methodology. This is not to say that black feminist thought will not be read and examined as a theory; rather, it is to say that black feminist thought has always been more than a simple theory. It is a project of revolutionary praxis—it is not merely a concept, *it is supposed to be meaningful and applicable*. Martin Luther King Jr. famously stated:

> Any religion that professes to be concerned about the souls of men and is not concerned about the slums that damn them, the economic conditions that strangle them and the social conditions that cripple them is a spiritually moribund religion awaiting burial.[9]

King's words may be harsher than what is intended here, but they do drive home the point I am making, which is that theory must be concerned with the world as it *is*, not as it *was*. How can black feminist theory directly confront in a way that is historically sensitive questions that are complicated and uncomfortable, questions asked by Joan Morgan, for example? Questions that are often cited by some as if Joan Morgan is really throwing down—and she is—but, I would submit that Morgan's questions are rarely if ever answered out loud. To explain this further, Morgan's cheeky questions typically elicit smiles, claps, hollers, remarks like "Oh my, she is really going there," but no real critical engagement because deep down her questions are troubling and gray and messy—and this makes them (Morgan's questions) uncomfortable, and they should. Some of the richer ones include (and I'm paraphrasing)[10]:

1   Is it ok to say that gender equality ain't all that sexy?
2   Is it ok to get dressed up in a hot outfit and feel bad if not one single man objectified you?
3   Why can't women just be honest and say that hip-hop is sexy?
4   Can you be a feminist and still appreciate and even desire being taken care of by a man?

I would be lying to myself if I did not admit that these questions make me uncomfortable because an affirmative response to any of them poses a threat to the black feminism that raised me. An affirmative response makes me question whether I am really down for the struggle or if there is something inside me that desires objectification, total care, and protection by a man—I grew up in a house where my mother frequently reminded me that I did not need a man, a lesson I have passed on to my own daughter. And, what about the undertone of violence that seem to be embedded in some of her questions? Nevertheless, despite the trepidation that I and others might have, Morgan's questions are not rhetorical, nor are they easily dismissible. To answer a resounding *no* to any of these questions places black feminist thought in the precarious position of potentially alienating black women who answer in the affirmative to these and other gray questions, and in the long term, losing the next generation, whose job it is to carry the voice of black feminism forward. Thus, what I'd like to suggest is that answering Morgan's questions in the *affirmative* or allowing black women to answer such questions in the affirmative—without shame or shade—opens up radical possibilities not only for a new articulation of black feminism but for black women's ever evolving agencies.

Black Feminism and Disidentification

There are few theorists better at troubling normative and binary thinking and saying "yes" to questions and actions that many may read as disturbing than José Estaban Muñoz. Muñoz, I believe, offers a more fully developed picture of Judith Butler's disidentification, as he focuses on queer people of color. Muñoz's examination of disidentification attempts to trouble the fixedness of identity as well as the way that social scripts overlay the body, imbuing it with signification that restricts its functionality and freedoms. This reading of Muñoz calls to mind the way that stereotypes function. To stereotype another is to draw upon simple and often misleading perceptions that we use to paint an incomplete picture. We use stereotypes for our own convenience and for expedience, since they provide a way to quickly form an opinion and response to those we encounter, particularly those deemed as different. Sartre's *Antisemite and Jew*, for example, is as much about stereotypes as it is about trying to discern the actions of those who engage in irrational racial hated. Take,, for instance, Sartre's account of the woman who is upset because her fur was ruined and then states, "Well, they [the people who handled her fur] are all Jews." Sartre rightly asks, "But why did she choose to hate Jews rather than furriers? Why Jews or furriers rather than such and such a Jew or such and such a furrier?"[11] In this example, we see how this woman falls back on a simple, misguided, and potentially dangerous stereotype of Jewish people. And, since she is part of the majority, her perceptions about Jewish bodies have real implications for how Jewish people are treated or mistreated within society. Returning to Muñoz, thus, disidentification is crucial because it allows not only for another avenue to theorize the multiple pressures that marginalized bodies are subjected to, but also provides a way to resist such marginalization by creating spaces (grayness) and pockets for new oppositional identities to form—identities that define stereotypes and signification. Andrew Huston's work speaks to the functionality and usefulness of disidentification for marginalized identities when he sees identity formation as a "process that takes place at the point of collision ... this collision is precisely the moment of negotiation when hybrid, racially predicated, and defiantly gendered identities arrive at representation."[12] Disidentification is Foucauldian in that it allows for resistance to knowledge that forces bodies to become docile, and it accomplishes this pushback or force vis-à-vis rhetoric or language force.

In this way, terms like queer and hybrid are examples used by Muñoz that, I would argue, constitute a type of rhetorical force used to resist powers bent on determining bodies that are read as marginal and non-normative. Consequently, whereas the queer body can be (and often is) read as a place that invites violence due to its inability to orient the spectator because it does not fit neatly into a binary gender role, disidentification via rhetoric reclaims queerness as a site of radical possibility *precisely because it does not fit into binary gender roles*; its grayness is a form of strength, a resistance which opens up real and diverse ways of being. As previously mentioned, disidentification creates a space of wonder, creativity, and agency that can happen in the grays or that area created when binaries collide. In celebration of queerness the hybrid, Muñoz writes:

> Hybridity helps one understand how queer lives are fragmented into various identity bits: some of them adjacent, some of them complementary, some of them antagonistic. The hybrid—and terms that can be roughly theorized as equivalents, such as the Creole or the mestizo—are paradigms that help account for the complexities and impossibilities of identity, but, except a certain degree of dependence on institutional frames, what a subject can do from her or his position of hybridity is, basically, open-ended.[13]

"Queer lives" are not the only ones "fragmented into various identity bits" so too, as I have attempted to show, are the identities of younger black women caught between their mothers' and grandmothers' struggles and their current cultural context. What are the tensions associated with being stimulated (sexually, mentally) by the male gaze while at the same time being objectified by it? Or, being comforted by patriarchal power—the kind that wraps you up in a blanket of protection—while at the same time it limits your potential? How do you understand embracing womanist principles of loving other women including sexually, yet find yourself uncontrollably attracted to the most dominant, pants sagging, hard-core, badass butch in the room—the one who drips male sexual energy more than any man you've ever met? For this part, Muñoz takes up the desire one may feel toward contradictory and conflicting identities when he discusses Robert Mapplethorpe's *Black Book*.[14]

Black Book/Black Body/White Gaze

Mapplethorpe's *Black Book* is a collection of black and white photos of nude black gay male bodies. The nude bodies displayed in the book are simply stunning, erotic, and tell us something (I think) about how some of us identify with black male bodies. At the time they were displayed, the photos caused a great deal of controversy not simply because they were taken by Mapplethorpe—a master of controversy—but mainly because they seem to commodify and reify the black male body. There is a colonial aspect to the photos that simply cannot be denied—where we have well-chiseled black male bodies on display. The way they are posed signify their availability for both work and pleasure. And, because the men in the photographs are gay during the early area of AIDS, this adds yet another level of meaning to the photos. Speaking of this, Muñoz states:

> Mapplethorpe's pictures cannot, after the grim carnival of controversy around them, be seen any longer without a deep conversation of AIDS and both the gay and black communities' current crisis of mourning. In a *Vanity Fair* interview right before his death, Mapplethorpe commented that most of the black men who appeared in *Black Book* are now dead because of their poverty, lack of insurance, and the very high price of health care and medications such as AZT.[15]

How then do we come to understand Mapplethorpe's project, given the history of exploitation surrounding the black male body, the history AIDS that left (and currently leaves) poor communities of color devastated, and Mapplethorpe's hungry and potentially exploitative eye? To complicate these questions a bit further, how do we make sense and even come to terms with our own desire and hunger in the face of such images?

For those of us trained as traditional black feminist scholars and race theorists, I see one of two possible paths we may take in addressing these questions. The first is to condemn Mapplethorpe's colonizing gaze. Much like early colonial imagery, Mapplethorpe places the black body on display. In his images, especially those that explore the underground BDSM culture in New York City and those of the black male body, Mapplethorpe desires to make visible what is taboo and, if possible, it seems that he wants to humanize his subjects. The problem for many critical race and critical sexuality folks is that Mapplethorpe's images seems to (intentionally or otherwise) have a *didactic* function in the sense that they instruct the viewer to see the world and others in a particular way. Because his images are consumed mainly by European audiences, they train European viewers to regard black men as *other* by emphasizing their difference from white male bodies. Yet, in addition, we should pay special attention to those images that not only show black men as *other* but show them as sexually available and exploitable *others*. These images are examples of what I will call *didactic pornography*, inasmuch as they not only present the black male body as *other* but do so in a way that presents the black male body as available for sexual possession even as it represents a danger.[16] I have written elsewhere about the difference between pornography and didactic pornography, particularly when the subject matter is that of black colonized women. There is always something more going on in these images than simply an objective documentation of different body types or medical conditions. Sander Gilman gets at this by raising the broader question, "How do we organize our perceptions of the world?"[17] Whereas Gilman takes this question in the direction of how "specific individual realities are thus given mythic extension though association with the qualities of a class,"[18] here I am interested in following a slightly different path. That is, I want to examine how the photographic images of colonized black female bodies came to organize European perceptions of black women and how they continue to shape our perceptions today. Such images, I contend, thus have a didactic function in the sense that they instruct the viewer to see the world and others in a particular way. Many of the images of colonized women—could be said to have this didactic function. They train European viewers to regard black women as *other* by emphasizing their difference from white women. Yet, in addition, I want to call special attention to those images that not only show black women as *other* but show them as sexually available and exploitable *others*. These images are examples of what I will call didactic pornography, inasmuch as they not only present the black female body as *other* but do so in a way that presents the black female body as available for sexual possession.

Mapplethorpe's images in *Black Book* function in strikingly similar ways. Take, for example, the image of the very dark complexioned black man with his right arm outstretched pointing a gun. Although the man is fully dressed, his erect penis sticks out of his pants and is pointing in the same direction as the gun. This man represents to very distinct controlling images—the gun-wielding, black male menace *and* the sexually available or sexually menacing black man. Taken in this way, traditional black feminist scholars would condemn this image not only for being stereotypical but also we should condemn it for being didactic because it trains society how to treat black men—as dangerous and sexually exploitable.

The second way that critical race and critical sexuality scholars might frame these images is as having the potential to be reclaimed. The act of reclamation, I would argue, is a part of the larger postmodern project which calls for a decentering of the subject. Interestingly, the view might be tempted to see the black men highlighted throughout Mapplethorpe's *Black Book* as the subjects because it is their image that seems to sit at the center. Yet, the black men in the book are really merely objects of Mapplethorpe, who is really the subject—it is through his eye that the black male body is framed. What postmodernity then challenges us to do is *decenter* the subject or spectator. Meaning we are asked to displace or not focus on Mapplethorpe—another way to say this is to disempower Mapplethorpe's colonial gaze—and see how the black male bodies tell their own stories. We may call this the death of the photographer, but it might be more helpful to disassociate the images of the black men from the life, history, desire of Mapplethorpe. What this means is that we can read the images *on their own* without Mapplethorpe being the point of reference we use to understand the images. To do so does not mean that the black men become the subjects, what it means is that the photographs are open for wider interpretation and their meaning is expanded. Doing so disrupts Mapplethorpe's framing of the black male body. Both interpretations are valid, but what neither fully does is deal with *the desire of the nonconventional*.

The work of Josà Estaban Muñoz presents us with this third option—*the desire of the nonconventional*—that takes us outside of these two tried and true responses to the commodification of bodies of color. Instead of looking at Mapplethorpe's photography and beginning our analysis from the standpoint that the images are a "colonial fantasy,"[19] we might instead begin by asking about *pleasure*; specifically the pleasure that black gay men "and other gay men of color experience when consuming Mapplethorpe's images…"[20] Muñoz argues that the pleasure felt from these images:

> Is a disidentificatory pleasure, one that acknowledges what is disturbing about the familiar practices of black male objectification that Mapplethorpe participated in, while at the same time it understands that this pleasure cannot easily be dismissed even though it is politically dangerous.[21]

Disidentification allows us to recognize and own the sensations and, yes, pleasures that we feel in situations that our critical frameworks call us to disavow. Muñoz is correct when he argues that it is politically dangerous to do so because it can be argued that we place our theory, perhaps even our liberation in jeopardy if we find-acknowledge-pleasure in what is simultaneously read as painful and dehumanizing. But to *not* recognize the sometimes twin feelings/sensations that accompany forms of objectification, I think, limits the creative power of our theory by making it denialist, one-dimensional, and even essentialist. Muñoz continues: "Like melancholia, disidentification is an ambivalent structure of feeling that works to retain the problematic object and tap into the energies that are produced by contradictions and ambivalences."[22] Consuming the images in Mapplethorpe's *Black Book* draws one into the "racist exploitation" but through the lens of disidentification, we the viewer are at the same time allowed to experience "a powerful validation of the black male body."[23] As viewers—and by this I mean those of us who are directly implicated by such images, meaning that we can look at such images and on a visceral/lived experience level and utter "c'est moi"—we cannot and should not be blind to this radical reimagining of seemingly commodified images nor should we deny ourselves the feeling of pleasure we receive by consuming such images. Muñoz explains this radical reimaging or "making over" rather eloquently, writing:

> The object that is desired is reformatted so that dignity and grace are not eclipsed by racist exploitation. Disidentification is this "making over"; it is the way a subject looks at an image that has been constructed to exploit and deny identity and instead finds pleasure, both erotic and self-affirming.[24]

This is easier said than done especially when we are confronted with images like the one in video for "Tip Drill" that shows a black woman bending over and Nelly swiping a credit card down her ass. This shocking image is constructed to exploit black women. It is intentional. It is degrading. But, it is also pleasurable, titillating, and sexy. Disidentification allows us to look at the woman and the action being done to her (that she is allowing) and hold pleasure and commodification in tension. In the messy middle caused by the tension, we may come to understand the complexity of sexuality—Nelly's, the woman's and our own; Mapplethorpe, the men's, and our own. Disidentification disrupts the virgin–whore dichotomy, allowing for new forms of sexuality to emerge. In a world that is structured on good–bad; acceptable–unacceptable and one that has historically reduced black bodies, Disidentification is a difficult move to make, but it may also necessary.

The Objectified Agent

I use the example of Mapplethorpe, Nelly's "Tip Drill" video, and the theory of disidentification to challenge black feminist theory to take us beyond conventional applications and critiques, to provide us with a way to directly address Morgan's unsettling questions. Finally, I want to challenge black feminism to be open to a new form of agency—*objectified agency*—that without question is fully emerging among younger black women today. Disidentification does a few key things; first, it gives us a way to hold these contradictions—objectification and agency—in tension and not have to choose between pleasure and pain or ignore the pleasure some of us may find in pain. Thus, taking up Morgan's questions—"Can you be a good feminist and admit out loud that there are things you kinda dig about patriarchy?" Just like Muñoz and other critics of Mapplethorpe's work are able to see the harm his images cause to black bodies, and as critical folks acting out of a theory of liberation and resistance, they are trained to resist Mapplethorpe's colonizing gaze, we too completely understand why patriarchy is harmful and detrimental to all people, regardless of gender. But, on the other hand, we *should* follow up by critically interrogating what Morgan and other women might "dig about patriarchy." We might begin by asking another set of uncomfortable questions:

- What is the allure of this thing we've been trained to demonize?
- Is it possible to find pleasure in patriarchy?

Such questions might help us understand and come to terms with why patriarchy, for instance, has been so difficult to dismantle. Can we say without judgment that for some women, patriarchy just *works*, and that some women find not merely security but pleasure in it? We need to disidentify—hold this idea in tension with the way that patriarchy damages the lives of all people. I'm calling for grayness and even accepting the discomfort associated it.

Importantly, we should resist asking questions about Morgan and other women who ask difficult questions. We should not question their mental state or their background. Doing so is tantamount to directing focus away from disturbing questions, being dismissive, and pathologizing what I feel is a legitimate position. As a black feminist, to say that there is something that you "dig" about patriarchy and for other black feminists to take this statement seriously and to admit that there *is* maybe something appealing about patriarchy is to engage in the process of disidentification—it is to engage in a reorganization of our theory and practice. And maybe, just maybe, disidentification will allows black women to *displace* all others as the standard of agency. Black feminist theory, like postmodernism, is both adequate and indeed robust enough to provide salient critiques to conventional questions. I'll say it again, unlike mainstream feminism, black feminism has not quite found a way make a space for the unconventional, the problematic, the exploitive to exist as a valid and affirmed position within its theoretical structure. Disidentification allows us to *fuck with the grays* and in so doing provides us with a chance to extend the reach of black feminist agency.

Notes

1 Merriam Webster's Dictionary online at: www.merriam-webster.com/dictionary/gray
2 http://style.time.com/2012/11/20/male-models-the-female-of-the-species/
3 Ibid.
4 J. Longman, "Understanding the Controversy over Caster Semenya," *The New York Times*, August 18, 2016.
5 Tyler Kinkaid, "Oklahoma Frat Boys Caught Singing 'There Will Never Be a N*****
   in SAE'," *The Huffington Post*, March 8, 2015. Available at: www.huffingtonpost.
   com/2015/03/0hotmai+-8/frat-racist-sae-oklahoma_n_6828212.html (accessed July
   21, 2015).
6 I am a faculty member at the University of Oklahoma.
7 Joan Morgan, When Chickenheads Come Home to Roost: A Hip Hop Feminist
   Breaks it Down (New York: Simon & Schuster, 1999), p. 59.
8 Ibid., p. 57.
9 Martin Luther King, Address at the Religious Leaders Conference, May 11, 1959.
10 Morgan, When Chickenheads Come Home, pp. 57–58.
11 Jean-Paul Sartre, *Antisemite and Jew: An Exploration of the Etiology of Hate* (New
   York: Schocken, 1995) (in German), p. 273.
12 Andrew Huston. "Dis-ing the Main Drag and Walking Toward the Public Good in
   Here Be Dragons: Mapping Queer, Asian-Canadian Identity in Kitchener, Ontario."
   Theater Research in Canada 36(2) (2015): 282.
13 José Esteban Muñoz, *Disidentifications: Queers of Color and the Performance of Politics* (Minneapolis: University of Minnesota Press, 1999), p. 79.
14 Robert Mapplethorpe, *Black Book* (München: Schirmer-Mosel, 1986).
15 Muñoz, *Disidentifications*, p. 79.
16 My use of the term "didactic pornography" is in line with the idea of *controlling-images*—a phrase coined by Patricia Hill Collins. In *Black Feminist Thought*, Hill
   Collins argues that there are four images found throughout American history and
   culture that serve to "type" black women—the mammy, the matriarch, the jezebel,
   and the welfare mother. These images define, to a great extent, the black female body,
   and most importantly, teach society how to interact with black women. Likewise,
   many of the images in the "Colonial Conquest" section of Willis and Williams's book
   function as controlling images. Deborah Willis and Carla Williams. *The Black Female
   Body: A Photographic History* (Philadelphia, PA: Temple University Press, 2002).
17 Sander L. Gilman, "Black Bodies, White Bodies: Toward a Iconography of Female
   Sexuality in Late Nineteenth-Century Art, Medicine, and Literature," in Henry Louis
   Gates, ed., *"Race," Writing, and Difference* (Chicago: University of Chicago Press,
   1985), p. 223.
18 Ibid.

19 Muñoz, *Disidentifications*, p. 70.
20 Ibid. These images are not just pleasurable for gay men, many people from multiple sexual orientations would also find these images pleasurable.
21 Ibid., p. 71.
22 Ibid.
23 Ibid.
24 Ibid., p. 72.

Bibliography

Abel, Elizabeth, Barbara Christian, and Helene Moglen. "The Occult of True Black Womanhood: Critical Demeanor and Black Feminist Studies," in *Female Subjects in Black and White: Race, Psychoanalysis, Feminism*. Berkeley, CA: University of California, 1997.

Ahmed, Sara. "A Phenomenology of Whiteness," *Feminist Theory*, 8(2) (1993): 149–168.

Austin, Sierra *et al.* "Anita Hill Roundtable," *Frontiers*, 35(3) (2014): 65.

Beran, Michael Knox. *Jefferson's Demons: Portrait of a Restless Mind*. New York: Free Press, 2003.

Berman, D., L. L. Martin, and L. J. Kajfez, "County Home Rule: Does Where You Stand Depend on Where You Sit?" *State & Local Government Review*, 17(2), (Spring, 1985): 232

Blassingame, John W. *Slave Testimony: Two Centuries of Letters, Speeches, Interviews, and Autobiographies*. Baton Rouge, LA: Louisiana State University Press, 1977.

Bobo, Jacqueline, Cynthia Hudley, and Claudine Michel, eds., *The Black Studies Reader*. New York: Routledge, 2004.

Bridges, Khiara M. *Reproducing Race: An Ethnography of Pregnancy as a Site of Racialization*. Berkeley, CA: University of California Press, 2011.

Campt, Tina. *Other Germans*. Ann Arbor, MI: University of Michigan Press, 2004.

Cannon, Katie Geneva. "Slave Ideology and Biblical Interpretation," in Jacqueline Bobo and Cynthia Hudley, eds., *The Black Studies Reader*. New York: Routledge, 2004.

Chancer, Lynn S. *Reconcilable Differences: Confronting Beauty, Pornography, and the Future of Feminism*. Berkeley, CA: University of California Press, 1998.

Chancer, L. S. "From Pornography to Sadomasochism: Reconciling Feminist Differences," *The ANNALS of the American Academy of Political and Social Science* 571(1) (2000): 77–88. doi:10.1177/0002716200571001006.

Chisholm, Shirley. *Unbought and Unbossed*. Boston: Houghton Mifflin, 1970.

Clammer, John. "Performing Ethnicity: Performance, Gender, Body and Belief in the Construction and Signalling of Identity," *Ethnic and Racial Studies*, 38(13) (2015): 2159–2166. doi:10.1080/01419870.2015.1045305.

Collins, Lisa. "Economies of Flesh: Respecting the Black Female Body in Art," in Kimberly Wallace-Sanders, ed., *Skin Deep, Spirit Strong: The Black Female Body in American Culture*. Ann Arbor, MI: University of Michigan Press, 2002.

Combahee River Collective. "A Black Feminist Statement," *WSQ: Women's Studies Quarterly*, 42(3–4) (2014): 271–280.

Crenshaw, Kimberlé Williams. "Mapping the Margins: Intersectionality, Identity Politics, and Violence Against Women of Color," in Martha Albertson Fineman, and Rixanne

Mykitiuk, eds., *The Public Nature of Violence*. New York: Routledge, 1994, pp. 93–118.

Cruz, Ariane. "Beyond Black and Blue: BDSM, Internet Pornography, and Black Female Sexuality," *Feminist Studies*, 41(2) (2015): 409–436.

Dance, Daryl Cumber. *Shuckin' and Jivin': Folklore from Contemporary Black Americans*. Bloomington, IN: Indiana University Press, 1978.

Davidson, Maria del Guadalupe. "Rethinking Black Feminist Subjectivity: Ann duCille and Gilles Deleuze," in *Convergences: Black Feminism and Continental Philosophy* (Albany, NY: SUNY Press, 2010), pp 121–133.

Davidson, Maria del Guadalupe. "Deflection from the (Real) Issues," in *The American Mosaic: The African American Experience*. New York: ABC-CLIO, 2016a. Web. 28 April 2016.

Davidson, Maria del Guadalupe. "Black Women's Bodies, Ideology, and the Rhetoric of the Pro- and Anti Choice Movements in the US," *Gender and Education* (2016b) online.

Deetz, Stanley. "Conceptualizing Human Understanding: Gadamer's Hermeneutics and American Communication Studies," *Communication Quarterly*, 26(2) (1978): 12–23.

Deleuze, Gilles. "Foldings, or the Inside of Thought (Subjectivation)," in Michael Kelly, ed., *Critique and Power: Recasting the Foucault/Habermas Debate*. Cambridge, MA: MIT Press, 1994, pp. 315–346.

Donaldson, Mike. "What is Hegemonic Masculinity?" *Theory & Society*, 22(5) (1993): 643–657.

Dow, D. M. "Negotiating 'The Welfare Queen' and 'The Strong Black Woman': African American Middle-Class Mothers' Work and Family Perspectives," *Sociological Perspectives*, 58(1) (2014): 36–55. doi:10.1177/0731121414556546.

Du Bois, W. E. B. *The Souls of Black Folks*. New York: W.W. Norton, 1999.

duCille, Ann. "The Occult of True Black Womanhood: Critical Demeanor and Black Feminist Studies," *Signs: Journal of Women in Culture and Society*, 19(3) (1994): 591–629. doi:10.1086/494914.

Elam, Diane. "Sisters are Doing it to Themselves," in D. Looser and A. Kaplan, eds., *Generations: Academic Feminists in Dialogue*. Minneapolis: University of Minnesota Press, 1997, pp. 55–68.

Fanon, Frantz. *Black Skin, White Mask*. New York: Grove Press, 1967.

Fineman, Martha, and Roxanne Mykitiuk, eds., *The Public Nature of Private Violence: The Discovery of Domestic Abuse*. New York: Routledge, 1994.

Foss, Sonja. *Rhetorical Criticism*. Long Grove, IL: Waveland Press, 1996.

Freud, Sigmund. *Collected Papers*, vol. IV. London: Hogarth Press, 1949.

Friedan, Betty. *The Feminist Critique*. New York: W.W. Norton, 1997.

Gadamer, Hans-Georg. *Truth and Method*. London: Sheed and Ward, 1979.

Gates, Henry Louis, and Jennifer Burton, eds., *Call and Response: Key Debates in African American Studies*. New York: W.W. Norton, 2011.

Giddings, Paula. *When and Where I Enter: The Impact of Black Women on Race and Sex in America*. New York: W. Morrow, 1984.

Gillis, Stacy, Gillian Howie, and Rebecca Munford, eds., *Third Wave Feminism: A Critical Exploration*. Basingstoke: Palgrave Macmillan, 2004.

Gilman, Sander L. "Black Bodies, White Bodies: Toward a Iconography of Female Sexuality in Late Nineteenth-Century Art, Medicine, and Literature," in Henry Louis Gates, ed., *"Race," Writing, and Difference*. Chicago: University of Chicago Press, pp. 223–261.

Gossett, Thomas F. *Race: The History of an Idea in America*. New York: Oxford University Press, 1997.

Guy-Sheftall, Beverly. *Words of Fire: An Anthology of African-American Feminist Thought*. New York: New Press, 1995.

Heckman, Susan. "Reconstituting the Subject: Feminism, Modernism, and Postmodernism." *Hypatia*, 6(2) (1991): 44–63. doi:10.1111/j.1527–2001.1991.tb01392.x.

Heywood, Leslie and Jennifer Drake. "'It's All About the Benjamins': Economic Determinants of Third Wave Feminism in the United States," in *Third Wave Feminism: A Critical Exploration* (New York: Palgrave Macmillan, 2004).

Hill Collins, Patricia. "The Social Construction of Black Feminist Thought," in Beverly Guy-Sheftall, ed., *Words of Fire: An Anthology of African American Feminist Thought*. New York: The New Press, 1995.

Hill. Collins, Patricia. *Black Feminist Thought: Knowledge, Consciousness, and the Politics of Empowerment*. New York: Routledge, 2000.

Hill Collins, Patricia. "Intersecting Oppressions." Available at: www.sagepub.com/sites/default/files/upm-binaries/13299_Chapter_16_Web_Byte_Patricia_Hill_Collins.pdf

Hogeland, Lisa Marie. "Fear of Feminism: Why Young Women Get the Willies," in Susan M. Shaw and Janet Lee, eds., *Women's Voices/Feminist Visions: Classic and Contemporary Readings*. New York: McGraw-Hill, 2014.

hooks, bell. *Ain't I a Woman: Black Women and Feminism*. Boston South End Press, 1981.

hooks, bell. *Talking Back: Thinking Feminist, Thinking Black*. Boston: South End Press, 1989.

hooks, bell. "Moving Beyond Pain," blog, May 9, 2016. Available at: www.bellhooksinstitute.com/blog/2016/5/9/moving-beyond-pain

Hull, Gloria T., Patricia Bell-Scott, and Barbara Smith, eds., *All the Women Are White, All the Blacks Are Men, but Some of Us Are Brave: Black Women's Studies*. Old Westbury, NY: Feminist Press, 1982.

Hunter, Margaret. "Shake It, Baby, Shake It: Consumption and the New Gender Relation in Hip-Hop," *Sociological Perspectives*, 54(1) (2011): 15–36. doi:10.1525/sop.2011.54.1.15.

Huston, Andrew. "Dissing the Main Drag and Walking Toward the Public Good in *Here Be Dragons*: Mapping Queer, Asian-Canadian Identity in Kitchener, Ontario," *Theater Research in Canada*, 36(2) (2015): 274–289.

James, Joy. *Shadowboxing: Representations of Black Feminist Politics*. New York: St. Martin's Press, 1999.

James, Stanlie M., Frances Smith Foster, and Beverly Guy-Sheftall, eds., *Still Brave: The Evolution of Black Women's Studies*. New York: Feminist Press, 2009.

Johnson, Charles. "A Phenomenology of the Black Body," in Beverly Guy-Sheftall, ed., *Traps: African American Men on Gender and Sexuality*. Bloomington, IN: Indiana University Press, 2001.

Jones Royster, Jacqueline. "When the First Voice Your Hear is Not Your Own," in Cheryl Gunn and Andrea A. Lunsford, eds., *On Rhetoric and Feminism 1973–2000*. New York: Routledge, 2015.

Kapsalis, Terri, "Mastering the Female Pelvis: Race and the Tools of Reproduction," in T. Kapsalis, *Public Privates: Performing Gynecology from Both Ends of the Speculum* (Durham, NC: Duke University Press, 2002).

Kessler, Glenn. *The Confidante: Condoleezza Rice and the Creation of the Bush Legacy*. New York: St Martin's Press, 2007.

Kincheloe, Joe L. "The Struggle to Define and Reinvent Whiteness: A Pedagogical Analysis," *College English*, 26(3) (1999): 162–194.

Lévinas, Emmanuel, and Alphonso Lingis. *Totality and Infinity*. Pittsburgh, PA: Duquesne University Press, 1969.

Li, Stephanie. "Motherhood as Resistance in Harriet Jacobs's *Incidents in the Life of a Slave Girl*," *Legacy* 23(1) (2006): 14–29.

Lloyd, Maya. *Judith Butler*. Cambridge: Polity Press, 2007.

MacIntosh, Peggy. "White Privilege: Unpacking the Invisible Knapsack," *Peace and Freedom Magazine* July/August, 1989, pp 10–12.

Mapplethorpe, Robert. *Black Book*. München: Schirmer-Mosel, 1986.

Marable, Manning. "Grounding with my Sisters," in Beverley Guy-Sheftall, ed., *Traps: African American Men on Gender and Sexuality*. Bloomington, IN: Indiana University Press, 2001, pp. 119–152.

McBride, Cillian. *Recognition*. Cambridge: Polity, 2013.

Mills, Charles W. *The Racial Contract*. Ithaca, NY: Cornell University Press, 1997.

Moraga, Cherríe, and Gloria Anzaldúa. *This Bridge Called My Back: Writings by Radical Women of Color*. New York: Kitchen Table, Women of Color Press, 1983.

Moran, Dermot. *Introduction to Phenomenology*. London: Routledge, 2000.

Morgan, Joan. *When Chickenheads Come Home to Roost: My Life as a Hip-hop Feminist*. New York: Simon & Schuster, 1999.

Muñoz, José Esteban. *Disidentifications: Queers of Color and the Performance of Politics*. Minneapolis: University of Minnesota Press, 1999.

Nagourney, Adam. "A Defiant Rancher Savors the Audience That Rallied to His Side," *The New York Times*, April 23, 2014.

Napier, Winston. *African American Literary Theory: A Reader*. New York: New York University Press, 2000.

Nicholson, Linda. "Feminism in 'Waves': Useful Metaphor or Not?," *New Politics*, XII–4 (48) (2010). Available at: http://newpol.org/content/feminism-waves-useful-metaphor-or-not

Ohlheiser, Abby. "The Changing Context of Who Gets Called a 'Thug' in America," *The Washington Post*, April 28, 2015.

Omi, Michael, and Howard Winant. *Racial Formation in the United States*. New York: Routledge, 2015.

Parry-Giles, Shawn J. *Hillary Clinton in the News: Gender and Authenticity in American Politics*. Urbana, IL: University of Illinois Press, 2014.

Richardson, Elaine. "She Was Workin Like Foreal: Critical Literacy and Discourse Practices of African American Females in the Age of Hip Hop," *Discourse and Society*, 18 (2007).

Roberts, Dorothy. *Killing the Black Body: Race, Reproduction, and the Meaning of Liberty*. New York: Vintage Books, 1999.

Rosewarne, Lauren. *Cheating on the Sisterhood: Infidelity and Feminism*. Santa Barbara, CA: Praeger/ABC-CLIO, 2009.

Roy, Abhik and Bayo Oluda. "Hans-Georg Gadamer's *Praxis*: Implications for Connection and Action in Communication Studies," *Communication, Culture, and Critique*, 2(3) (September 2009): 255–273. doi:10.1111/j.1753-9137.2009.01038.x.

Sartre, Jean-Paul. *Antisemite and Jew: An Exploration of the Etiology of Hate*. New York: Schocken, 1995 (in German).

Schep, Dennis. "The Limits of Performativity: A Critique of Hegemony in Gender Theory," *Hypatia*, 27(4) (2011): 864–880. doi:10.1111/j.1527-2001.2011.01230.x.

Sharpley-Whiting, T. Denean. *Pimps Up, Ho's Down: Hip Hop's Hold on Young Black Women.* New York: New York University Press, 2007.

Smith, Barbara. "Toward a Black Feminist Criticism," in Winston Napier, ed., *African American Literary Theory*. New York: NYU Press, 2000.

Song, Miri. "Introduction: Who's at the Bottom? Examining Claims about Racial Hierarchy." *Ethnic and Racial Studies*, 27(6) (2004): 859–877. doi:10.1080/014198704200 0268503.

Stivale, Charles J., ed., *Gilles Deleuze: Key Concepts.* Montreal: McGill-Queen's University Press, 2005.

Szymanski, Dawn M., and Jioni A. Lewis. "Gendered Racism, Coping, Identity Centrality, and African American College Women's Psychological Distress," *Psychology of Women Quarterly*, 40(2) (2015): 229–243. doi:10.1177/0361684315616113.

Taylor, Charles, and Amy Gutmann, eds., *Multiculturalism: Examining the Politics of Recognition*. Princeton, NJ: Princeton University Press, 1994.

Tong, Rosemarie. *Feminist Thought: A More Comprehensive Introduction.* Boulder, CO: Westview Press, 2009.

Wallace, Michelle. "A Black Feminist Search for Sisterhood," in Gloria T. Hull, Patricia Bell Scott, and Barbara Smith, eds., *But Some of Us Are Brave*. New York: The Feminist Press, 1982.

Wallace-Sanders, Kimberly. *Skin Deep, Spirit Strong: The Black Female Body in American Culture*. Ann Arbor, MI: University of Michigan Press, 2002.

Wander, P. "The Ideological Turn in Modern Criticism," *Central States Speech Journal*, 34 (1983): 1–18.

Welter, Barbara. "The Cult of True Womanhood: 1820–1816," *American Quarterly*, 18(2) (Summer 1966): 151–174.

Wheatley, Phillis. *Poems on Various Subjects, Religious and Moral.* New York: AMS Press, 1976 [1773].

Willis, Deborah, and Carla Williams. *The Black Female Body: A Photographic History*, Philadelphia, PA: Temple University Press, 2002.

Wise, Tim. *White Like Me: Reflections on Race from a Privileged Son*, 3rd rev. edn. Berkeley, CA: Soft Skull Press, 2011.

Wood, Julia T. "Feminist Standpoint Theory," in *Encyclopedia of Communication Theory.* Thousand Oaks, CA: SAGE, 2009, pp. 397–399.

Wray, Matt. *Not Quite White: White Trash and the Boundaries of Whiteness.* Durham, NC: Duke University Press, 2006.

Yancy, George. *Black Bodies, White Gazes: The Continuing Significance of Race.* Lanham, MD: Rowman & Littlefield, 2008.

Index

Page numbers in **bold** denote figures.